Learning TypeScript

Exploit the features of TypeScript to develop and maintain captivating web applications with ease

Remo H. Jansen

[PACKT] open source ✳

PUBLISHING

community experience distilled

BIRMINGHAM - MUMBAI

Learning TypeScript

First published: September 2015

Production reference: 1230915

Published by Packt Publishing Ltd.
Livery Place
35 Livery Street
Birmingham B3 2PB, UK.

ISBN 978-1-78398-554-8

www.packtpub.com

Credits

Author
Remo H. Jansen

Reviewers
Liviu Ignat
Jakub Jedryszek
Andrew Leith Macrae
Brandon Mills
Ivo Gabe de Wolff

Commissioning Editor
Amarabha Banerjee

Acquisition Editor
Manish Nainani

Content Development Editor
Kirti Patil

Technical Editor
Vivek Arora

Copy Editor
Puja Lalwani

Project Coordinator
Nidhi Joshi

Proofreader
Safis Editing

Indexer
Rekha Nair

Graphics
Jason Monteiro

Production Coordinator
Manu Joseph

Cover Work
Manu Joseph

About the Author

Remo H. Jansen is a web development engineer, open source contributor, entrepreneur, technology lover, gamer, and Internet enthusiast.

He is originally from Seville, Spain, but currently lives in Dublin, Ireland, where he has a full-time job in the financial services industry. Remo has been working on large-scale JavaScript applications for the last few years, from flight booking engines to investment and portfolio management solutions.

Remo is an active member of the TypeScript community. He is the organizer of the Dublin TypeScript Meet-up and the creator of InversifyJS (an inversion of control container for TypeScript applications) and AtSpy (a test spies framework for TypeScript applications). He also writes a blog about TypeScript and other web technologies at `http://blog.wolksoftware.com/`.

Remo has previously worked as a technical reviewer on *Mastering TypeScript* written by *Nathan Rozentals* and published by Packt Publishing.

If you wish to contact him, you can do so at `http://www.remojansen.com/`.

Acknowledgments

This is my first book. It has been a really long journey to get to this day, and, along the way, I had the pleasure of learning a lot from some amazing people who deserve a big thank you.

I would like to start by thanking my teachers from the school of computer science at Salesians of St. Peter in Triana (Seville, Spain) because they made me appreciate the value of education.

To the team at Packt Publishing for their support and hard work; it has been an absolute pleasure to work with you guys.

To the technical reviewers of this book, because their invaluable feedback and hard work really helped to improve the contents of this book.

To my work colleagues and housemates, Sergio Pacheco Gimenez and Adolfo Blanco Diez, for the long technical conversations at midnight and the constant supply of caffeinated beverages.

To my girlfriend, Lorraine, I'm so privileged for your unconditional support and patience. You are simply the best and keep getting better.

Finally, to my family, for always believing in me, for your advice, for being the best listeners, for all your hard work, for forgiving my mistakes, and for all that you have taught me. Thanks for the laughs and thanks for the tears, I'm really proud of being your grandson, son, and brother.

About the Reviewers

Liviu Ignat is a full-stack developer and architect, technology geek, and entrepreneur, and has been writing commercial software since 2004. He started with VB6, soon moved to .NET Java and then continued moving to frontend web development. He has fun with everything that is a functional language, such as F#, Scala, Swift, JavaScript, and so on. He has been using Typescript for some of his latest projects together with Node.js on the server or with most of the popular frontend frameworks on the client side.

Currently, he is also involved in a number of projects, the most relevant being `http://giftdoodle.com/`, where he is the CTO of the company, where most of the JavaScript software stack written is also Typescript. During his work experience, he has been involved in building distributed backend services, mostly with .NET and then complex single-page web applications. Recently, he has become a big fan of micro-services with Node.js and Docker, single-page web applications, and native applications for Android and iOS.

When he is not coding, Liviu loves snowboarding during winter, sailing in exotic places during summer, or just traveling the world. You can find and contact Liviu at `http://www.ignat.email/`.

Jakub Jedryszek works for Microsoft as a software engineer. At the time of reviewing this book, he was working on the Azure Portal—the largest and most complex single-page web application in the world written in TypeScript. He is a cofounder of dotNetConfPL—online conference for .NET Developers. His blog is at `http://jj09.net/`.

Andrew Leith Macrae first cut his programming teeth on an Apple, poking bytes into RAM. Over the years, he has developed interactive applications with Hypercard, Director, Flash, and, more recently, Adobe AIR for mobile. He has also worked in HTML since there was HTML to work in, and is currently working as a senior frontend developer at Rogers Communications Inc. in Toronto, in an Agile environment using AngularJS and SASS.

He is convinced that TypeScript is the future of JavaScript, bringing the structure and discipline of strongly typed object oriented language to facilitate efficient, intentional coding for the development of large scale applications for the Web.

You can contact Andrew at `http://adventmedia.net/`.

Brandon Mills was first introduced to programming more than a decade ago, kicking off a career which has taken him to companies as small as two-person start-ups and as large as Microsoft, where he helped build Visual Studio 2013, Azure Tools, and the developer tools in the new Edge browser that shipped with Windows 10. He is a member of the core development team for ESLint, a customizable, open source linter for JavaScript and JSX. Node.js is his platform of choice, on top of which he authors applications and services in JavaScript or TypeScript. You can follow him on GitHub at `https://github.com/btmills`.

Thanks to Scott for his impetus and inspiration, Linda for her unconditional love, Abby for his patience, and Ashlynn for her support.

Ivo Gabe de Wolff is a freelance developer under the name of *ivogabe*, founded in 2012, and he is studying mathematics and computing sciences at Utrecht University. When he was 11, he started programming games with Game Maker. After learning various languages, such as C# and JavaScript, he now uses TypeScript for almost all his projects. In the last few years, he has used TypeScript in lots of different environments, including for mobile apps. Now, he mainly specializes in Node.js programming.

Furthermore, he is the author of various open source projects, including gulp-typescript. You can find his projects on `https://github.com/ivogabe`. If you want to read more about TypeScript, JavaScript, Gulp, or mathematical backgrounds, you can take a look at his blog at `http://dev.ivogabe.com/`.

www.PacktPub.com

Support files, eBooks, discount offers, and more

For support files and downloads related to your book, please visit www.PacktPub.com.

Did you know that Packt offers eBook versions of every book published, with PDF and ePub files available? You can upgrade to the eBook version at www.PacktPub.com and as a print book customer, you are entitled to a discount on the eBook copy. Get in touch with us at service@packtpub.com for more details.

At www.PacktPub.com, you can also read a collection of free technical articles, sign up for a range of free newsletters and receive exclusive discounts and offers on Packt books and eBooks.

https://www2.packtpub.com/books/subscription/packtlib

Do you need instant solutions to your IT questions? PacktLib is Packt's online digital book library. Here, you can search, access, and read Packt's entire library of books.

Why subscribe?

- Fully searchable across every book published by Packt
- Copy and paste, print, and bookmark content
- On demand and accessible via a web browser

Free access for Packt account holders

If you have an account with Packt at www.PacktPub.com, you can use this to access PacktLib today and view 9 entirely free books. Simply use your login credentials for immediate access.

Table of Contents

Preface

Over the past few years, the JavaScript code base of an average web application has been exponentially growing. However, the current JavaScript specification (ECMAScript 5 or ES5) was designed several years ago and lacks some features that are necessary to cope with the complexity that we can find in large-scale JavaScript applications today. As a result of these missing features, maintainability problems have arisen.

The upcoming JavaScript version (ECMAScript 6 or ES6) is meant to solve some of the maintainability issues of JavaScript, but its implementation is in progress and many incompatible web browsers are still in use today. For these reasons, the wide adoption of the ES6 specification is expected to be a slow process.

Microsoft spent two years developing TypeScript with the goal of resolving the maintainability and scalability problems of JavaScript and publicly announced it in October 2012:

> *"We designed TypeScript to meet the needs of the JavaScript programming teams that build and maintain large JavaScript programs. TypeScript helps programming teams to define interfaces between software components and to gain insight into the behavior of existing JavaScript libraries. TypeScript also enables teams to reduce naming conflicts by organizing their code into dynamically loadable modules. Typescript's optional type system enables JavaScript programmers to use highly-productive development tools and practices: static checking, symbol-based navigation, statement completion, and code re-factoring."*

> *- TypeScript Language Specification 1.0*

Some developers with years of experience in the field find it challenging to define what is a large-scale JavaScript application. When referring to this term, we will avoid taking into account the number of lines of code in the application. It is much better to consider the number of modules, dependencies between modules as measures of the application's scale. We will define large-scale applications as non-trivial applications that require significant developer effort to be maintained.

Learning TypeScript introduces many of the TypeScript features in a simple and easy-to-understand format. This book will teach you everything you need to know in order to implement large-scale JavaScript applications using TypeScript. Not only does it teach TypeScript's core features, which are essential to implement a web application, but it also explores the power of some tools, design principles, best practices, and it also demonstrates how to apply them in a real-life application.

What this book covers

Chapter 1, Introducing TypeScript, introduces the core features of TypeScript, including the optional static type notation system, operators, functions, interfaces, and modules. The chapter also demonstrates how to apply these features in a real-life example.

Chapter 2, Automating Your Development Workflow, introduces some automation tools, such as Gulp and Karma, to maximize your productivity as a developer. This chapter also introduces some tools that facilitate the usage of third-party libraries in the development of TypeScript applications.

Chapter 3, Working with Functions, provides an in-depth look at the functions in TypeScript. This chapter also teaches you everything you need to know about asynchronous programming in order to become a proficient TypeScript developer.

Chapter 4, Object-Oriented Programming with TypeScript, provides an in-depth look at object-oriented programming in TypeScript, including classes, interfaces, and modules and encourages adherence to good practices (SOLID principles). It also covers features such as inheritance, mixings, and generics, which facilitate the reusability of our code.

Chapter 5, Runtime, helps you understand how the runtime works. Understanding how the runtime works can help us identify potential performance issues and allow us to be much more effective as TypeScript developers.

Chapter 6, Application Performance, provides the necessary knowledge to make effective use of the available resources of a system. This chapter teaches you how to test the performance of a TypeScript web application and how to automate some common tasks in the performance optimization process of a TypeScript application.

Chapter 7, Application Testing, demonstrates how to use the behavior-driven development methodology together with the leading TypeScript testing tools to create bug-free applications. In this chapter, you will learn how to write TypeScript unit tests with Karma, Mocha, Chai, and Sinon.JS, how to create end-to-end tests using Nightwatch.js, and how to generate test coverage reports using Istanbul.

Chapter 8, Decorators, provides an in-depth look at decorators, including class, property, parameter, and method decorators. This chapter also includes an introduction to the reflection metadata API.

Chapter 9, Application Architecture, demonstrates some of the core architecture principles of a modern web application. The chapter introduces the concept of the single-page web application and its common components and features (models, views, controllers, routers, templates, and so on). This chapter will teach you everything you need to know in order to understand the majority of single-page web application frameworks by implementing a real-life single-page web application framework from scratch.

Chapter 10, Putting Everything Together, demonstrates how to apply the majority of the concepts exposed in this book by implementing a real-life single-page web application using TypeScript.

What you need for this book

The examples in this book are written using TypeScript 1.5. You will need the TypeScript compiler and a text editor. This book explains how to use Atom, but it is also possible to use other editors, such as Visual Studio 2015, Visual Studio Code, or Sublime Text.

You also need an Internet connection to download the required references and online packages and libraries, such as jQuery, Mocha, and Gulp. Depending on your operating system, you will need a user account with administrative privileges in order to install some of the tools used in this book.

Chapter 2, Automating Your Development Workflow, describes the setup of a development environment.

Who this book is for

If you are an intermediate-level JavaScript developer aiming to learn TypeScript to build beautiful web applications, then this book is for you. No prior knowledge of TypeScript is required but a basic understanding of jQuery is expected.

The book introduces TypeScript from basic to advanced language constructs and object-oriented techniques for getting the most out of the TypeScript language and compiler. This book will show you how to incorporate strong typing, object-oriented principles, design patterns, and the best practices for managing the complexity of large-scale JavaScript applications with ease.

Conventions

In this book, you will find a number of text styles that distinguish between different kinds of information. Here are some examples of these styles and an explanation of their meaning.

Code words in text, database table names, folder names, filenames, file extensions, pathnames, dummy URLs, user input, and Twitter handles are shown as follows: "We can include other contexts through the use of the `include` directive."

A block of code is set as follows:

```
class Greeter {
    greeting: string;
    constructor(message: string) {
        this.greeting = message;
    }
    greet() {
        return "Hello, " + this.greeting;
    }
}
```

When we wish to draw your attention to a particular part of a code block, the relevant lines or items are set in bold:

```
function MathHelper() { /* ... */ }

// class method
MathHelper.areaOfCircle = function(radius) {
  return radius * radius * this.PI;
}

// class property
MathHelper.PI = 3.14159265359;
```

Any command-line input or output is written as follows:

```
git clone https://github.com/user-name/repository-name.git
```

New terms and **important words** are shown in bold. Words that you see on the screen, for example, in menus or dialog boxes, appear in the text like this: "In this tab, we can select **Create JavaScript CPU Profile** and then click on the **Start** button to start recording the CPU usage."

> Warnings or important notes appear in a box like this.

> Tips and tricks appear like this.

Reader feedback

Feedback from our readers is always welcome. Let us know what you think about this book—what you liked or disliked. Reader feedback is important for us as it helps us develop titles that you will really get the most out of.

To send us general feedback, simply e-mail feedback@packtpub.com, and mention the book's title in the subject of your message.

If there is a topic that you have expertise in and you are interested in either writing or contributing to a book, see our author guide at www.packtpub.com/authors.

Customer support

Now that you are the proud owner of a Packt book, we have a number of things to help you to get the most from your purchase.

Downloading the example code

You can download the example code files from your account at http://www.packtpub.com for all the Packt Publishing books you have purchased. If you purchased this book elsewhere, you can visit http://www.packtpub.com/support and register to have the files e-mailed directly to you.

Errata

Although we have taken every care to ensure the accuracy of our content, mistakes do happen. If you find a mistake in one of our books—maybe a mistake in the text or the code—we would be grateful if you could report this to us. By doing so, you can save other readers from frustration and help us improve subsequent versions of this book. If you find any errata, please report them by visiting http://www.packtpub.com/submit-errata, selecting your book, clicking on the **Errata Submission Form** link, and entering the details of your errata. Once your errata are verified, your submission will be accepted and the errata will be uploaded to our website or added to any list of existing errata under the Errata section of that title.

To view the previously submitted errata, go to https://www.packtpub.com/books/content/support and enter the name of the book in the search field. The required information will appear under the **Errata** section.

Piracy

Piracy of copyrighted material on the Internet is an ongoing problem across all media. At Packt, we take the protection of our copyright and licenses very seriously. If you come across any illegal copies of our works in any form on the Internet, please provide us with the location address or website name immediately so that we can pursue a remedy.

Please contact us at copyright@packtpub.com with a link to the suspected pirated material.

We appreciate your help in protecting our authors and our ability to bring you valuable content.

Questions

If you have a problem with any aspect of this book, you can contact us at questions@packtpub.com, and we will do our best to address the problem.

1
Introducing TypeScript

This book focuses on TypeScript's object-oriented nature and how it can help you to write better code. Before diving into the object-oriented programing features of TypeScript, this chapter will give you an overview of the history behind TypeScript and introduce you to some of the basics.

In this chapter, you will learn about the following concepts:

- The TypeScript architecture
- Type annotations
- Variables and primitive data types
- Operators
- Flow control statements
- Functions
- Classes
- Interfaces
- Modules

The TypeScript architecture

In this section, we will focus on the TypeScript's internal architecture and its original design goals.

Design goals

In the following points, you will find the main design goals and architectural decisions that shaped the way the TypeScript programming language looks like today:

- Statically identify JavaScript constructs that are likely to be errors. The engineers at Microsoft decided that the best way to identify and prevent potential runtime issues was to create a strongly typed programming language and perform static type checking at compilation time. The engineers also designed a language services layer to provide developers with better tools.

- High compatibility with the existing JavaScript code. TypeScript is a superset of JavaScript; this means that any valid JavaScript program is also a valid TypeScript program (with a few small exceptions).

- Provide a structuring mechanism for larger pieces of code. TypeScript adds class-based object orientation, interfaces, and modules. These features will help us structure our code in a much better way. We will also reduce potential integration issues within our development team and our code will become more maintainable and scalable by adhering to the best object-oriented principles and practices.

- Impose no runtime overhead on emitted programs. It is common to differentiate between design time and execution time when working with TypeScript. We use the term *design time code* to refer to the TypeScript code that we write while designing an application; we use the terms *execution time code* or *runtime code* to refer to the JavaScript code that is executed after compiling some TypeScript code.

  TypeScript adds features to JavaScript but those features are only available at design time. For example, we can declare interfaces in TypeScript but since JavaScript doesn't support interfaces, the TypeScript compiler will not declare or try to emulate this feature in the output JavaScript code.

  The Microsoft engineers provided the TypeScript compiler with mechanisms such as code transformations (converting TypeScript features into plain JavaScript implementations) and type erasure (removing static type notation) to generate really clean JavaScript code. Type erasure removes not only the type annotations but also all the TypeScript exclusive language features such as interfaces.

Furthermore, the generated code is highly compatible with web browsers as it targets the ECMAScript 3 specification by default but it also supports ECMAScript 5 and ECMAScript 6. In general, we can use the TypeScript features when compiling to any of the available compilation targets, but there are some features that will require ECMAScript 5 or higher as the compilation target.

- Align with the current and future ECMAScript proposals. TypeScript is not just compatible with the existing JavaScript code; it will also potentially be compatible with future versions of JavaScript. The majority of Typescript's additional features are based on the future ECMAScript proposals; this means many TypeScript files will eventually become valid JavaScript files.

- Be a cross-platform development tool. Microsoft released TypeScript under the open source Apache license and it can be installed and executed in all major operating systems.

TypeScript components

The TypeScript language is internally divided into three main layers. Each of these layers is, in turn, divided into sublayers or components. In the following diagram, we can see the three layers (green, blue, and orange) and each of their internal components (boxes):

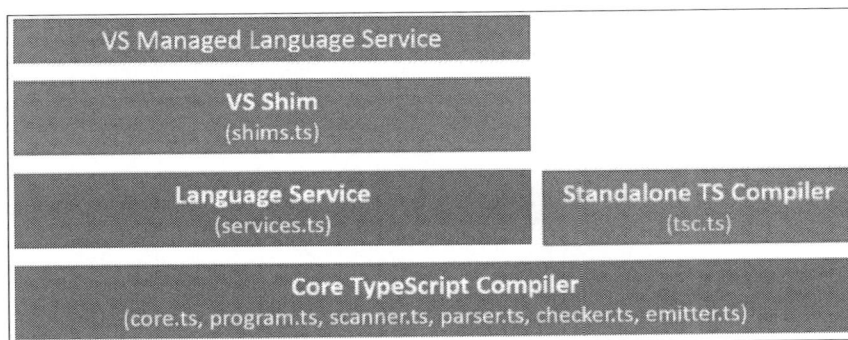

In the preceding diagram, the acronym **VS** refers to Microsoft's Visual Studio, which is the official integrated development environment for all the Microsoft products (including TypeScript). We will learn more about this and the other IDEs in the next chapter.

Each of these main layers has a different purpose:

- The language: It features the TypeScript language elements.
- The compiler: It performs the parsing, type checking, and transformation of your TypeScript code to JavaScript code.
- The language services: It generates information that helps editors and other tools provide better assistance features such as IntelliSense or automated refactoring.
- IDE integration: In order to take advantages of the TypeScript features, some integration work is required to be done by the developers of the IDEs. TypeScript was designed to facilitate the development of tools that help to increase the productivity of JavaScript developers. As a result of these efforts, integrating TypeScript with an IDE is not a complicated task. A proof of this is that the most popular IDEs these days include a good TypeScript support.

> In other books and online resources, you may find references to the term transpiler instead of compiler. A **transpiler** is a type of compiler that takes the source code of a programming language as its input and outputs the source code into another programming language with more or less the same level of abstraction.

We don't need to go into any more detail as understanding how the TypeScript compiler works is out of the scope of this book; however, if you wish to learn more about this topic, refer to the TypeScript language specification, which can be found online at `http://www.typescriptlang.org/`.

TypeScript language features

Now that you have learned about the purpose of TypeScript, it's time to get our hands dirty and start writing some code.

Before you can start learning how to use some of the basic TypeScript building blocks, you will need to set up your development environment. The easiest and fastest way to start writing some TypeScript code is to use the online editor available on the official TypeScript website at `http://www.typescriptlang.org/Playground`, as you can see in the following screenshot:

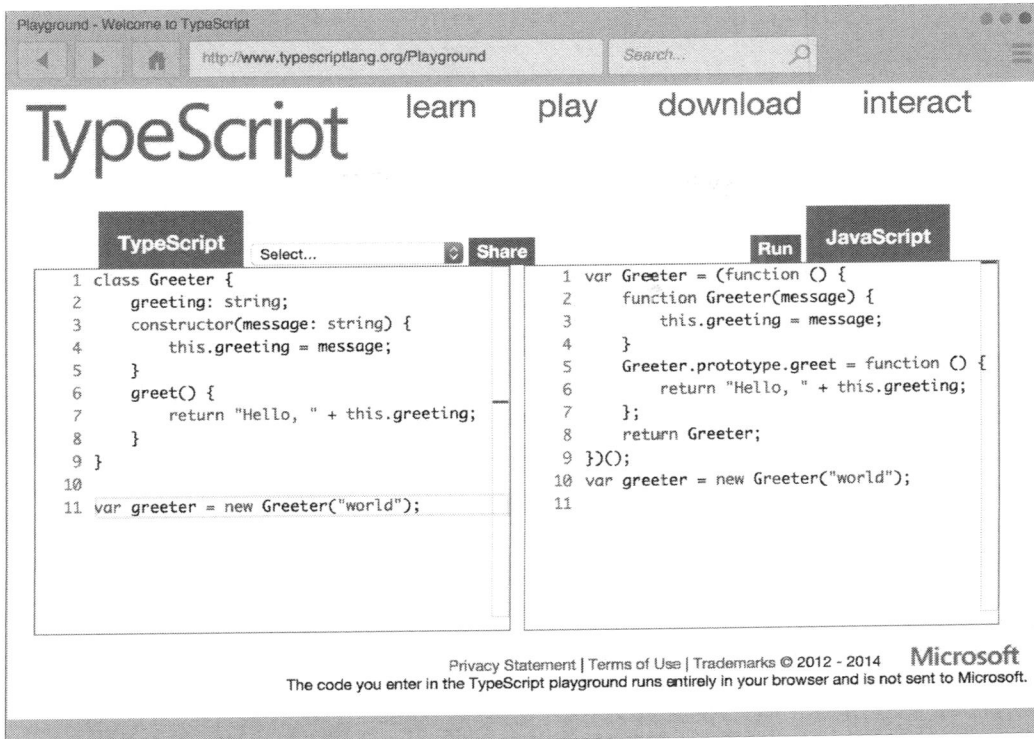

In the preceding screenshot, you will be able to use the text editor on the left-hand side to write your TypeScript code. The code is automatically compiled to JavaScript and the output code will be inserted in the text editor located on the right-hand side of the screen. If your TypeScript code is invalid, the JavaScript code on the right-hand side will not be refreshed.

Alternatively, if you prefer to be able to work offline, you can download and install the TypeScript compiler. If you work with Visual Studio, you can download the official TypeScript extension (version 1.5 beta) from `https://visualstudiogallery.msdn.microsoft.com/107f89a0-a542-4264-b0a9-eb91037cf7af`. If you are working with Visual Studio 2015, you don't need to install the extension as Visual Studio 2015 includes TypeScript support by default.

If you use a different code editor or you use the OS X or Linux operating systems, you can download an npm module instead. Don't worry if you are not familiar with npm. For now, you just need to know that it stands for Node Package Manager and is the default Node.js package manager.

> There are TypeScript plugins available for many popular editors such as Sublime `https://github.com/Microsoft/TypeScript-Sublime-Plugin` and Atom `https://atom.io/packages/atom-typescript`.

In order to be able to use npm, you will need to first install Node.js in your development environment. You will be able to find the Node.js installation files on the official website at `https://nodejs.org/`.

Once you have installed Node.js in your development environment, you will be able to run the following command in a console or terminal:

```
npm install -g typescript
```

OS X users need to use the `sudo` command when installing global (`-g`) npm packages. The `sudo` command will prompt for user credentials and install the package using administrative privileges:

```
sudo npm install -g typescript
```

Create a new file named `test.ts` and add the following code to it:

```
var t : number = 1;
```

Save the file into a directory of your choice and once you have saved the file open the console, select the directory where you saved the file, and execute the following command:

```
tsc test.ts
```

The tsc command is a console interface for the TypeScript compiler. This command allows you to compile your TypeScript files into JavaScript files. The compiler features many options that will be explored in the upcoming chapters of this book.

In the preceding example, we used the `tsc` command to transform the `test.ts` file into a JavaScript file.

If everything goes right, you will find a file named `test.js` in the same directory in which the `test.ts` file was located. Now, you know how to compile your TypeScript code into JavaScript and we can start learning about the TypeScript features.

> You will be able to learn more about editors and other tools in *Chapter 2, Automating Your Development Workflow*.

Types

As we have already learned, TypeScript is a typed superset of JavaScript. TypeScript added optional static type annotations to JavaScript in order to transform it into a strongly typed programming language. The optional static type annotations are used as constraints on program entities such as functions, variables, and properties so that compilers and development tools can offer better verification and assistance (such as IntelliSense) during software development.

Strong typing allows the programmer to express his intentions in his code, both to himself and to others in the development team.

Typescript's type analysis occurs entirely at compile time and adds no runtime overhead to program execution.

Optional static type notation

The TypeScript language service is really good at inferring types, but there are certain cases where it is not able to automatically detect the type of an object or variable. For these cases, TypeScript allows us to explicitly declare the type of a variable. The language element that allows us to declare the type of a variable is known as **optional static type notation**. For a variable, the type notation comes after the variable name and is preceded by a colon:

```
var counter;                // unknown (any) type
var counter = 0;            // number (inferred)
var counter : number;       // number
var counter : number = 0;   // number
```

As you can see, the type of the variable is declared after the name, this style of type notation is based on type theory and helps to reinforce the idea of types being optional. When no type annotations are available, TypeScript will try to guess the type of the variable by examining the assigned values. For example, in the second line in the preceding code snippet, we can see that the variable counter has been identified as a numeric variable because the numeric value 0 was assigned as its value. This process in which types are automatically detected is known as **Type inference**, when a type cannot be inferred the especial type any is used as the type of the variable.

Variables, basic types, and operators

The basic types are the Boolean, number, string, array, void types, and all user defined Enum types. All types in TypeScript are subtypes of a single top type called the **Any type**. The `any` keyword references this type. Let's take a look at each of these primitive types:

Data Type	Description
Boolean	Whereas the string and number data types can have a virtually unlimited number of different values, the Boolean data type can only have two. They are the literals `true` and `false`. A Boolean value is a truth value; it specifies whether the condition is true or not. `var isDone: boolean = false;`
Number	As in JavaScript, all numbers in TypeScript are floating point values. These floating-point numbers get the type `number`. `var height: number = 6;`

String	You use the string data type to represent text in TypeScript. You include string literals in your scripts by enclosing them in single or double quotation marks. Double quotation marks can be contained in strings surrounded by single quotation marks, and single quotation marks can be contained in strings surrounded by double quotation marks.
	
	`var name: string = "bob";`
	`name = 'smith';`

Array	TypeScript, like JavaScript, allows you to work with arrays of values. Array types can be written in one of the two ways. In the first, you use the type of the elements followed by `[]` to denote an array of that element type:
	
	`var list:number[] = [1, 2, 3];`
	The second way uses a generic array type, `Array`:
	
	`var list:Array<number> = [1, 2, 3];`

Enum	An enum is a way of giving more friendly names to sets of numeric values. By default, enums begin numbering their members starting at 0, but you can change this by manually setting the value of one to its members.
	
	`enum Color {Red, Green, Blue};`
	`var c: Color = Color.Green;`

Data Type	Description

Any	The any type is used to represent any JavaScript value. A value of the any type supports the same operations as a value in JavaScript and minimal static type checking is performed for operations on any values.
	
	```\nvar notSure: any = 4;\nnotSure = "maybe a string instead";\nnotSure = false; // okay, definitely a boolean\n```
	
	The any type is a powerful way to work with existing JavaScript, allowing you to gradually opt in and opt out of type checking during compilation. The any type is also handy if you know some part of the type, but perhaps not all of it. For example, you may have an array but the array has a mix of different types:
	
	```\nvar list:any[] = [1, true, "free"];\nlist[1] = 100;\n```

Void	The opposite in some ways to any is void, the absence of having any type at all. You will see this as the return type of functions that do not return a value. ```\nfunction warnUser(): void {\n alert("This is my warning message");\n}\n```

JavaScript's primitive types also include undefined and null. In JavaScript, undefined is a property in the global scope that is assigned as a value to variables that have been declared but have not yet been initialized. The value null is a literal (not a property of the global object). It can be assigned to a variable as a representation of no value.

```
var TestVar;            // variable is declared but not initialized
alert(TestVar);         // shows undefined
alert(typeof TestVar);  // shows undefined

var TestVar = null;     // variable is declared and value null is
assigned as value
alert(TestVar);         // shows null
alert(typeof TestVar);  // shows object
```

In TypeScript, we will not be able to use null or undefined as types:

```
var TestVar : null;      // Error, Type expected
var TestVar : undefined; // Error, cannot find name undefined
```

Since null or undefined cannot be used as types, both the variable declarations in the preceding code snippet are invalid.

Var, let, and const

When we declare a variable in TypeScript, we can use the var, let, or const keywords:

```
var mynum : number = 1;
let isValid : boolean = true;
const apiKey : string = "0E5CE8BD-6341-4CC2-904D-C4A94ACD276E";
```

Variables declared with var are scoped to the nearest function block (or global, if outside a function block).

Variables declared with let are scoped to the nearest enclosing block (or global if outside any block), which can be smaller than a function block.

The const keyword creates a constant that can be global or local to the block in which it is declared. This means that constants are block scoped. You will learn more about scopes in *Chapter 5, Runtime*.

> The let and const keywords have been available since the release of TypeScript 1.4 but only when the compilation target is ECMAScript 6. However, they will also work when targeting ECMAScript 3 and ECMAScript 5 once TypeScript 1.5 is released.

Union types

TypeScript allows you to declare union types:

```
var path : string[]|string;
path = '/temp/log.xml';
path = ['/temp/log.xml', '/temp/errors.xml'];
path = 1; // Error
```

Union types are used to declare a variable that is able to store a value of two or more types. In the preceding example, we have declared a variable named path that can contain a single path (string), or a collection of paths (array of string). In the example, we have also set the value of the variable. We assigned a string and an array of strings without errors; however, when we attempted to assign a numeric value, we got a compilation error because the union type didn't declare a number as one of the valid types of the variable.

Type guards

We can examine the type of an expression at runtime by using the `typeof` or `instanceof` operators. The TypeScript language service looks for these operators and will change type inference accordingly when used in an `if` block:

```
var x: any = { /* ... */ };
if(typeof x === 'string') {
  console.log(x.splice(3, 1)); // Error, 'splice' does not exist
on 'string'
}
// x is still any
x.foo(); // OK
```

In the preceding code snippet, we have declared an x variable of type `any`. Later, we check the type of x at runtime by using the `typeof` operator. If the type of x results to be string, we will try to invoke the method splice, which is supposed to a member of the x variable. The TypeScript language service is able to understand the usage of `typeof` in a conditional statement. TypeScript will automatically assume that x must be a string and let us know that the `splice` method does not exist on the type string. This feature is known as **type guards**.

Type aliases

TypeScript allows us to declare type aliases by using the `type` keyword:

```
type PrimitiveArray = Array<string|number|boolean>;
type MyNumber = number;
type NgScope = ng.IScope;
type Callback = () => void;
```

Type aliases are exactly the same as their original types; they are simply alternative names. Type aliases can help us to make our code more readable but it can also lead to some problems.

If you work as part of a large team, the indiscriminate creation of aliases can lead to maintainability problems. In the book, *Maintainable JavaScript, Nicholas C. Zakas*, the author recommends to avoid modifying objects you don't own. Nicholas was talking about adding, removing, or overriding methods in objects that have not been declared by you (DOM objects, BOM objects, primitive types, and third-party libraries) but we can apply this rule to the usage of aliases as well.

Ambient declarations

Ambient declaration allows you to create a variable in your TypeScript code that will not be translated into JavaScript at compilation time. This feature was designed to facilitate integration with the existing JavaScript code, the **DOM (Document Object Model)**, and **BOM (Browser Object Model)**. Let's take a look at an example:

```
customConsole.log("A log entry!");   // error
```

If you try to call the member log of an object named customConsole, TypeScript will let us know that the customConsole object has not been declared:

```
// Cannot find name 'customConsole'
```

This is not a surprise. However, sometimes we want to invoke an object that has not been defined, for example, the console or window objects.

```
console.log("Log Entry!");
var host = window.location.hostname;
```

When we access DOM or BOM objects, we don't get an error because these objects have already been declared in a special TypeScript file known as **declaration files**. You can use the declare operator to create an ambient declaration.

In the following code snippet, we will declare an interface that is implemented by the customConsole object. We then use the declare operator to add the customConsole object to the scope:

```
interface ICustomConsole {
    log(arg : string) : void;
}
declare var customConsole : ICustomConsole;
```

> Interfaces are explained in greater detail later in the chapter.

We can then use the customConsole object without compilation errors:

```
customConsole.log("A log entry!"); // ok
```

TypeScript includes, by default, a file named lib.d.ts that provides interface declarations for the built-in JavaScript library as well as the DOM.

Declaration files use the file extension .d.ts and are used to increase the TypeScript compatibility with third-party libraries and run-time environments such as Node.js or a web browser.

[![notes] We will learn how to work with declaration files in *Chapter 2, Automating Your Development Workflow*.]

Arithmetic operators

There following arithmetic operators are supported by the TypeScript programming language. In order to understand the examples, you must assume that variable A holds 10 and variable B holds 20.

Operator	Description	Example
+	This adds two operands	A + B will give 30
-	This subtracts the second operand from the first	A - B will give -10
*	This multiplies both the operands	A * B will give 200
/	This divides the numerator by the denominator	B / A will give 2
%	This is the modulus operator and remainder after an integer division	B % A will give 0
++	This is the increment operator that increases the integer value by 1	A++ will give 11
--	This is the decrement operator that decreases the integer value by 1	A-- will give 9

Comparison operators

The following comparison operators are supported by the TypeScript language. In order to understand the examples, you must assume that variable A holds 10 and variable B holds 20.

Operator	Description	Example
==	This checks whether the values of two operands are equal or not. If yes, then the condition becomes true.	(A == B) is false. A == "10" is true.
===	This checks whether the value and type of two operands are equal or not. If yes, then the condition becomes true.	A === B is false. A === "10" is false.
!=	This checks whether the values of two operands are equal or not. If the values are not equal, then the condition becomes true.	(A != B) is true.

Operator	Description	Example
>	This checks whether the value of the left operand is greater than the value of the right operand; if yes, then the condition becomes true.	(A > B) is false.
<	This checks whether the value of the left operand is less than the value of the right operand; if yes, then the condition becomes true.	(A < B) is true.
>=	This checks whether the value of the left operand is greater than or equal to the value of the right operand; if yes, then the condition becomes true.	(A >= B) is false.
<=	This checks whether the value of the left operand is less than or equal to the value of the right operand; if yes, then the condition becomes true.	(A <= B) is true.

Logical operators

The following logical operators are supported by the TypeScript language. In order to understand the examples, you must assume that variable A holds 10 and variable B holds 20.

Operator	Description	Example
&&	This is called the logical AND operator. If both the operands are nonzero, then the condition becomes true.	(A && B) is true.
||	This is called logical OR operator. If any of the two operands are nonzero, then the condition becomes true.	(A || B) is true.
!	This is called the logical NOT operator. It is used to reverse the logical state of its operand. If a condition is true, then the logical NOT operator will make it false.	!(A && B) is false.

Bitwise operators

The following bitwise operators are supported by the TypeScript language. In order to understand the examples, you must assume that variable A holds 2 and variable B holds 3.

Operator	Description	Example
&	This is called the Bitwise AND operator. It performs a Boolean AND operation on each bit of its integer arguments.	(A & B) is 2
|	This is called the Bitwise OR operator. It performs a Boolean OR operation on each bit of its integer arguments.	(A | B) is 3.

Operator	Description	Example
^	This is called the Bitwise XOR operator. It performs a Boolean exclusive OR operation on each bit of its integer arguments. Exclusive OR means that either operand one is true or operand two is true, but not both.	(A ^ B) is 1.
~	This is called the Bitwise NOT operator. It is a unary operator and operates by reversing all bits in the operand.	(~B) is -4
<<	This is called the Bitwise Shift Left operator. It moves all bits in its first operand to the left by the number of places specified in the second operand. New bits are filled with zeros. Shifting a value left by one position is equivalent to multiplying by 2, shifting two positions is equivalent to multiplying by 4, and so on.	(A << 1) is 4
>>	This is called the Bitwise Shift Right with sign operator. It moves all bits in its first operand to the right by the number of places specified in the second operand.	(A >> 1) is 1
>>>	This is called the Bitwise Shift Right with zero operators. This operator is just like the >> operator, except that the bits shifted in on the left are always zero,	(A >>> 1) is 1

One of the main reasons to use bitwise operators in languages such as C++, Java, or C# is that they're extremely fast. However, bitwise operators are often considered not that efficient in TypeScript and JavaScript. Bitwise operators are less efficient in JavaScript because it is necessary to cast from floating point representation (how JavaScript stores all of its numbers) to a 32-bit integer to perform the bit manipulation and back.

Assignment operators

The following assignment operators are supported by the TypeScript language.

Operator	Description	Example
=	This is a simple assignment operator that assigns values from the right-side operands to the left-side operand.	C = A + B will assign the value of A + B into C
+=	This adds the AND assignment operator. It adds the right operand to the left operand and assigns the result to the left operand.	C += A is equivalent to C = C + A

Operator	Description	Example
-=	This subtracts the AND assignment operator. It subtracts the right operand from the left operand and assigns the result to the left operand.	C -= A is equivalent to C = C - A
*=	This multiplies the AND assignment operator. It multiplies the right operand with the left operand and assigns the result to the left operand.	C *= A is equivalent to C = C * A
/=	This divides the AND assignment operator. It divides the left operand with the right operand and assigns the result to the left operand.	C /= A is equivalent to C = C / A
%=	This is the modulus AND assignment operator. It takes the modulus using two operands and assigns the result to the left operand.	C %= A is equivalent to C = C % A

Flow control statements

This section describes the decision-making statements, the looping statements, and the branching statements supported by the TypeScript programming language.

The single-selection structure (if)

The following code snippet declares a variable of type Boolean and name isValid. Then, an if statement will check whether the value of isValid is equal to true. If the statement turns out to be true, the Is valid! message will be displayed on the screen.

```
var isValid : boolean = true;

if(isValid) {
  alert("is valid!");
}
```

The double-selection structure (if...else)

The following code snippet declares a variable of type Boolean and name isValid. Then, an if statement will check whether the value of isValid is equal to true. If the statement turns out to be true, the message Is valid! will be displayed on the screen. On the other side, if the statement turns out to be false, the message Is NOT valid! will be displayed on the screen.

```
var isValid : boolean = true;

if(isValid) {
  alert("Is valid!");
```

```
}
else {
  alert("Is NOT valid!");
}
```

The inline ternary operator (?)

The inline ternary operator is just an alternative way of declaring a double-selection structure.

```
var isValid : boolean = true;
var message = isValid ? "Is valid!" : "Is NOT valid!";
alert(message);
```

The preceding code snippet declares a variable of type Boolean and name `isValid`. Then it checks whether the variable or expression on the left-hand side of the operator `?` is equal to true.

If the statement turns out to be true, the expression on the left-hand side of the character will be executed and the message `Is valid!` will be assigned to the message variable.

On the other hand, if the statement turns out to be false, the expression on the right-hand side of the operator will be executed and the message, `Is NOT valid!` will be assigned to the message variable.

Finally, the value of the message variable is displayed on the screen.

The multiple-selection structure (switch)

The `switch` statement evaluates an expression, matches the expression's value to a case clause, and executes statements associated with that case. A `switch` statement and enumerations are often used together to improve the readability of the code.

In the following example, we will declare a function that takes an enumeration `AlertLevel`. Inside the function, we will generate an array of strings to store e-mail addresses and execute a `switch` structure. Each of the options of the enumeration is a case in the `switch` structure:

```
enum AlertLevel{
  info,
  warning,
  error
}
```

```
function getAlertSubscribers(level : AlertLevel){
  var emails = new Array<string>();
  switch(level){
    case AlertLevel.info:
        emails.push("cst@domain.com");
        break;
    case AlertLevel.warning:
        emails.push("development@domain.com");
        emails.push("sysadmin@domain.com");
        break;
    case AlertLevel.error:
        emails.push("development@domain.com");
        emails.push("sysadmin@domain.com");
        emails.push("management@domain.com");
        break;
    default:
        throw new Error("Invalid argument!");
  }
  return emails;
}

getAlertSubscribers(AlertLevel.info); // ["cst@domain.com"]
getAlertSubscribers(AlertLevel.warning); //
["development@domain.com", "sysadmin@domain.com"]
```

The value of the level variable is tested against all the cases in the switch. If the variable matches one of the cases, the statement associated with that case is executed. Once the case statement has been executed, the variable is tested against the next case.

Once the execution of the statement associated to a matching case is finalized, the next case will be evaluated. If the break keyword is present, the program will not continue the execution of the following case statement.

If no matching case clause is found, the program looks for the optional default clause, and if found, it transfers control to that clause and executes the associated statements.

If no default clause is found, the program continues execution at the statement following the end of switch. By convention, the default clause is the last clause, but it does not have to be so.

The expression is tested at the top of the loop (while)

The `while` expression is used to repeat an operation while a certain requirement is satisfied. For example, the following code snippet, declares a numeric variable `i`. If the requirement (the value of `i` is less than 5) is satisfied, an operation takes place (increase the value of `i` by 1 and display its value in the browser console). Once the operation has completed, the accomplishment of the requirement will be checked again.

```
var i : number = 0;
while (i < 5) {
  i += 1;
  console.log(i);
}
```

In a `while` expression, the operation will take place only if the requirement is satisfied.

The expression is tested at the bottom of the loop (do...while)

The `do-while` expression is used to repeat an operation until a certain requirement is not satisfied. For example, the following code snippet declares a numeric variable `i` and repeats an operation (increase the value of `i` by 1 and display its value in the browser console) for as long as the requirement (the value of `i` is less than 5) is satisfied.

```
var i : number = 0;
do {
  i += 1;
  console.log(i);
} while (i < 5);
```

Unlike the `while` loop, the `do-while` expression will execute at least once regardless of the requirement value as the operation will take place before checking if a certain requirement is satisfied or not.

Iterate on each object's properties (for...in)

The `for-in` statement by itself is not a *bad practice*; however, it can be misused, for example, to iterate over arrays or array-like objects. The purpose of the `for-in` statement is to enumerate over object properties.

```
var obj : any = { a:1, b:2, c:3 };
for (var key in obj) {
  console.log(key + " = " + obj[key]);
}

// Output:
// "a = 1"
// "b = 2"
// "c = 3"
```

The following code snippet will go up in the prototype chain, also enumerating the inherited properties. The `for-in` statement iterates the entire prototype chain, also enumerating the inherited properties. When you want to enumerate only the object's own properties (the ones that aren't inherited), you can use the `hasOwnProperty` method:

```
for (var key in obj) {
  if (obj.hasOwnProperty(prop)) {
    // prop is not inherited
  }
}
```

Counter controlled repetition (for)

The `for` statement creates a loop that consists of three optional expressions, enclosed in parentheses and separated by semicolons, followed by a statement or a set of statements executed in the loop.

```
for (var i: number = 0; i < 9; i++) {
  console.log(i);
}
```

The preceding code snippet contains a `for` statement, it starts by declaring the variable `i` and initializing it to `0`. It checks whether `i` is less than `9`, performs the two succeeding statements, and increments `i` by 1 after each pass through the loop.

Functions

Just as in JavaScript, TypeScript functions can be created either as a named function or as an anonymous function. This allows us to choose the most appropriate approach for an application, whether we are building a list of functions in an API or a one-off function to hand over to another function.

```
// named function
function greet(name? : string) : string {
  if (name) {
    return "Hi! " + name;
  }
  else
  {
    return "Hi!";
  }
}

// anonymous function
var greet = function(name? : string) : string {
  if (name) {
    return "Hi! " + name;
  }
  else
  {
    return "Hi!";
  }
}
```

As we can see in the preceding code snippet, in TypeScript we can add types to each of the parameters and then to the function itself to add a return type. TypeScript can infer the return type by looking at the return statements, so we can also optionally leave this off in many cases.

There is an alternative function syntax, which uses the arrow (=>) operator after the function's return type and skips the usage of the function keyword.

```
var greet = (name : string) : string => {
    if (name) {
      return "Hi! " + name;
    }
    else
    {
      return "Hi! my name is " + this.fullname;
    }
};
```

The functions declared using this syntax are commonly known as **arrow functions**. Let's return to the previous example in which we were assigning an anonymous function to the `greet` variable. We can now add the type annotations to the `greet` variable to match the anonymous function signature.

```
var greet : (name : string) => string = function(name : string) :
string {
    if(name){
      return "Hi! " + name;
    }
    else
    {
      return "Hi!";
    }
};
```

> Keep in mind that the arrow function (=>) syntax changes the way the `this` operator works when working with classes. We will learn more about this in the upcoming chapters.

Now you know how to add type annotations to force a variable to be a function with a specific signature. The usage of this kind of annotations is really common when we use a call back (functions used as an argument of another function).

```
function sume(a : number, b : number, callback : (result:number)
=> void){
  callback(a+b);
}
```

In the preceding example, we are declaring a function named `sume` that takes two numbers and a `callback` as a function. The type annotations will force the callback to return void and take a number as its only argument.

> We will focus on functions in *Chapter 3, Working with Functions*.

Classes

ECMAScript 6, the next version of JavaScript, adds class-based object orientation to JavaScript and, since TypeScript is based on ES6, developers are allowed to use class-based object orientation today, and compile them down to JavaScript that works across all major browsers and platforms, without having to wait for the next version of JavaScript.

Let's take a look at a simple TypeScript class definition example:

```typescript
class Character {
  fullname : string;
  constructor(firstname : string, lastname : string) {
    this.fullname = firstname + " " + lastname;
  }
  greet(name? : string) {
    if(name)
    {
      return "Hi! " + name + "! my name is " + this.fullname;
    }
    else
    {
      return "Hi! my name is " + this.fullname;
    }
  }
}

var spark = new Character("Jacob","Keyes");
var msg = spark.greet();
alert(msg); // "Hi! my name is Jacob Keyes"
var msg1 = spark.greet("Dr. Halsey");
alert(msg1); // "Hi! Dr. Halsey! my name is Jacob Keyes"
```

In the preceding example, we have declared a new class `Character`. This class has three members: a property called `fullname`, a `constructor`, and a method `greet`. When we declare a class in TypeScript, all the methods and properties are public by default.

You'll notice that when we refer to one of the members of the class (from within itself) we prepend the `this` operator. The `this` operator denotes that it's a member access. In the last lines, we construct an instance of the `Character` class using a `new` operator. This calls into the constructor we defined earlier, creating a new object with the `Character` shape, and running the constructor to initialize it.

TypeScript classes are compiled into JavaScript functions in order to achieve compatibility with ECMAScript 3 and ECMAScript 5.

> We will learn more about classes and other object-oriented programming concepts in *Chapter 4, Object-Oriented Programming with TypeScript.*

Interfaces

In TypeScript, we can use interfaces to enforce that a class follow the specification in a particular contract.

```
interface LoggerInterface{
  log(arg : any) : void;
}

class Logger implements LoggerInterface{
  log(arg){
    if(typeof console.log === "function"){
      console.log(arg);
    }
    else
    {
      alert(arg);
    }
  }
}
```

In the preceding example, we have defined an interface loggerInterface and a class Logger, which implements it. TypeScript will also allow you to use interfaces to declare the type of an object. This can help us to prevent many potential issues, especially when working with object literals:

```
interface UserInterface{
  name : string;
  password : string;
}

var user : UserInterface = {
  name : "",
  password : "" // error property password is missing
};
```

> We will learn more about interfaces and other object-oriented programming concepts in *Chapter 4, Object-Oriented Programming with TypeScript*.

Namespaces

Namespaces, also known as internal modules, are used to encapsulate features and objects that share a certain relationship. Namespaces will help you to organize your code in a much clearer way. To declare a namespace in TypeScript, you will use the `namespace` and `export` keywords.

```
namespace Geometry{
    interface VectorInterface {
        /* ... */
    }
    export interface Vector2dInterface {
        /* ... */
    }
    export interface Vector3dInterface {
        /* ... */
    }
    export class Vector2d implements VectorInterface,
    Vector2dInterface {
      /* ... */
    }
    export class Vector3d implements VectorInterface,
    Vector3dInterface {
      /* ... */
    }
}

var vector2dInstance : Geometry.Vector2dInterface = new
Geometry.Vector2d();
var vector3dInstance : Geometry.Vector3dInterface = new
Geometry.Vector3d();
```

In the preceding code snippet, we have declared a namespace that contains the classes `vector2d` and `vector3d` and the interfaces `VectorInterface`, `Vector2dInterface`, and `Vector3dInterface`. Note that the first interface is missing the keyword `export`. As a result, the interface `VectorInterface` will not be accessible from outside the namespace's scope.

> In *Chapter 4, Object-Oriented Programming with TypeScript*, we'll be covering namespaces (internal modules) and external modules and we'll discuss when each is appropriate and how to use them.

Putting everything together

Now that we have learned how to use the basic TypeScript building blocks individually, let's take a look at a final example in which we will use modules, classes, functions, and type annotations for each of these elements:

```typescript
module Geometry{
  export interface Vector2dInterface {
    toArray(callback : (x : number[]) => void) : void;
    length() : number;
    normalize();
  }
  export class Vector2d implements Vector2dInterface {
    private _x: number;
    private _y : number;
    constructor(x : number, y : number){
      this._x = x;
      this._y = y;
    }
    toArray(callback : (x : number[]) => void) : void{
      callback([this._x, this._y]);
    }
    length() : number{
      return Math.sqrt(this._x * this._x + this._y * this._y);
    }
    normalize(){
      var len = 1 / this.length();
      this._x *= len;
      this._y *= len;
    }
  }
}
```

The preceding example is just a small portion of a basic 3D engine written in JavaScript. In 3D engines, there are a lot of mathematical calculations involving matrices and vectors. As you can see, we have defined a module `Geometry` that will contain some entities; to keep the example simple, we have only added the class `Vector2d`. This class stores two coordinates (x and y) in 2d space and performs some operations on the coordinates. One of the most used operations on vectors is normalization, which is one of the methods in our `Vector2d` class.

3D engines are complex software solutions, and as a developer, you are much more likely to use a third-party 3D engine than create your own. For this reason, it is important to understand that TypeScript will not only help you to develop large-scale applications, but also to work with large-scale applications. In the following code snippet, we will use the module declared earlier to create a `Vector2d` instance:

```
var vector : Geometry.Vector2dInterface = new
Geometry.Vector2d(2,3);
vector.normalize();
vector.toArray(function(vectorAsArray : number[]){
  alert(' x :' + vectorAsArray[0] + ' y : '+ vectorAsArray[1]);
});
```

The type checking and IntelliSense features will help us create a `Vector2d` instance, normalize its value, and convert it into an array to finally show its value on screen with ease.

```
28  var vector : Geometry.Vector2dInterface = new Geometry.Vector2d(2,3);
29  vector.
30         ⊗ length (method) Geometry.Vector2dInterface.length(): number
           ⊗ normalize
           ⊗ toArray
```

Summary

In this chapter, you have learned about the purposes of TypeScript. You have also learned about some of the design decisions made by the TypeScript engineers at Microsoft.

Towards the end of this chapter, you learned a lot about the basic building blocks of a TypeScript application .You started to write some TypeScript code for the first time and you can now work with type annotations, variables and primitive data types, operators, flow control statements, functions, and classes.

In the next chapter, you will learn how to automate your development workflow.

2
Automating Your Development Workflow

After taking a first look at the main TypeScript language features, we will now learn how to use some tools to automate our development workflow. These tools will help us to reduce the amount of time that we usually spend on simple and repetitive tasks.

In this chapter, we will learn about the following topics:

- An overview of the development workflow
- Source control tools
- Package management tools
- Task runners
- Test runners
- Integration tools
- Scaffolding tools

A modern development workflow

Developing a web application with high quality standards has become a time-consuming activity. If we want to achieve a great user experience, we will need to ensure that our applications can run as smoothly as possible on many different web browsers, devices, Internet connection speeds, and screen resolutions. Furthermore, we will need to spend a lot of our time working on quality assurance and performance optimization tasks.

As developers, we should try to minimize the time spent on simple and repetitive tasks. This might sound familiar as we have been doing this for years. We started by writing build scripts (such as makefiles) or automated tests and today, in a modern web development workflow, we use many tools to try to automate as many tasks as we can. These tools can be categorized into the following groups:

- Source control tools
- Package management tools
- Task runners
- Test runners
- Continuous integration tools
- Scaffolding tools

Prerequisites

You are about to learn how to write a script, which will automate many tasks in your development workflow; however, before that, we need to install a few tools in our development environment.

Node.js

Node.js is a platform built on V8 (Google's open source JavaScript engine). Node.js allows us to run JavaScript outside a web browser. We can write backend and desktop applications using JavaScript with Node.js.

We are not going to write server-side JavaScript applications but we are going to need Node.js because many of the tools used in this chapter are Node.js applications.

If you didn't install Node.js in the previous chapter, you can visit `https://nodejs.org` to download the installer for your operating system.

Atom

Atom is an open source editor developed by the GitHub team. The open source community around this editor is really active and has developed many plugins and themes. You can download Atom from `https://atom.io/`.

Once you have completed the installation, open the editor and go to the preferences window. You should be able to find a section within the preferences window to manage packages and another to manage themes just like the ones that we can see in the following screenshot:

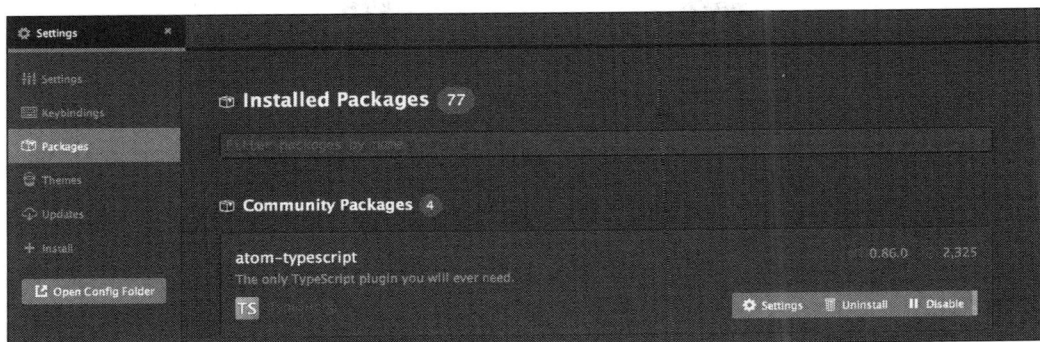

> The Atom user interface is slightly different from the other operating systems. Refer to the Atom documentation at `https://atom.io/docs` if you need additional help to manage packages and themes.

We need to search for the `atom-typescript` package in the package management section and install it. We can additionally visit the themes section and install a theme that makes us feel more comfortable with the editor.

> We will use Atom instead of Visual Studio because Atom is available for Linux, OS X, and Windows, so it will suit most readers.
>
> Unfortunately, we will not cover Visual Studio Code because it was announced when this book was about to be published. Visual Studio Code is a lightweight IDE developed by Microsoft and available for free for Windows, OS X, and Linux. You can visit `https://code.visualstudio.com/` if you wish to learn more about it.
>
> If you want to work with Visual Studio, you will be able to find the extension to enable Typescript support in Visual Studio at `https://visualstudiogallery.msdn.microsoft.com/2d42d8dc-e085-45eb-a30b-3f7d50d55304`.

One of the highest rated themes is called `seti-ui` and is particularly useful because it uses a really good set of icons to help us to identify each file in our application. For example, the `gulpfile.js` or `bower.json` files (we will learn about these files later) are just JavaScript and JSON files but the `seti-ui` theme is able to identify that they are the Gulp and Bower configuration files respectively and will display their icons accordingly.

```
'use strict';

var browserify = require('browserify'),
    gulp       = require('gulp'),
    run        = require('gulp-run'),
    uglify     = require('gulp-uglify'),
    sourcemaps = require('gulp-sourcemaps'),
    ts         = require('gulp-typescript'),
    tslint     = require('gulp-tslint'),
    sass       = require('gulp-sass'),
    scsslint = require('gulp-scss-lint');

var paths = {
    ts : './source/ts/**/**.ts',
    jsDest : './build/source/js/',
    dtsDest : './build/source/definitions/',
    scss : './source/scss/**/**.scss',
    scssDest : './build/source/css/'
};

var tsProject = ts.createProject({
```

We can install this theme by opening the console of our operating system and running the following commands:

```
cd ~/.atom/packages
git clone https://github.com/jesseweed/seti-ui --depth=1
```

You need to install Git to be able to run the preceding command. You will find some information about the Git installation later on in this chapter.

Once we have installed the theme and TypeScript plugin, we will need to close the Atom editor and open it again to make the changes effective. If everything goes well, we will get a confirmation message in the top-right corner of the editor window.

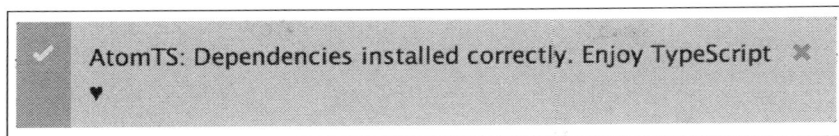

> ✓ AtomTS: Dependencies installed correctly. Enjoy TypeScript ✕
>   ♥

Git and GitHub

Towards the end of this chapter, we will learn how to configure a continuous integration build server. The build server will observe changes in our application's code and ensure that the changes don't break the application.

In order to be able to observe the changes in the code, we will need to use a source control system. There are a few source control systems available. Some of the most widely used ones are Subversion, Mercurial and Git.

Source control systems have many benefits. First, they enable multiple developers to work on a source file without any work being overridden.

Second, source control systems are also a good way of keeping previous copies of a file or auditing its changes. These features can be really useful, for example, when trying to find out when a new bug was introduced for the first time.

While working through the examples, we will perform some changes to the source code. We will use Git and GitHub to manage these changes. To install Git, go to `http://git-scm.com/downloads` and download the executable for your operating system. Then, go to `https://github.com/` to create a GitHub account. While creating the GitHub account, you will be offered a few different subscription plans, the free plan offers everything we need to follow the examples in this chapter.

Source control tools

Now that we have installed Git and created a GitHub account, we will use GitHub to create a new code repository. A repository is a central file storage location. It is used by the source control systems to store multiple versions of files. While a repository can be configured on a local machine for a single user, it is often stored on a server, which can be accessed by multiple users.

GitHub offers free source control repositories for open source projects. GitHub is really popular within the open source community and many popular projects are hosted on GitHub (including TypeScript). However, GitHub is not the only option available and you can use a local Git repository or another source control service provider such as Bitbucket. If you wish to learn more about these alternatives, refer to the official Git documentation at `https://git-scm.com/doc` or the BitBucket website at `https://bitbucket.org/`.

To create a new repository on GitHub, log in to your GitHub account and click on the link to create a new repository, which we can find in the top-right corner of the screen.

A web form similar to the one in the following screenshot will then appear. This form contains some fields, which allow us to set the repository's name, description, and privacy settings.

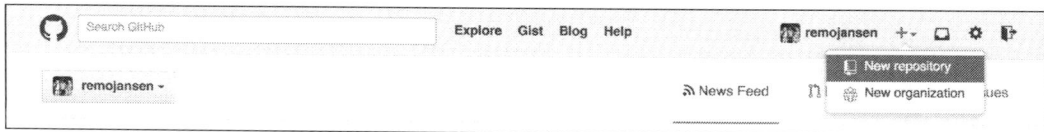

We can also add a README.md file, which uses markdown syntax and is used to add whatever text we want to the repository's home page on GitHub. Furthermore, we can add a default .gitignore file, which is used to specify files that we would like to be ignored by Git and therefore not saved into the repository.

Last but not least, we can also select a software license to cover our source code. Once we have created the repository, we will navigate to our profile page on GitHub, find the repository that we have just created, and go to the repository's page. On the repository's page, we will be able to find the clone URL at the bottom-right corner of the page.

We need to copy the repository's clone URL, open a console, and use the URL as an argument of the git clone command:

```
git clone https://github.com/user-name/repository-name.git
```

> Sometimes the Windows command-line interface is not able to find the Git and Node.js commands.
>
> The easiest way to get around this issue is to use the Git console (installed with Git) rather than using the Windows command line.
>
> If you want to use the Windows console, you will need to manually add the Git and Node installation paths to the Windows PATH environment variable.
>
> Also, note that we will use the UNIX path syntax in all the examples.
>
> If you are working with OS X or Linux, the default command-line interface should work fine.

The command output should look similar to this:

```
Cloning into 'repository-name'...
remote: Counting objects: 3, done.
remote: Compressing objects: 100% (3/3), done.
remote: Total 3 (delta 2), reused 0 (delta 0), pack-reused 0
Unpacking objects: 100% (3/3), done.
Checking connectivity... done.
```

We can then move inside the repository by using the change directory command (cd) and use the `git status` command to check the local repository's status:

```
cd repository-name
git status
On branch master
Your branch is up-to-date with 'origin/master'.
nothing to commit, working directory clean
```

> We will use GitHub throughout this book. However, if you want to use a local repository, you can use the Git `init` command to create an empty repository.
>
> Refer to the Git documentation at http://git-scm.com/docs/git-init to learn more about the `git init` command and working with a local repository.

The `git status` command is telling us that there are no changes in our working directory. Let's open the repository folder in Atom and create a new file called `gulpfile.js`. Now, run the `git status` command again, and we will see that there are some new untracked files:

```
On branch master
Your branch is up-to-date with 'origin/master'.

Untracked files:
  (use "git add <file>..." to include in what will be committed)

  gulpfile.js

nothing added to commit but untracked files present (use "git add" to
track)
```

> The files in the Atom project explorer are displayed using a
> color code, which will help us to identify whether a file is new,
> or has changed since we cloned the repository.

When we make some changes, such as adding a new file or changing an existing
file, we need to execute the `git add` command to indicate that we want to add that
change to a snapshot:

```
git add gulpfile.js
git status
On branch master
Your branch is up-to-date with 'origin/master'.

Changes to be committed:
  (use "git reset HEAD <file>..." to unstage)


  new file:   gulpfile.js
```

Now that we have staged the content we want to snapshot, we have to run the `git
commit` command to actually record the snapshot. Recording a snapshot requires a
commentary field, which can be provided using the `git commit` command together
with its `-m` argument:

```
git commit -m "added the new gulpfile.js"
```

If everything has gone well, the command output should be similar to the following:

```
[master 2a62321] added the new file gulpfile.js
 1 file changed, 1 insertions(+)
 create mode 100644 gulpfile.js
```

To share the commit with other developers, we need to push our changes to the
remote repository. We can do this by executing the `git push` command:

```
git push
```

The `git push` command will ask for our GitHub username and password and
then send the changes to the remote repository. If we visit the repository's page on
GitHub, we will be able to find the recently created file. We will return to GitHub
later in this chapter to configure our continuous integration server.

> If you are working in a large team, you might encounter some file conflicts when attempting to push some changes to the remote repository. Resolving a file conflict is out of the scope of this book; however, if you need further information about Git, you will find an extensive user manual at `https://www.kernel.org/pub/software/scm/git/docs/user-manual.html`.

Package management tools

Package management tools are used for dependency management, so that we no longer have to manually download and manage our application's dependencies. We will learn how to work with three different package management tools: Bower, npm, and tsd.

npm

The npm package manager was originally developed as the default Node.js package management tool, but today it is used by many tools. Npm uses a configuration file, called `package.json`, to store references to all the dependencies in our application. It is important to remember that we will normally use npm to install dependencies that we will use on the server side, in a desktop application, or with development tools.

Before we install any packages, we should add a `package.json` file to our project. We can do it by executing the following command:

```
npm init
```

The `npm init` command will ask for some basic information about our project, including its name, version, description, entry point, test command, Git repository, keywords, author and license.

> Refer to the official npm documentation at `https://docs.npmjs.com/files/package.json` if you are unsure about the purposes of some of the `package.json` fields mentioned earlier.

The `npm` command will then show us a preview of the `package.json` file that is about to be generated and ask for our final confirmation.

> Remember that you need to have Node.js installed to be able to use the npm command tool.

After creating the project's `package.json` file, run the `npm install` command to install our first dependency. The `npm install` command takes the name of one or multiple dependencies separated by a single space as an argument and a second argument to indicate the scope of the installation.

The scope can be:

- A dependency at development time (testing frameworks, compilers, and so on)
- A dependency at runtime (a web framework, database ORMs, and so on)

We will use the `gulp-typescript` npm package to compile our TypeScript code; so, let's install it as a development dependency (using the `--save-dev` argument):

```
npm install gulp-typescript --save-dev
```

To install a global dependency, we will use the `-g` argument:

```
npm install typescript -g
```

> We might need administrative privileges to install packages with global scope in our development environment, as we already learned in the previous chapter.
>
> Also, note that npm will not add any entries to our `package.json` file when installing packages with global scope but it is important that we manually add the right dependencies to the `devDependencies` and `peerDependencies` sections in the `package.json` file to guarantee that the continuous integration build server will resolve all our project's dependencies correctly. We will learn about the continuous integration build server in detail later in this chapter.

To install a runtime dependency, use the `--save` argument:

```
npm install jquery --save
```

> JQuery is probably the most popular JavaScript framework or library ever created. It is used to facilitate the usage of some browser APIs without having to worry about some vendor-specific differences in the APIs. JQuery also provides us with many helpers that will help us reduce the amount of code necessary to perform tasks such as selecting an HTML node within the tree of nodes in an HTML document.
>
> It is assumed that the readers of this book have a good understanding of JQuery. If you need to learn more about JQuery, refer to the official documentation at https://api.jquery.com/.

Once we have installed some dependencies in the `package.json` file, the contents should look similar to this:

```json
{
  "name": "repository-name",
  "version": "1.0.0",
  "description": "example",
  "main": "index.html",
  "scripts": {
    "test": "test"
  },
  "repository": {
    "type": "git",
    "url": "https://github.com/username/repository-name.git"
  },
  "keywords": [
    "typescript",
    "demo",
    "example"
  ],
  "author": "Name Surname",
  "contributors": [],
  "license": "MIT",
  "bugs": {
    "url": "https://github.com/username/repository-name/issues"
  },
  "homepage": "https://github.com/username/repository-name",
  "engines": {},
  "dependencies": {
    "jquery" : "^2.1.4"
  },
  "devDependencies": {
    "gulp-typescript": "^2.8.0"
  }
}
```

Some fields in the `package.json` file must be configured manually. To learn more about the available `package.json` configuration fields, visit `https://docs.npmjs.com/files/package.json`.

The versions of the npm packages used throughout this book may have been updated since the publication of this book. Refer to the packages documentation at `https://npmjs.com` to find out potential incompatibilities and learn about new features.

All the npm packages will be saved under the `node_modules` directory. We should add the `node_modules` directory to our `.gitignore` file as it is recommended to avoid saving the application's dependencies into source control. We can do this by opening the `.gitignore` file and adding a new line that contains the name of the folder (`node_modules`).

The next time we clone our repository, we will need to download all our dependencies again, but to do so, we will only need to execute the `npm install` command without any additional parameters:

```
npm install
```

The package manager will then search for the `package.json` file and install all the declared dependencies.

> If, in the future, we need to find an npm package name, we will be able to use the npm search engines at `https://www.npmjs.com` in order to find it.

Bower

Bower is another package management tool. It is really similar to npm but it was designed specifically to manage frontend dependencies. As a result, many of the packages are optimized for its usage in a web browser.

We can install Bower by using npm:

```
npm install -g bower
```

Instead of the `package.json` file, Bower uses a configuration file named `bower.json`. We can use the majority of the npm commands and arguments in Bower. For example, we can use the `bower init` command to create the initial bower configuration file:

```
bower init
```

> The initial configuration file is quite similar to the `package.json` file. Refer to the official documentation at `http://bower.io/docs/config/` if you want to learn more about the `bower.json` configuration fields.

We can also use the `bower install` command to install a package:

```
bower install jquery
```

Furthermore, we can also use the install scope arguments:

```
bower install jquery --save
bower install jasmine --save-dev
```

All the Bower packages will be saved under the `bower_components` directory. As you have already learned, it is recommended to avoid saving your application's dependencies in your remote repository, so you should also add the `bower_components` directory to your `.gitignore` file.

tsd

In the previous chapter, we learned that TypeScript by default includes a file `lib.d.ts` that provides interface declarations for the built-in JavaScript objects as well as the **Document Object Model (DOM)** and **Browser Object Model (BOM)** APIs. The TypeScript files with the extension `.d.ts` are a special kind of TypeScript file known as **type definition files** or **declaration files**.

The type definition files usually contain the type declarations of third-party libraries. These files facilitate the integration between the existing JavaScript libraries and TypeScript. If, for example, we try to invoke the JQuery in a TypeScript file, we will get an error:

```
$.ajax({ / **/ }); // cannot find name '$'
```

To resolve this issue, we need to add a reference to the JQuery type definition file in our TypeScript code, as shown in the following line of code:

```
///<reference path="jquery.d.ts">
```

Fortunately, we don't need to create the type definition files because there is an open source project known as **DefinitelyTyped** that already contains type definition files for many JavaScript libraries. In the early days of TypeScript development, developers had to manually download and install the type definition files from the DefinitelyTyped project website, but those days are gone, and today we can use a much better solution known as `tsd`.

The `tsd` acronym stands for **TypeScript Definitions** and it is a package manager that will help us to manage the type definition files required by our TypeScript application. Just like npm and bower, `tsd` uses a configuration file named `tsd.json` and stores all the downloaded packages under a directory named `typings`.

Run the following command to install tsd:

```
npm install tsd -g
```

We can use the `tsd init` command to generate the initial `tsd.json` file and the `tsd install` command to download and install dependencies:

```
tsd init // generate tsd.json
tsd install jquery --save // install jquery type definitions
```

You can visit the DefinitelyTyped project website at https://github.com/borisyankov/DefinitelyTyped to search for tsd packages.

Task runners

A task runner is a tool used to automate tasks in the development process. The task can be used to perform a wide variety of operations such as the compilation of TypeScript files or the compression of JavaScript files. The two most popular JavaScript task runners these days are Grunt and Gulp.

Grunt started to become popular in early 2012 and since then the open source community has developed a large number of Grunt-compatible plugins.

On the other hand, Gulp started to become popular in late 2013; therefore, there are less plugins available for Gulp, but it is quickly catching up with Grunt.

Besides the number of plugins available, the main difference between Gulp and Grunt is that while in Grunt we will work using files as the input and output of our tasks, in Gulp we will work with streams and pipes instead. Grunt is configured using some configuration fields and values. However, Gulp prefers code over configuration. This approach makes the Gulp configuration somehow more minimalistic and easier to read.

> In this book, we will work with Gulp; however, if you want to learn more about Grunt, you can do so at http://gruntjs.com/.

In order to gain a good understanding of Gulp, we can use the project that we have already created and add some extra folders and files to it. Alternatively, we can start a new project from scratch. We will configure some tasks, which will reference paths, folders, and files numerous times, so the following directory tree structure should help us understand each of these tasks:

```
├── LICENSE
├── README.md
├── index.html
├── gulpfile.js
├── karma.conf.js
```

```
├── tsd.json
├── package.json
├── bower.json
├── source
│    └── ts
│        └── *.ts
├── test
│    └── main.test.ts
├── data
│    └── *.json
├── node_modules
│    └── ...
├── bower_components
│    └── ...
└── typings
     └── ...
```

> A copy of a finished example project is provided in the companion source code. The code is provided to help you follow the content. You can use the finished project to help improve the understanding of the concepts discussed in the rest of this chapter.

Let's start by installing gulp globally with npm:

npm install -g gulp

Then install gulp in our package.json devDependencies:

npm install --save-dev gulp

Create a JavaScript file named gulpfile.js inside the root folder of our project, which should contain the following piece of code:

```javascript
var gulp = require('gulp');

gulp.task('default', function() {
  console.log('Hello Gulp!');
});
```

And, finally, run gulp (we must execute this command from where the gulpfile.js file is located):

gulp

We have created our first Gulp task, which is named `default`. When we run the `gulp` command, it will automatically try to search for the `gulpfile.js` file in the current directory, and once found, it will try to find the default task.

Checking the quality of the TypeScript code

The `default` task is not performing any operations in the preceding example, but we will normally use a Gulp plugin in each task. We will now add a second task, which will use the `gulp-tslint` plugin to check whether our TypeScript code follows a series of recommended practices.

We need to install the plugin with npm:

```
npm install gulp-tslint --save-dev
```

We can then load the plugin in to our `gulpfile.js` file and add a new task:

```
var tslint = require('gulp-tslint');
gulp.task('lint', function() {
  return gulp.src([
    './source/ts/**/**.ts', './test/**/**.test.ts'
  ]).pipe(tslint())
    .pipe(tslint.report('verbose'));
});
```

We have named the new task `lint`. Let's take a look at the operations performed by the `lint` task, step by step:

1. The `gulp src` function will fetch the files in the directory located at `./source/ts` and its subdirectories with the file extension `.ts`. We will also fetch all the files in the directory located at `./test` and its subdirectories with the file extension `.test.ts`.

2. The output stream of the `src` function will be then redirected using the `pipe` function to be used as the `tslint` function input.

3. Finally, we will use the output of the `tslint` function as the input of the `tslint.report` function.

Now that we have added the `lint` task, we will modify the `gulpfile.js` file to indicate that we want to run `lint` as a subtask of the default task:

```
gulp.task('default', ['lint']);
```

> Many plugins allow us to indicate that some files should be ignored by adding the exclamation symbol (!) before a path. For example, the path !path/*.d.ts will ignore all files with the extension .d.ts; this is useful when the declaration files and source code files are located in the same directory.

Compiling the TypeScript code

We will now add two new tasks to compile our TypeScript code (one for the application's logic and one for the application's unit tests).

We will use the gulp-typescript plugin, so remember to install it as a development dependency using the npm package manager, just as we did previously in this chapter:

```
npm install -g gulp-typescript
```

We can then create a new gulp-typescript project object:

```
var ts = require('gulp-typescript');
var tsProject = ts.createProject({
    removeComments : true,
    noImplicitAny : true,
    target : 'ES3',
    module : 'commonjs',
    declarationFiles : false
});
```

> It has been announced that the gulp-typescript plugin will soon support the usage of a special JSON file named tsconfig.json. This file is used to store the TypeScript compiler configuration. When the file is available, it is used by the compiler during the compilation process.
>
> The tsconfig.json file is useful because it prevents us from having to write all the desired compiler parameters when using its console interface. Refer to the gulp-typescript documentation, which can be found at https://www.npmjs.com/package/gulp-typescript, to learn more about this feature.

In the preceding code snippet, we have loaded the TypeScript compiler as a dependency and then created an object named `tsProject`, which contains the settings to be used by the TypeScript compiler during the compilation of our code. We are now ready to compile our application's source code:

```
gulp.task('tsc', function() {
return gulp.src('./source/ts/**/**.ts')
        .pipe(ts(tsProject))
        .js.pipe(gulp.dest('./temp/source/js'));
});
```

The `tsc` task will fetch all the `.ts` files in the directory located at `./source/ts` and its subdirectories and pass them as a stream to the TypeScript compiler. The compiler will use the compilation settings passed as the `tsProject` argument and then save the output JavaScript files into the path `./temp/sources/js`.

We also need to compile some unit tests written in TypeScript. The tests are located in the `test` folder and we want the output JavaScript files to be stored under `temp/test`. Using the same project configuration object in a different task and with different input files can result in bad performance and unexpected behavior; so we need to initialize another gulp-typescript project object. This time we will name the object `tsTestProject`:

```
var tsTestProject = ts.createProject({
    removeComments : true,
    noImplicitAny : true,
    target : 'ES3',
    module : 'commonjs',
    declarationFiles : false
});
```

The `tsc-test` task is almost identical to the `tsc` task, but instead of compiling the application's code, it will compile the application's tests. Since the source and test are located in different directories, we have used different paths in this task:

```
gulp.task('tsc-tests', function() {
   return gulp.src('./test/**/**.test.ts')
            .pipe(ts(tsTestProject ))
            .js.pipe(gulp.dest('./temp/test/'));
});
```

We will update the default task once more in order to perform the new tasks:

```
gulp.task('default', ['lint', 'tsc', 'tsc-tests']);
```

Optimizing a TypeScript application

When we compile our Typescript code, the compiler will generate a JavaScript file for each compiled TypeScript file. If we run the application in a web browser, these files won't really be useful on their own because the only way to use them would be to create an individual HTML script tag for each one of them.

Alternatively, we could follow two different approaches:

- We could use a tool, such as the RequireJS library, to load each of those files on demand using AJAX. This approach is known as asynchronous module loading. To follow this approach, we will need to change the configuration of the TypeScript compiler to use the **asynchronous module definition (AMD)** notation.

- We could configure the TypeScript compiler to use the CommonJS module notation and use a tool, such as Browserify, to trace the application's modules and dependencies and generate a highly optimized single file, which will contain all the application's modules.

In this book, we will use the CommonJS method because it is highly integrated with Browserify and Gulp.

> If you have never worked with AMD or CommonJS modules before, don't worry too much about it for now. We will focus on modules in *Chapter 4, Object-Oriented Programming with TypeScript*.

We can find the application's root module (named `main.ts` in our example) in the companion code. This file contains the following code:

```
///<reference path="./references.d.ts" />

import { headerView }  from './header_view';
import { footerView } from './footer_view';
import { loadingView } from './loading_view';

headerView.render();
footerView.render();
loadingView.render();
```

> The preceding `import` statements are used to access the contents of some external modules. We will learn more about external modules in *Chapter 4, Object-Oriented Programming with TypeScript*.

When compiled (using the CommonJS module notation), the output JavaScript code will look like this:

```
var headerView = require('./header_view');
var footerView = require('./footer_view');
var loadingView = require('./loading_view');
headerView.render();
footerView.render();
loadingView.render();
```

As we can see in the first three lines, the `main.js` file depends on the other three JavaScript files: `header_view.js`, `footer_view.js`, and `loading_view.js`. If we check the companion code, we will see that these files also have some dependencies.

We will normally refer to these dependencies as modules. Importing a module allows us to use the public parts (also known as the exported parts) of a module from another module.

Browserify is able to trace the full tree of dependencies and generate a highly optimized single file, which will contain all the application's modules and dependencies.

We will now add two new tasks to our automated build (`gulpfile.js`). In the first one, we will configure Browserify to trace the dependencies of our application's modules. In the second one, we will configure Browserify to trace the dependencies of our application's unit tests.

We need to install some packages before implementing the new task:

npm install browserify vinyl-transform gulp-uglify gulp-sourcemaps

We can then import the modules and write some initialization code:

```
Var browserify  = require('browserify'),
    transform   = require('vinyl-transform'),
    uglify      = require('gulp-uglify'),
    sourcemaps  = require('gulp-sourcemaps');

var browserified = transform(function(filename) {
  var b = browserify({ entries: filename, debug: true });
  return b.bundle();
});
```

In the preceding code snippet, we have loaded the required plugins and declared a function named `browserified`, which is required for compatibility reasons. The `browserified` function will transform a regular Node.js stream into a Gulp (buffered vinyl) stream.

Let's proceed to implement the actual task:

```
gulp.task('bundle-js', function () {
  return gulp.src('./temp/source/js/main.js')
             .pipe(browserified)
             .pipe(sourcemaps.init({ loadMaps: true }))
             .pipe(uglify())
             .pipe(sourcemaps.write('./'))
             .pipe(gulp.dest('./dist/source/js/'));
});
```

The task we just defined will take the file `main.js` as the entry point of our application and trace all the application's modules and dependencies from this point. It will then generate one single stream containing a highly optimized JavaScript.

We will then use the `uglify` plugin to minimize the output size. The reduced file size will reduce the application's loading time, but will make it harder to debug. We will also generate a source map file to facilitate the debugging process.

> Uglify removes all line breaks and whitespaces and reduces the length of some variable names. The source map files allow us to map the reduced file to its original code while debugging.
>
> A source map provides a way of mapping code within a compressed file back to its original position in a source file. This means we can easily debug an application even after its assets have been optimized. The Chrome and Firefox developer tools both ship with built-in support for source maps.

The `bundle-test` task is really similar to the previous task. This time, we will avoid using uglify and source maps because usually we won't need to optimize the download times of our unit tests. As you can see, we don't have a single entry point because we will allow the existence of multiple entry points (each entry point will be liked to a collection of automated tests known as test suite. Don't worry if you are not familiar with this term, as we will learn more about it in *Chapter 7, Application Testing*):

```
gulp.task('bundle-test', function () {
  return gulp.src('./temp/test/**/**.test.js')
             .pipe(browserified)
             .pipe(gulp.dest('./dist/test/'));
});
```

Finally, we have to update the default task to also perform the new tasks:

```
gulp.task('default', ['lint', 'tsc', 'tsc-tests', 'bundle-js',
'bundle-test']);
```

We have created a task to compile the TypeScript files into JavaScript files. The JavaScript files are stored in a temporary folder and a second task bundles all the JavaScript files into a single file. In a real corporate environment, it is not recommended to store files temporarily when working with Gulp. We can perform all these operations with one single task by passing the output stream of an operation as the input of the following operation. However, in this book, we will try to split the tasks to facilitate the understanding of each task.

If we try to execute the default task after adding these changes, we will probably experience some issues because the tasks are executed in parallel by default. We will now learn how to control the task's execution order to avoid this kind of issue.

Managing the Gulp tasks' execution order

Sometimes we will need to run our tasks in a certain order (for example, we need to compile our TypeScript into JavaScript before we can execute our unit tests). Controlling the tasks' execution order can be challenging since in Gulp all the tasks are asynchronous by default.

There are three ways to make a task synchronous:

- Passing in a callback
- Returning a stream
- Returning a promise

Refer to *Chapter 3, Working with Functions* to learn more about the usage callbacks and promises.

Let's take a look at the first two ways (we will not cover the usage of promises in this chapter):

```
// Passing a callback (cb)
gulp.task('sync', function (cb) { // note the cb argument
    // setTimeout could be any async task
    setTimeout(function () {
        cb(); // note the cb usage here
    }, 1000);
});

// Returning a stream
gulp.task('sync', function () {
```

```
    return gulp.src('js/*.js') // note the return keyword here
        .pipe(concat('script.min.js')
        .pipe(uglify())
        .pipe(gulp.dest('../dist/js');
});
```

Now that we have a synchronous task, we can combine it with the task dependency notation to manage the execution order:

```
gulp.task('secondTask', ['sync'], function () {
    // this task will not start until
    // the sync task is all done!
});
```

In the preceding code snippet, the secondTask task will not start until the sync task is done. Now, let's imagine that there is a third task named thirdTask. We will write the following code snippet hoping that it will execute the sync task before the thirdTask task and finally the default task, but it will in fact run the sync task and thirdTask task in parallel:

```
gulp.task('default', ['sync', 'thirdTask'], function () {
    // do stuff
});
```

Fortunately, we can install the run-sequence Gulp plugin via npm, which will allow us to have better control over the task execution order:

```
var runSequence = require('run-sequence');
gulp.task('default', function(cb) {
  runSequence(
    'lint',                          // lint
    ['tsc', 'tsc-tests'],            // compile
    ['bundle-js','bundle-test'],     // optimize
    'karma'                          // test
    'browser-sync',                  // serve
    cb                               // callback
  );
});
```

The preceding code snippet will run in the following order:

1. lint.
2. tsc and tsc-tests in parallel.
3. bundle-js and bundle-test in parallel.
4. karma.
5. browser-sync.

> The Gulp development team announced plans to improve the management of the task execution order without the need for external plugins when this book was about to be published. Refer to the Gulp documentation and release notes on future releases to learn more about it. The documentation can be found at `https://github.com/gulpjs/gulp/blob/master/docs/README.md`.

Test runners

A test runner is a tool that allows us to automate the execution of our application's unit tests.

> Unit testing refers to the practice of testing certain functions and areas (units) of our code. This gives us the ability to verify that our functions work as expected. It is assumed that the reader has some understanding of the unit test process, but the topics explored here will be covered in a much higher level of detail in *Chapter 7, Application Testing.*

We can use a test runner to automatically execute our application's test suites in multiple browsers instead of having to manually open each web browser in order to execute the tests.

We will use a test runner known as Karma. Karma is compatible with multiple unit testing frameworks, but we will use the Mocha testing framework together with two libraries: Chai (an assertion library) and Sinon (a mocking framework).

> You don't need to worry too much about these libraries right now because we will focus on their usage in *Chapter 7, Application Testing.*

Let's start by using npm to install the testing framework that we are going to use:

```
npm install mocha chai sinon --save-dev
```

We will continue by installing the `karma` test runner and some dependencies:

```
npm install karma karma-mocha karma-chai karma-sinon karma-coverage
karma-phantomjs-launcher gulp-karma --save-dev
```

After installing all the necessary packages, we have to add a new Gulp task to the `gulpfile.js` file. The new task will run the application's unit tests using Karma:

```
Var karma = require("gulp-karma");

gulp.task('karma', function(cb) {
  gulp.src('./dist/test/**/**.test.js')
      .pipe(karma({
        configFile: 'karma.conf.js',
        action: 'run'
      }))
      .on('end', cb)
      .on('error', function(err) {
        // Make sure failed tests cause gulp to exit non-zero
        throw err;
      });
});
```

In the preceding code snippet, we are fetching all the files with the extension `.test.js` under the directory located at `./dist/test/` and all its subdirectories. We will then pass the files to the Karma plugin together with the location of the `karma.conf.js` file, which contains the Karma configuration. We will create a new JavaScript file named `karma.conf.js` in the project's root directory and copy the following code into it:

```
module.exports = function (config) {
    'use strict';
    config.set({
        basePath: '',
        frameworks: ['mocha', 'chai', 'sinon'],
        browsers: ['PhantomJS'],
        reporters: ['progress', 'coverage'],
        plugins : [
          'karma-coverage',
          'karma-mocha',
          'karma-chai',
          'karma-sinon',
          'karma-phantomjs-launcher'
        ],
        preprocessors: {
          './dist/test/*.test.js' : ['coverage']
        },
        port: 9876,
        colors: true,
        autoWatch: false,
        singleRun: false,
        logLevel: config.LOG_INFO
    });
};
```

The configuration file tells Karma about the application's base path, frameworks (Mocha, Chai, and Sinon.JS), browsers (PhantomJS), plugins, and reporters that we want to use during the tests' execution. PhantomJS is a headless web browser, it is useful because it can execute the unit test without actually having to open a web browser.

> We should run the tests in real web browsers along with PhantomJS before doing a production deployment. There are Karma plugins, such as karma-firefox-launcher and karma-chrome-launcher, which will allow us to run the unit tests in the browsers of our choice.

Karma uses the progress reporter by default to let us know the status of the test execution process. We added the coverage reporter as well because we want to have an idea of what percentage of our application's code has been tested with unit tests. After adding the coverage reporter and running our unit tests we will be able to find the coverage report under a folder named coverage, which should be located in the same directory where the karma.conf.js file was located.

If we look at the Karma configuration documentation at http://karma-runner. github.io/0.8/config/configuration-file.html, we will notice that we are missing the files field in our karma.conf.js file. We didn't indicate the location of our unit tests because the Gulp task will pass the stream, which contains the unit tests', files to Karma, and then the Karma task is executed.

Synchronized cross-device testing

We will add one last task to the gulpfile.js file, which will allow us to run our application in a web browser. We need to install the browser-sync package by using npm:

```
npm install -g browser-sync
```

We will then create two new tasks. These tasks are just used to group a few tasks into one main task. We are doing this because sometimes we want to refresh a webpage to see the effect of changing some TypeScript code and we need to run a number of tasks (compilation, bundling, and so on) before we can actually see the changes in a web browser. By grouping all these tasks into higher-level tasks, we can save some time and make our configuration files more readable:

```
gulp.task('bundle', function(cb) {
  runSequence('build', [
```

```
      'bundle-js', 'bundle-test'
   ], cb);
});

gulp.task('test', function(cb) {
   runSequence('bundle', ['karma'], cb);
});
```

The preceding two tasks are used to group all the build-related tasks into a
higher-level task (named `bundle`) and to group all the test-related tasks into
a higher-level task (named `test`).

After installing the package and implementing the preceding two tasks, we can
add a new Gulp task to the `gulpfile.js` file:

```
var browserSync = require('browser-sync');
gulp.task('browser-sync', ['test'], function() {
   browserSync({
      server: {
         baseDir: "./dist"
      }
   });

   return gulp.watch([
      "./dist/source/js/**/*.js",
      "./dist/source/css/**.css",
      "./dist/test/**/**.test.js",
      "./dist/data/**/**",
      "./index.html"
   ], [browserSync.reload]);
});
```

In this task, we are configuring `BrowserSync` to host in the local web server all the
static files under the `dist` directory. We then use the `gulp watch` function to indicate
that, if the content of any of the files under the `dist` directory changes, `BrowserSync`
should automatically refresh our web browser.

When some changes are detected, the `test` task is invoked. Because the `test` task
invokes the bundle tasks, any changes will trigger the entire process (`build` and
`test`) before refreshing the webpage and displaying the new files in a web browser.

`BrowserSync` is a really powerful tool, it allows us to test in one device and
automatically repeat our actions (clicks, scrolls, and so on) on as many devices as we
want. It will also allow us to debug our applications remotely, which can be really
useful when we are testing an application on mobile devices.

Synchronizing devices is really simple. If we run the `browser-sync` task, the application will be launched in the default web browser. If we look at the console output, we will see that the application is running in one URL (`http://localhost:3000`) and the `BrowserSync` tools are available in a second URL (`http://localhost:3001`):

```
[BS] Access URLs:
 --------------------------------------
       Local: http://localhost:3000
    External: http://192.168.241.17:3000
 --------------------------------------
          UI: http://localhost:3001
 UI External: http://192.168.241.17:3001
 --------------------------------------
[BS] Serving files from: ./dist
```

If we open another tab in our browser pointing to the `BrowserSync` tools URL (`http://localhost:3001`, in the example), we will access the `BrowserSync` tools user interface:

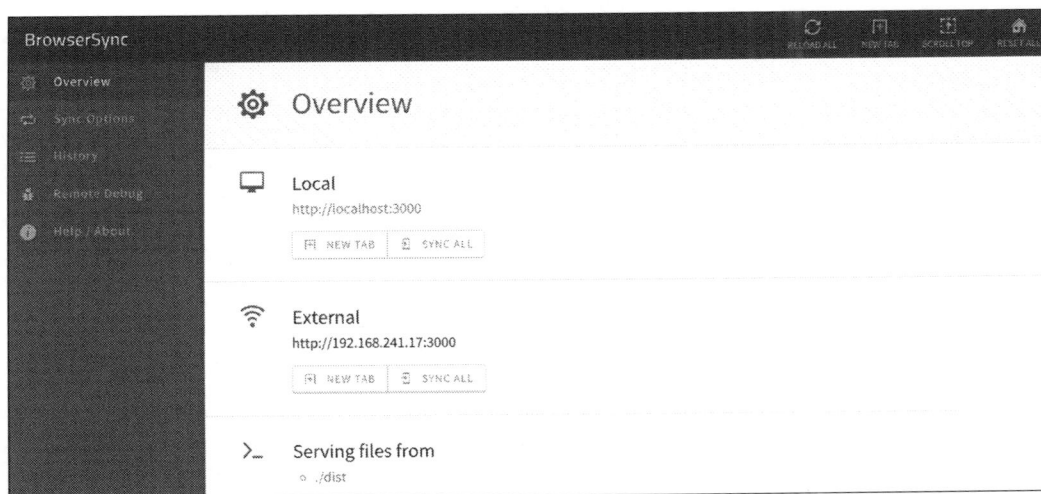

We can use the `BrowserSync` tools user interface to access the remote debugging options and device synchronization options. To synchronize a new device, we just need to use a phone or tablet connected to the same local area network and open the indicated external URL in the device's web browser.

If you wish to learn more about `BrowserSync`, visit the official project documentation at `http://www.browsersync.io/docs/`.

Continuous Integration tools

Continuous Integration (CI) is a development practice that helps to prevent potential integration issues. Software integration issues refers to the difficulties that may arise during the practice of combining individually tested software components into an integrated whole. Software is integrated when components are combined into subsystems or when subsystems are combined into products.

Components may be integrated after all of them are implemented and tested, as in a waterfall model or a big bang approach. On the other hand, CI requires developers to commit their code daily into a remote code repository. Each commit is then verified by an automated build, allowing teams to detect integration issues earlier.

In this chapter, we have created a remote code repository and an automated build, but we haven't configured a tool to observe our commits and run the automate build accordingly. We need a CI server. There are many options when it comes to choosing a CI server, but exploring these options is out of the scope of this book. We will work with Travis CI because it is highly integrated with GitHub and is free for open source projects and learning purposes.

To configure Travis CI, we need to visit the website `https://travis-ci.org` and log in using our GitHub credentials. Once we have logged in, we will be able to see a list of our public GitHub repositories and will also be able to enable the CI.

username/repository-name	ON

To finish the configuration, we need to add a file named `travis.yml` to our application's root directory, which contains the Travis CI configuration:

```
language: node_js
node_js:
  - "0.10""
```

> There are many other available TravisCI configuration options. Refer to `http://docs.travis-ci.com/` to learn more about the available options.

After completing these two small configuration steps, Travis CI will be ready to observe the commits to our remote code repository.

If the build works in the local development environment, but fails in the CI server, we will have to check the build error log and try to figure out what went wrong. Chances are that the software versions in our environment will be ahead of the ones in the CI server and we will need to indicate to Travis CI that a dependency needs to be installed or updated. We can find the Travis CI documentation at `http://docs.travis-ci.com/user/build-configuration/` to learn how to resolve this kind of issue.

Scaffolding tools

A scaffolding tool is used to autogenerate the project structure, build scripts, and much more. The most popular scaffolding tool these days is Yeoman. Yeoman uses an internal command known as `yo`, a package manager, and a task runner of our choice to generate projects based on templates.

The project templates are known as generators and the open source community has already published many of them, so we should be able to find one that more or less suits our needs. Alternatively, we can write and publish our own Yeoman generator.

We will now create a new project to showcase how Yeoman can help us to save some time. Yeoman will generate the `package.json` and `bower.json` files and automatically install some dependencies for us.

The `yo` command can be installed using npm:

```
npm install -g yo
```

After installing the `yo` command, we will need to install at least one generator. We need to find a generator for the kind of project that we wish to create.

We are going create a new project using Gulp as the task runner and TypeScript to showcase the usage of Yeoman. We can use a generator called `generator-typescript`. The list of available generators can be found online at `http://yeoman.io/generators/`.

We can install a generator by using npm:

```
npm install -g generator-typescript
```

After installing the generator, we can use it with the help of the `yo` command:

```
yo typescript
```

If, for example, we also wanted to use Sass, we could use the `generator-gulp-sass-typescript` generator instead:

```
npm install -g generator-gulp-sass-typescript
```

Some of the generators are interactive and will allow us to select whether we want to add some optional third-party libraries to the project or not. Let's run the generator to see what it looks like:

```
yo generator-gulp-sass-typescript
```

The screen that is displayed contains a series of steps to guide us through the process of creating a new project, which includes Gulp as the task runner, Sass as the CSS preprocessor, and TypeScript as the programming language:

Downloading the example code

You can download the example code files from your account at http://www.packtpub.com for all the Packt Publishing books you have purchased. If you purchased this book elsewhere, you can visit http://www.packtpub.com/support and register to have the files e-mailed directly to you.

After executing the generator, the project template will generate a directory tree similar to the following one:

```
├── app
│   ├── index.html
│   ├── sass
│   │   └── styles.scss
│   ├── scripts
│   │   └── main.js
│   ├── styles
│   │   └── styles.css
│   └── ts
│       └── main.ts
├── bower.json
├── bower_components
│   └── ...
├── gulpfile.js
├── node_modules
│   └── ...
└── package.json
```

The `bower.json`, `package.json`, and `gulpfile.js` files (the Gulp task runner configuration) are autogenerated and will save us a considerable amount of time.

> It is never a good idea to let a tool generate some code for us if we don't really understand what that code does. While in the future you should definitely consider using Yeoman to generate a new project, it is recommended to gain a good understanding of task and test runners before using a scaffolding tool.

Summary

In this chapter, you learned how to work with a source control repository and how to use Gulp to manage the tasks in an automated build. The automated build helps us to validate the quality of the TypeScript code, compile it, test it, and optimize it. You also learned how to install third-party packages and TypeScript type definitions for those third-party components.

Towards the end of the chapter, you learned how to use the automated build and a continuous integration server to reduce the impact of potential integration issues.

In the next chapter, you will learn about functions.

3
Working with Functions

In *Chapter 1, Introducing TypeScript*, we took a first look at the usage of functions. Functions are the fundamental building block of any application in TypeScript, and they are powerful enough to deserve the dedication of an entire chapter to explore their potential.

In this chapter, we will learn to work with functions in depth. The chapter is divided into two main sections. In the first section, we will start with a quick recap of some basic concepts and then move onto some less commonly known function features and use cases. The first section includes the following concepts:

- Function declaration and function expressions
- Function types
- Functions with optional parameters
- Functions with default parameters
- Functions with rest parameters
- Function overloading
- Specialized overloading signature
- Function scope
- Immediately invoked functions
- Generics
- Tag functions and tagged templates

The second section focuses on TypeScript asynchronous programming capabilities and includes the following concepts:

- Callbacks and higher order functions
- Arrow functions
- Callback hell
- Promises
- Generators
- Asynchronous functions (async and await)

Working with functions in TypeScript

In this section, we will focus on the declaration and usage of functions, parameters, and arguments. We will also introduce one of the most powerful features of TypeScript: Generics.

Function declarations and function expressions

In the first chapter, we introduced the possibility of declaring functions with (named function) or without (unnamed or anonymous function) explicitly indicating its name, but we didn't mention that we were also using two different types of function.

In the following example, the named function `greetNamed` is a function declaration while `greetUnnamed` is a function expression. Ignore the first two lines, which contain two console log statements, for now:

```
console.log(greetNamed("John"));
console.log(greetUnnamed("John"));

function greetNamed(name : string) : string {
  if(name) {
    return "Hi! " + name;
  }
}

var greetUnnamed = function(name : string) : string {
  if(name){
    return "Hi! " + name;
  }
}
```

We might think that these preceding functions are really similar, but they will behave differently. The interpreter can evaluate a function declaration as it is being parsed. On the other hand, the function expression is part of an assignment and will not be evaluated until the assignment has been completed.

> The main cause of the different behavior of these functions is a process known as variable hoisting. We will learn more about the variable hoisting process later in this chapter.

If we compile the preceding TypeScript code snippet into JavaScript and try to execute it in a web browser, we will observe that the first alert statement will work because JavaScript knows about the declaration function and can parse it before the program is executed.

However, the second alert statement will throw an exception, which indicates that `greetUnnamed` is not a function. The exception is thrown because the `greetUnnamed` assignment must be completed before the function can be evaluated.

Function types

We already know that it is possible to explicitly declare the type of an element in our application by using the optional type declaration annotation:

```
function greetNamed(name : string) : string {
  if(name) {
    return "Hi! " + name;
  }
}
```

In the preceding function, we have specified the type of the parameter name (string) and its return type (string). Sometimes, we will need to not just specify the types of the function elements, but also the function itself. Let's take a look at an example:

```
var greetUnnamed : (name : string) => string;

greetUnnamed = function (name : string) : string {
  if(name) {
    return "Hi! " + name;
  }
}
```

In the preceding example, we have declared the variable greetUnnamed and its type. The type of greetUnnamed is a function type that takes a string variable called name as its only parameter and returns a string after being invoked. After declaring the variable, a function, whose type must be equal to the variable type, is assigned to it.

We can also declare the greetUnnamed type and assign a function to it in the same line rather than declaring it in two separate lines like we did in the previous example:

```
var greetUnnamed : (name : string) => string = function(name : string)
: string {
  if(name){
    return "Hi! " + name;
  }
}
```

Just like in the previous example, the preceding code snippet also declares a variable greetUnnamed and its type. We will assign a function to this variable in the same line in which it is declared. The assigned function must be equal to the variable type.

> In the preceding example, we have declared the type of the greetUnnamed variable and then assigned a function as its value. The type of the function can be inferred from the assigned function, and for this reason, it is unnecessary to add a redundant type annotation. We have done this to facilitate the understanding of this section, but it is important to mention that adding redundant type annotations can make our code harder to read, and it is considered bad practice.

Functions with optional parameters

Unlike JavaScript, the TypeScript compiler will throw an error if we attempt to invoke a function without providing the exact number and type of parameters that its signature declares. Let's take a look at a code sample to demonstrate it:

```
function add(foo : number, bar : number, foobar : number) : number {
  return foo + bar + foobar;
}
```

The preceding function is called `add` and will take three numbers as parameters: named `foo`, `bar`, and `foobar`. If we attempt to invoke this function without providing exactly three numbers, we will get a compilation error indicating that the supplied parameters do not match the function's signature:

```
add();        // Supplied parameters do not match any signature
add(2, 2);    // Supplied parameters do not match any signature
add(2, 2, 2); // returns 6
```

There are scenarios in which we might want to be able to call the function without providing all its arguments. TypeScript features optional parameters in functions to help us to increase the flexibility of our functions. We can indicate to TypeScript that we want a function's parameter to be optional by appending the character `?` to its name. Let's update the previous function to transform the required parameter `foobar` into an optional parameter:

```
function add(foo : number, bar : number, foobar? : number) : number {
  var result =  foo + bar;
  if(foobar !== undefined){
    result += foobar;
  }
  return result;
}
```

Note how we have changed the `foobar` parameter name into `foobar?`, and how we are checking the type of `foobar` inside the function to identify if the parameter was supplied as an argument to the function or not. After doing these changes, the TypeScript compiler will allow us to invoke the function without errors when we supply two or three arguments to it:

```
add();        // Supplied parameters do not match any signature
add(2, 2);    // returns 4
add(2, 2, 2); // returns 6
```

It is important to note that the optional parameters must always be located after the required parameters in the function's parameters list.

Functions with default parameters

When a function has some optional parameters, we must check if an argument has been passed to the function (just like we did in the previous example).

There are some scenarios in which it would be more useful to provide a default value for a parameter when it is not supplied than to make it an optional parameter. Let's rewrite the add function (from the previous section) using the inline `if` structure:

```
function add(foo : number, bar : number, foobar? : number) :
number {
    return foo + bar + (foobar !== undefined ? foobar : 0);
}
```

There is nothing wrong with the preceding function, but we can improve its readability by providing a default value for the `foobar` parameter instead of flagging it as an optional parameter:

```
function add(foo : number, bar : number, foobar : number = 0) :
number {
    return foo + bar + foobar;
}
```

To indicate that a function parameter is optional, we just need to provide a default value using the = operator when declaring the function's signature. The TypeScript compiler will generate an `if` structure in the JavaScript output to set a default value for the `foobar` parameter if it is not passed as an argument to the function:

```
function add(foo, bar, foobar) {
    if (foobar === void 0) { foobar = 0; }
    return foo + bar + foobar;
}
```

Void 0 is used by the TypeScript compiler to check if a variable is equal to undefined. While most developers use the undefined variable, most compilers use void 0.

Just like optional parameters, default parameters must be always located after any required parameters in the function's parameter list.

Functions with rest parameters

We have seen how to use optional and default parameters to increase the number of ways that we can invoke a function. Let's return one more time to the previous example:

```
function add(foo : number, bar : number, foobar : number = 0) :
number {
   return foo + bar + foobar;
}
```

We have seen how to make possible the usage of the add function with two or three parameters, but what if we wanted to allow other developers to pass four or five parameters to our function? We would have to add two extra default or optional parameters. And what if we wanted to allow them to pass as many parameters as they may need? The solution to this possible scenario is the use of rest parameters. The rest parameter syntax allows us to represent an indefinite number of arguments as an array:

```
function add(...foo : number[]) : number {
   var result = 0;
   for(var i = 0; i < foo.length; i++){
      result += foo[i];
   }
   return result;
}
```

As we can see in the following code snippet, we have replaced the function parameters foo, bar, and foobar with just one parameter: foo. Note that the name of the parameter foo is preceded by an ellipsis (a set of three periods—not the actual ellipsis character). A rest parameter must be of an array type or we will get a compilation error. We can now invoke the add function with as many parameters as we may need:

```
add();                 // returns 0
add(2);                // returns 2
add(2,2);              // returns 4
add(2,2,2);            // returns 6
add(2,2,2,2);          // returns 8
add(2,2,2,2,2);        // returns 10
add(2,2,2,2,2,2);      // returns 12
```

Although there is no specific limit to the theoretical maximum number of arguments that a function can take, there are, of course, practical limits. These limits are entirely implementation-dependent and, most likely, will also depend exactly on how we are calling the function.

JavaScript functions have a built-in object called the `arguments` object. This object is available as a local variable named arguments. The `arguments` variable contains an object similar to an array, which contains the arguments used when the function was invoked.

> The arguments object exposes some of the methods and properties provided by a standard array, but not all of them. Refer to the complete reference at `https://developer.mozilla.org/en-US/docs/Web/JavaScript/Reference/Functions/arguments` to learn more about its peculiarities.

If we examine the JavaScript output, we will notice that TypeScript iterates the arguments object in order to add the values to the `foo` variable:

```
function add() {
    var foo = [];
    for (var _i = 0; _i < arguments.length; _i++) {
        foo[_i - 0] = arguments[_i];
    }
    var result = 0;
    for (var i = 0; i < foo.length; i++) {
        result += foo[i];
    }
    return result;
}
```

We can argue that this is an extra, unnecessary iteration over the function's parameters. Even though is hard to imagine this extra iteration becoming a performance issue, if you think that this could be a problem for the performance of your application, you may want to consider avoiding using rest parameters and use an array as the only parameter of the function instead:

```
function add(foo : number[]) : number {
  var result = 0;
  for(var i = 0; i < foo.length; i++){
    result += foo[i];
  }
  return result;
}
```

The preceding function takes an array of numbers as its only parameter. The invocation API will be a little different from the rest parameters, but we will effectively avoid the extra iteration over the function's argument list:

```
add();        // Supplied parameters do not match any signature
add(2);       // Supplied parameters do not match any signature
add(2,2);     // Supplied parameters do not match any signature
add(2,2,2);   // Supplied parameters do not match any signature

add([]);      // returns 0
add([2]);     // returns 2
add([2,2]);   // returns 4
add([2,2,2]); // returns 6
```

Function overloading

Function overloading or method overloading is the ability to create multiple methods with the same name and a different number of parameters or types. In TypeScript, we can overload a function by specifying all function signatures of a function, followed by a signature known as the implementation signature. Let's take a look at an example:

```
function test(name: string) : string;       // overloaded signature
function test(age: number) : string;         // overloaded signature
function test(single: boolean) : string;     // overloaded signature
function test(value: (string | number | boolean) : string { //
implementation signature
  switch(typeof value){
    case "string":
      return `My name is ${value}.`;
    case "number":
      return `I'm ${value} years old.`;
    case "boolean":
      return value ? "I'm single." : "I'm not single.";
    default:
      console.log("Invalid Operation!");
  }
}
```

> You might not be familiar with the syntax used in some of the strings in the preceding code snippet. This syntax is known as **Template Strings**. Template strings are enclosed by the backtick (` ` `) character instead of double or single quotes. Template strings can contain placeholders. These are indicated by the dollar sign and curly braces (${expression}). The expressions in the placeholders and the text between them get passed to a function. The default function just concatenates the parts into a single string.

As we can see in the preceding example, we have overloaded the function test three times by adding a signature that takes a string as its only parameter, another function that takes a number, and a final signature that takes a Boolean as its unique parameter. It is important to note that all function signatures must be compatible; so if, for example, one of the signatures tries to return a number while another tries to return a string, we will get a compilation error.

The implementation signature must be compatible with all the overloaded signatures, always be the last in the list, and take any or a union type as the type of its parameters.

Invoking the implementation signature directly will cause a compilation error:

```
test("Remo");                    // returns "My name is Remo."
test(26);                        // returns "I'm 26 years old.";
test(false);                     // returns "I'm not single.";
test({ custom : "custom" }); // error
```

Specialized overloading signatures

We can use a specialized signature to create multiple methods with the same name and number of parameters but a different return type. To create a specialized signature, we must indicate the type of function parameter using a string. The string literal is used to identify which of the function overloads is invoked:

```
interface Document {
  createElement(tagName: "div"): HTMLDivElement; // specialized
  createElement(tagName: "span"): HTMLSpanElement;  // specialized
  createElement(tagName: "canvas"): HTMLCanvasElement; //
  specialized
  createElement(tagName: string): HTMLElement; // non-specialized
}
```

In the preceding example, we have declared three specialized overloaded signatures and one non-specialized signature for the function named createElement.

When we declare a specialized signature in an object, it must be assignable to at least one non-specialized signature in the same object. This can be observed in the preceding example, as the `createElement` property belongs to a type that contains three specialized signatures, all of which are assignable to the non-specialized signature in the type.

When writing overloaded declarations, we must list the non-specialized signature last.

> Remember that, as seen in *Chapter 1, Introducing TypeScript*, we can also use union types to create a method with the same name and number of parameters but a different type.

Function scope

Low-level languages such as C have low-level memory management features. In programming languages with a higher level of abstraction such as TypeScript, values are allocated when variables are created and automatically cleared from memory when they are not used anymore. The process that cleans the memory is known as **garbage collection** and is performed by the JavaScript runtime garbage collector.

The garbage collector generally does a great job, but it is a mistake to assume that it will always prevent us from facing a memory leak. The garbage collector will clear a variable from the memory whenever the variable is out of the scope. Is important to understand how the TypeScript scope works so we understand the lifecycle of the variables.

Some programming languages use the structure of the program source code to determine what variables we are referring to (lexical scoping), while others use the runtime state of the program stack to determine what variable we are referring to (dynamic scoping). The majority of modern programing languages use lexical scoping (including TypeScript). Lexical scoping tends to be dramatically easier to understand for both humans and analysis tools than dynamic scoping.

While in most lexical scoped programming languages, variables are scoped to a block (a section of code delimited by curly braces { }), in TypeScript (and JavaScript), variables are scoped to a function:

```
function foo() : void {
  if(true){
    var bar : number = 0;
  }
```

```
    alert(bar);
}


foo(); // shows 0
```

The preceding function named `foo` contains an `if` structure. We have declared a numeric variable named `bar` inside the `if` structure, and later we have attempted to show the value of the variable bar using the `alert` function.

We might think that the preceding code sample would throw an error in the fifth line because the `bar` variable should be out of the scope when the alert function is invoked. However, if we invoke the `foo` function, the alert function will be able to display the variable bar without errors because all the variables inside a function will be in the scope of the entire function body, even if they are inside another block of code (except a function block).

This might seem really confusing, but it is easy to understand once we know that, at runtime, all the variable declarations are moved to the top of a function before the function is executed. This behavior is called hoisting.

> TypeScript is compiled to JavaScript and then executed — this means that a TypeScript application is a JavaScript application at runtime, and for this reason, when we refer to the TypeScript runtime, we are talking about the JavaScript runtime. We will learn in depth about the runtime in *Chapter 5, Runtime*.

So, before the preceding code snippet is executed, the runtime will move the declaration of the variable bar to the top of our function:

```
function foo() : void {
  var bar :number;
  if(true){
    bar= 0;
  }
  alert(bar);
}
```

This means that we can use a variable before it is declared. Let's take a look at an example:

```
function foo2() : void {
  bar = 0;
  var bar : number;
  alert(bar);
}


foo2();
```

In the preceding code snippet, we have declared a function foo2, and in its body, we have assigned the value 0 to a variable named bar. At this point, the variable has not been declared. In the second line, we are actually declaring the variable bar and its type. In the last line, we are displaying the value of bar using the alert function.

Because declaring a variable anywhere inside a function (except another function) is equivalent to declaring it at the top of the function, the foo2 function is transformed into the following at runtime:

```
function foo2() : void {
  var bar : number;
  bar = 0;
  alert(bar);
}


foo2();
```

Because developers with a Java or C# background are not used to the function scope, it is one of the most criticized characteristics of JavaScript. The people in charge of the development of the ECMAScript 6 specification are aware of this and, as a result, they have introduced the keywords let and const.

The let keyword allows us to set the scope of a variable to a block (if, while, for...) rather than a function block. We can update the first example in this section to showcase how let works:

```
function foo() : void {
   if(true){
let bar : number = 0;
bar = 1;
   }
   alert(bar); // error
}
```

The bar variable is now declared using the let keyword and, as a result, it is only accessible inside the if block. The variable is not hoisted to the top of the foo function and cannot be accessed by the alert function outside the if statement.

While variables defined with const follow the same scope rules as variables declared with let, they can't be reassigned:

```
function foo() : void {
   if(true){
      const bar : number = 0;
      bar = 1; // error
```

```
    }
    alert(bar); // error
}
```

If we attempt to compile the preceding code snippet, we will get an error because the `bar` variable is not accessible outside the `if` statement (just like when we used the `let` keyword), and a new error occurs when we try to assign a new value to the `bar` variable. The second error is caused because it is not possible to assign a value to a constant variable once the variable has already been initialized.

Immediately invoked functions

An **immediately invoked function expression (IIFE)** is a design pattern that produces a lexical scope using function scoping. IIFE can be used to avoid variable hoisting from within blocks or to prevent us from polluting the global scope. For example:

```
var bar = 0; // global

(function() {
  var foo : number = 0; // in scope of this function
  bar = 1; // in global scope
  console.log(bar); // 1
  console.log(foo); // 0
})();

console.log(bar); // 1
console.log(foo); // error
```

In the preceding example, we have wrapped the declaration of two variables (`foo` and `bar`) with an IIFE. The `foo` variable is scoped to the IIFE function and is not available in the global scope, which explains the error when trying to access it in the last line.

We can also pass a variable to the IIFE to have better control over the creation of variables outside its own scope:

```
var bar = 0; // global

(function(global) {
  var foo : number = 0; // in scope of this function
  bar = 1; // in global scope
  console.log(global.bar); // 1
  console.log(foo); // 0
})(this);
```

```
console.log(bar); // 1
console.log(foo); // error
```

This time, the IIFE takes the `this` operator as its only argument, which points to the global scope, because we are not invoking the `this` operator from within a function. Inside the IIFE, the `this` operator is passed as a parameter named `global`. We can then achieve much better control over the objects we want to declare in the global scope (`bar`) and those we don't (`foo`).

Furthermore, IIFE can help us to simultaneously allow public access to methods while retaining privacy for variables defined within the function. Let's take a look at an example:

```
class Counter {
  private _i : number;
  constructor() {
    this._i = 0;
  }
  get() : number {
    return this._i;
  }
  set(val : number) : void {
    this._i = val;
  }
  increment() : void {
    this._i++;
  }
}
var counter = new Counter();
console.log(counter.get()); // 0
counter.set(2);
console.log(counter.get()); // 2
counter.increment();
console.log(counter.get()); // 3
console.log(counter._i); // Error: Property '_i' is private
```

> By convention, TypeScript and JavaScript developers usually name private variables with names preceded by an underscore (_).

We have defined a class named `Counter` that has a private numeric attribute named _i. The class also has methods to get and set the value of the private property _i. We have also created an instance of the `Counter` class and invoked the methods set, get, and increment to observe that everything is working as expected. If we attempt to access the _i property in an instance of `Counter`, we will get an error because the variable is private.

If we compile the preceding TypeScript code (only the class definition) and examine the generated JavaScript code, we will see the following:

```
var Counter = (function () {
    function Counter() {
        this._i = 0;
    }
    Counter.prototype.get = function () {
        return this._i;
    };
    Counter.prototype.set = function (val) {
        this._i = val;
    };
    Counter.prototype.increment = function () {
        this._i++;
    };
    return Counter;
})();
```

This generated JavaScript code will work perfectly in most scenarios, but if we execute it in a browser and try to create an instance of `Counter` and access its property `_i`, we will not get any errors because TypeScript will not generate runtime private properties for us. Sometimes we will need to write our functions in such a way that some properties are private at runtime, for example, if we release a library that will be used by JavaScript developers. We can use IIFE to simultaneously allow public access to methods while retaining privacy for variables defined within the function:

```
var Counter = (function () {
    var _i : number = 0;
    function Counter() {
    }
    Counter.prototype.get = function () {
        return _i;
    };
    Counter.prototype.set = function (val : number) {
        _i = val;
    };
    Counter.prototype.increment = function () {
        _i++;
    };
    return Counter;
})();
```

In the preceding example, everything is almost identical to TypeScript's generated JavaScript, except that the variable _i before was an attribute of the Counter class, and now it is an object in the Counter closure.

> Closures are functions that refer to independent (free) variables. In other words, the function defined in the closure *remembers* the environment (variables in the scope) in which it was created. We will discover more about closures in *Chapter 5, Runtime*.

If we run the generated output in a browser and try to invoke the _i property directly, we will notice that the property is now private at runtime:

```
var counter = new Counter();
console.log(counter.get()); // 0
counter.set(2);
console.log(counter.get()); // 2
counter.increment();
console.log(counter.get()); // 3
console.log(counter._i); // undefined
```

> In some cases, we will need to have really precise control over scope and closures, and our code will end up looking much more like JavaScript. Just remember that, as long as we write our application components (classes, modules, and so on) to be consumed by other TypeScript components, we will rarely have to worry about implementing runtime private properties. We will look in depth at the TypeScript runtime in *Chapter 5, Runtime*.

Generics

Andy Hunt and Dave Thomas formulated the **don't repeat yourself (DRY)** principle in the book *The Pragmatic Programmer*. The DRY principle aims to reduce the repetition of information of all kinds. We will now take a look at an example that will help us to understand what generics functions are and how they can help us follow the DRY principle.

We will start by declaring a really simple User class:

```
class User {
  name : string;
  age : number;
}
```

Now that we have our User class in place, let's write a function named getUsers that will request a list of users via AJAX:

```
function getUsers(cb : (users : User[]) => void) : void {
  $.ajax({
    url: "/api/users",
    method: "GET",
    success: function(data) {
      cb(data.items);
    },
    error : function(error) {
      cb(null);
    }
  });
}
```

> We will use jQuery in this example. Remember to create a package.
> json file and install the jQuery package using npm. You will also
> need to install the jQuery type definitions file using tsd. Refer to
> *Chapter 1, Introducing Typescript* and *Chapter 2, Automating Your
> Development Workflow* if you need additional help.

The getUsers function takes a function as a parameter that will be invoked if the AJAX request has been successful. It can be invoked as follows:

```
getUsers(function(users : User[]){
  for(var i; users.length; i++){
    console.log(users[i].name);
  }
});
```

Now let's imagine that we need an almost identical operation. But this time, we will use an Order entity instead:

```
class Order {
  id : number;
  total : number;
  items : any[]
}
```

The getOrders function is almost identical to the getUsers function. It uses a different URL and it will pass an array of Orders instead of a User array:

```
function getOrders(cb : (orders : Order[]) => void) : void {
  $.ajax({
```

```
        url: "/api/orders",
        method: "GET",
        success: function(data) {
          cb(data.items);
        },
        error : function(error) {
          cb(null);
        }
      });
    }

    getOrders(function(orders : Orders[]){
      for(var i; orders.length; i++){
        console.log(orders[i].total);
      }
    });
```

We can use generics to avoid this kind of repetition. Generic programming is a style of computer programming in which algorithms are written in terms of types to be specified later. These types are then instantiated when needed for specific types provided as parameters. We are going to write a generic function named getEntities that takes two parameters:

```
function getEntities<T>(url : string, cb : (list : T[]) => void) :
void {
  $.ajax({
    url: url,
    method: "GET",
    success: function(data) {
        cb(data.items);
    },
    error : function(error) {
      cb(null);
    }
  });
}
```

We have added angle brackets (<>) after the name of our functions to indicate that it is a generic function. Enclosed in the angle brackets is the character T, which is used to refer to a type. The first parameter is named url and is a string; the second parameter is a function named cb, which takes a parameter list of type T as its only parameter.

We can now use this generic function to indicate what type T will represent:

```
getEntities<User>("/api/users",function(users : Users[]) {
  for(var i; users.length; i++) {
    console.log(users[i].name);
  }
});

getEntities<Order>("/api/orders", function(orders : Orders[]) {
  for(var i; orders.length; i++) {
    console.log(orders[i].total);
  }
});
```

Tag functions and tagged templates

We have already seen how to work with template strings such as the following:

```
var name = 'remo';
var surname = jansen;
var html = `<h1>${name} ${surname}</h1>`;
```

However, there is one use of template strings that we deliberately skipped because it is closely related to the use of a special kind of function known as **tag function**.

We can use a tag function to extend or modify the standard behavior of template strings. When we apply a tag function to a template string, the template string becomes a **tagged template**.

We are going to implement a tag function named htmlEscape. To use a tag function, we must use the name of the function followed by a template string:

```
var html = htmlEscape `<h1>${name} ${surname}</h1>`;
```

A tag template must return a string and take the following arguments:

- An array which contains all the static literals in the template string (<h1> and </h1> in the preceding example) is passed as the first argument.

- A rest parameter is passed as the second parameter. The rest parameter contains all the values in the template string (name and surname in the preceding example).

We now know the signature of a tag function.

```
tag(literals : string[], ...values : any[]) : string
```

Let's implement the `htmlEscape` tag function:

```
function htmlEscape(literals, ...placeholders) {
    let result = "";
    for (let i = 0; i < placeholders.length; i++) {
        result += literals[i];
        result += placeholders[i]
            .replace(/&/g, '&amp;')
            .replace(/"/g, '&quot;')
            .replace(/'/g, '&#39;')
            .replace(/</g, '&lt;')
            .replace(/>/g, '&gt;');
    }
    result += literals[literals.length - 1];
    return result;
}
```

The preceding function iterates through the literals and values and ensures that the HTML code is escaped from the values to avoid possible code injection attacks.

The main benefit of using a tagged function is that it allows us to create custom template string processors.

> This feature will be available in the TypeScript 1.6 release.

Asynchronous programming in TypeScript

Now that we have seen how to work with functions, we will explore how we can use them, together with some native objects, to write asynchronous applications.

Callbacks and higher-order functions

In TypeScript, functions can be passed as arguments to another function. The function passed to another as an argument is known as a **callback**. Functions can also be returned by another function. The functions that accept functions as parameters (callbacks) or return functions as an argument are known as **higher-order functions**. Callbacks are usually anonymous functions.

```
var foo = function() { // callback
  console.log('foo');
```

```
  }

  function bar(cb : () => void) { // higher order function
    console.log('bar');
    cb();
  }

  bar(foo); // prints 'bar' then prints 'foo'
```

Arrow functions

In TypeScript, we can declare a function using a `function` expression or an arrow function. An arrow function expression has a shorter syntax compared to function expressions and lexically binds the value of the `this` operator.

The `this` operator behaves a little differently in TypeScript compared to other languages. When we define a class in TypeScript, we can use the `this` operator to refer to the class's own properties. Let's take a look at an example:

```
  class Person {
  name : string;
    constructor(name : string) {
      this.name = name;
    }
    greet() {
      alert(`Hi! My name is ${this.name}`);
    }
  }
  var remo = new Person("Remo");
  remo.greet(); // "Hi! My name is Remo"
```

We have defined a `Person` class that contains a property of type string called `name`. The class has a constructor and a method `greet`. We have created an instance named `remo` and invoked the method named `greet`, which internally uses the `this` operator to access the `remo` property's name. Inside the `greet` method, the `this` operator points to the object that encloses the `greet` method.

We must be careful when using the `this` operator because in some scenarios it can point to the wrong value. Let's add an extra method to the previous example:

```
  class Person {
  name : string;
    constructor(name : string) {
      this.name = name;
    }
```

```
  greet() {
    alert(`Hi! My name is ${this.name}`);
  }
  greetDelay(time : number) {
    setTimeout(function() {
      alert(`Hi! My name is ${this.name}`);
    }, time);
  }
}
var remo = new Person("remo");
remo.greet(); // "Hi! My name is remo"
remo.greetDelay(1000); // "Hi! My name is "
```

In the `greetDelay` method, we perform an almost identical operation to the one performed by the greet method. This time the function takes a parameter named `time`, which is used to delay the greet message.

In order to delay the message, we use the `setTimeout` function and a callback. As soon as we define an anonymous function (the callback), the `this` keyword changes its value and starts pointing to the anonymous function. This explains why the name `remo` is not displayed by the `greetDelay` message.

As mentioned, an arrow function expression lexically binds the value of the `this` operator. This means that it allows us to add a function without altering the value of this operator. Let's replace the function expression from the previous example with an arrow function:

```
class Person {
    name : string;
  constructor(name : string) {
    this.name = name;
  }
  greet() {
   alert(`Hi! My name is ${this.name}`);
  }
  greetDelay(time : number) {
   setTimeout(() => {
     alert(`Hi! My name is ${this.name}`);
   }, time);
  }
}

var remo = new Person("remo");
remo.greet(); // "Hi! My name is remo"
remo.greetDelay(1000); // "Hi! My name is remo"
```

By using an arrow function, we can ensure that the `this` operator still points to the `Person` instance and not to the `setTimeout` callback. If we execute the `greetDelay` function, the name property will be displayed as expected.

The following piece of code was generated by the TypeScript compiler. When compiling an arrow function, the TypeScript compiler will generate an alias for the `this` operator named _this. The alias is used to ensure that the `this` operator points to the right object.

```
Person.prototype.greetDelay = function (time) {
  var _this = this;
  setTimeout(function () {
    alert("Hi! My name is " + _this.name);
  }, time);
};
```

Callback hell

We have seen that callbacks and higher order functions are two powerful and flexible TypeScript features. However, the use of callbacks can lead to a maintainability issue known as **callback hell**. We will now write a real-life example to showcase what a callback hell is and how easily we can end up dealing with it.

> Remember that you can find the complete source code for this demo in the companion source code.

We are going to need handlebars and jQuery libraries, so let's install these two libraries and their respective type definition files using npm and tsd. We can then import their type definitions:

```
///<reference path="../typings/handlebars/handlebars.d.ts" />

///<reference path="../typings/jquery/jquery.d.ts" />
```

To make our code easier to read, we will create an alias for the callback type:

```
type cb = (json : any) => void;
```

Now we need to declare our `View` class. The `View` class has some properties that allow us to set the following properties:

- **Container**: The DOM selector where we want our view to be inserted
- **Template URL**: The URL that will return a handlebars template

- **Service URL**: The URL of a web service that will return some JSON data
- **Arguments**: The data to be send to the service

We can see the `View` class implementation as follows:

```
class View {
  private _container : string;
  private _templateUrl : string;
  private _serviceUrl : string;
  private _args : any;
  constructor(config){
    this._container = config.container;
    this._templateUrl = config.templateUrl;
    this._serviceUrl = config.serviceUrl;
    this._args = config.args;
  }
  //...
```

After defining the class constructor and its properties, we will add a private method named `_loadJson` to our class. This method takes the service URL, the arguments, a success callback, and an error callback as its arguments. Inside the method, we will send a jQuery AJAX request using the service URL and argument settings:

```
private _loadJson(url : string, args : any, cb : cb, errorCb :
cb) {
  $.ajax({
    url: url,
    type: "GET",
    dataType: "json",
    data: args,
    success: (json) => {
      cb(json);
    },
    error: (e) => {
      errorCb(e);
    }
  });
}
//...
```

Handlebars is a library that allows us to compile and render HTML templates in a browser. These templates help with JSON-to-HTML transformations. We will mention this library later a couple of times, but don't worry if you have never used it before; this section is not about handlebars.

This section is about a set of tasks and how we can control the execution flow of those tasks using callbacks. If you want to learn more about handlebars, visit http://handlebarsjs.com/.

This function is almost identical to the previous one, but instead of loading some JSON, we will load a handlebars template:

```
private _loadHbs(url : string, cb : cb, errorCb : cb) {
  $.ajax({
    url: url,
    type: "GET",
    dataType: "text",
    success: (hbs) => {
      cb(hbs);
    },
    error: (e) => {
      errorCb(e);
    }
  });
}
//...
```

This function takes a handlebar template code as input and tries to compile it using the handlebars compile function. Just like in the previous example, we use callbacks, which will be invoked after the success or failure of the operation:

```
private _compileHbs(hbs : string, cb : cb, errorCb : cb) {
  try
  {
    var template = Handlebars.compile(hbs);
    cb(template);
  }
  catch(e) {
    errorCb(e);
  }
}
//...
```

In this function, we take the already compiled template and the already loaded JSON data and put them together to transform JSON into HTML following the template formatting rules. Just like in the previous example, we use callbacks that will be invoked after the success or failure of the operation:

```
private _jsonToHtml(template : any, json : any, cb : cb, errorCb
: cb) {
  try
  {
    var html = template(json);
    cb(html);
  }
  catch(e) {
    errorCb(e);
  }
}
//...
```

The following function takes the HTML generated by the _jsonToHtml function and appends it to a DOM element:

```
private _appendHtml = function (html : string, cb : cb, errorCb
: cb) {
  try
  {
    if($(this._container).length === 0) {
      throw new Error("Container not found!");
    }
    $(this._container).html(html);
    cb($(this._container));
  }
  catch(e) {
    errorCb(e);
  }
}
//...
```

Now that we have a few functions that use callbacks, we will use all of them together in one single function named render. The render method controls the execution flow of the tasks, and executes them in the following order:

1. Loads the JSON data.

2. Loads the template.

3. Compiles the template.

4. Transforms JSON into HTML.

5. Appends HTML to the DOM.

Each task takes a success callback, which invokes the following tasks in the list if it is successful, and an error callback, which is invoked when something goes wrong:

```
public render (cb : cb, errorCb : cb) {
  try
  {
    this._loadJson(this._serviceUrl, this._args, (json) => {
      this._loadHbs(this._templateUrl, (hbs) => {
        this._compileHbs(hbs, (template) => {
          this._jsonToHtml(template, json, (html) => {
            this._appendHtml(html, cb);
          }, errorCb);
        }, errorCb);
      }, errorCb);
    }, errorCb);
  }
  catch(e){
    errorCb(e);
  }
}
```

In general, you should try to avoid nesting callbacks like in the preceding example because it will:

- Make the code harder to understand
- Make the code harder to maintain (refactor, reuse, and so on)
- Make exception handling more difficult

Promises

After seeing how the use of callbacks can lead to some maintainability problems, we will now look at promises and how they can be used to write better asynchronous code. The core idea behind promises is that a promise represents the result of an asynchronous operation. Promise must be in one of the three following states:

- **Pending**: The initial state of a promise
- **Fulfilled**: The state of a promise representing a successful operation
- **Rejected**: The state of a promise representing a failed operation

Once a promise is fulfilled or rejected, its state can never change again. Let's take a look at the basic syntax of a promise:

```
function foo() {
  return new Promise((fulfill, reject) => {
    try
    {
      // do something
      fulfill(value);
    }
    catch(e){
      reject(reason);
    }
  });
}

foo().then(function(value){ console.log(value); })
     .catch(function(e){ console.log(e); });
```

> A try...catch statement is used here to showcase how we can explicitly fulfill or reject a promise. The try...catch statement is not really needed in a Promise function because when an error is thrown in a promise, the promise will automatically be rejected.
>
> The preceding code snippet declares a function named foo that returns a promise. The promise contains a method named then, which accepts a function to be invoked when the promise is fulfilled. Promises also provide a method named catch, which is invoked when a promise is rejected.

We will now return to the callback hell example and make some changes in the code to use promises instead of callbacks.

Just like before, we are going to need handlebars and jQuery; so let's import their type definitions. In addition, this time, we will also need the declarations of a library known as **Q**:

```
///<reference path="../typings/handlebars/handlebars.d.ts" />
///<reference path="../typings/jquery/jquery.d.ts" />
///<reference path="../typings/q/q.d.ts" />
```

> We will use the Promise object from a library instead of the native object because the libraries implement fallbacks so our code can work in old browsers. We will use a promises library known as Q (version 1.0.1) in this example. If you want to learn more about it, visit https://github.com/kriskowal/q.

The class name has changed from `View` to `ViewAsync` but everything else is still identical to the previous example:

```
class ViewAsync {
  private _container : string;
  private _templateUrl : string;
  private _serviceUrl : string;
  private _args : any;
  constructor(config) {
    this._container = config.container;
    this._templateUrl = config.templateUrl;
    this._serviceUrl = config.serviceUrl;
    this._args = config.args;
  }
  //...
```

> Many developers append the word `Async` to the name of a function as a code convention, which is used to indicate that a function is an asynchronous function.

We will use our first promise in the function `_loadJsonAsync`. This function was named `_loadJson` in the callback example. We have removed the callbacks for success and error previously declared in the function signature. Finally, we have wrapped the function with a promise object and invoked the `resolve` and `reject` methods when the promise succeeds or fails respectively.

```
private _loadJsonAsync(url : string, args : any) {
  return Q.Promise(function(resolve, reject) {
    $.ajax({
      url: url,
      type: "GET",
      dataType: "json",
      data: args,
      success: (json) => {
        resolve(json);
      },
      error: (e) => {
        reject(e);
      }
    });
  });
}
//...
```

We will then refactor (rename, remove callbacks, wrap logic with a promise, and so on) each of the class functions (_loadHbsAsync, compileHbsAsync, and _appendHtmlAsync):

```
private _loadHbsAsync(url : string) {
  return Q.Promise(function(resolve, reject) {
    $.ajax({
      url: url,
      type: "GET",
      dataType: "text",
      success: (hbs) => {
        resolve(hbs);
      },
      error: (e) => {
        reject(e);
      }
    });
  });
}
private _compileHbsAsync(hbs : string) {
  return Q.Promise(function(resolve, reject) {
    try
    {
    var template : any = Handlebars.compile(hbs);
      resolve(template);
    }
    catch(e) {
      reject(e);
    }
  });
}
private _jsonToHtmlAsync(template : any, json : any) {
  return Q.Promise(function(resolve, reject) {
    try
    {
      var html = template(json);
      resolve(html);
    }
    catch(e) {
      reject(e);
    }
  });
}
```

```
private _appendHtmlAsync(html : string, container : string) {
  return Q.Promise((resolve, reject) => {
    try
    {
      var $container : any = $(container);
      if($container.length === 0) {
        throw new Error("Container not found!");
      }
      $container.html(html);
      resolve($container);
    }
    catch(e) {
      reject(e);
    }
  });
}
//...
```

The RenderAsync method (previously named render) will present some significant differences.

In the following function, we start by wrapping the function's logic with a promise, invoke the function _loadJsonAsync, and assign its return value to the variable getJson. If we return to the _loadJsonAsync function, we will notice that the return type is a promise. Therefore, the getJson variable is a promise that once fulfilled will return the JSON data required to render our view.

This time, we will invoke the then method, which belongs to the promise returned by the _loadHbsAsync method. This will allow us to pass the output of the function _loadHbsAsync to _compileHbsAsync when the promise's state changes to fulfilled.

```
public renderAsync() {
  return Q.Promise((resolve, reject) => {
    try
    {
      // assign promise to getJson
      var getJson = this._loadJsonAsync(this._serviceUrl,
      this._args);

      // assign promise to getTemplate
      var getTemplate = this._loadHbsAsync(this._templateUrl)
      .then(this._compileHbsAsync);

      // execute promises in parallel
      Q.all([getJson, getTemplate]).then((results) => {
```

```
        var json = results[0];
        var template = results[1];

        this._jsonToHtmlAsync(template, json)
        .then((html : string) => {
            return this._appendHtmlAsync(html, this._container);
        })
        .then(($container : any) => { resolve($container); });
        });
    }
    catch(error) {
        reject(error);
    }
    });
  }
}
```

Once we have declared the getJson and getTemplate variables (each containing a promise as a value) we will use the all method from the Q library to execute the getJson and getTemplate promises in parallel.

Q's all method takes a list of promises and a callback as input. Once all the promises in the list have been fulfilled, the callback is invoked and an array named results is passed to the fulfilment callback. The array contains the results of each of the promises in the same order that they were passed to the all method.

Inside Q's all method callback, we will use the loaded JSON and the compiled template and arguments when invoking the _jsonToHtmlAsync promise. We will finally use the then method to call the _appendHtmlAsync method and resolve the promise.

As observed in the example, using promises gives us better control over the execution flow of each of the operations in our render method. Remember that you can use four different types of asynchronous flow control:

- **Concurrent**: The tasks are executed in parallel. We saw this in the example when we used the all method in the getJson and getTemplate promises.
- **Series**: A group of tasks is executed in sequence but the preceding tasks do not pass arguments to the next task.
- **Waterfall**: A group of tasks is executed in sequence and each task passes arguments to the next task. This approach is useful when the tasks have dependencies on each other. In the preceding example, we find this asynchronous flow control approach when the _loadHbsAsync promise passes its output to the _compileHbsAsync promise.

- **Composite**: This is any combination of the previous concurrent, series, and waterfall approaches. The `render` method in the example uses a combination of all the asynchronous flow control approaches in this list.

Generators

If we invoke a function in TypeScript, we can assume that once the function starts running, it will always run to completion before any other code can run. This has been the case until now. However, a new kind of function which may be paused in the middle of execution—one or many times—and resumed later, allowing other code to run during these paused periods, is about to arrive in TypeScript and ES6. These new kinds of functions are known as **generators**.

A generator represents a sequence of values. The interface of a generator object is a just an iterator. The `next()` function can be invoked until it runs out of values.

We can define the constructor of a generator by using the `function` keyword followed by an asterisk (*). The `yield` keyword is used to stop the execution of the function and return a value. Let's take a look at an example:

```
function *foo() {
    yield 1;
    yield 2;
    yield 3;
    yield 4;
    return 5;
}

var bar = new foo();
bar.next(); // Object {value: 1, done: false}
bar.next(); // Object {value: 2, done: false}
bar.next(); // Object {value: 3, done: false}
bar.next(); // Object {value: 4, done: false}
bar.next(); // Object {value: 5, done: true}
bar.next(); // Object { done: true }
```

As you can see, this iterator has five steps. The first time we call `next`, the function will be executed until it reaches the first yield statement, and then it will return the value 1 and stop the execution of the function until we invoke the generator's `next` method again. As we can see, we are now able to stop the function's execution at a given point. This allows us to write infinite loops without causing a stack overflow as in the following example:

```
function* foo() {
  var i = 1;
```

```
  while (true) {
    yield i++;
  }
}

var bar = new foo();
bar.next(); // Object {value: 1, done: false}
bar.next(); // Object {value: 2, done: false}
bar.next(); // Object {value: 3, done: false}
bar.next(); // Object {value: 4, done: false}
bar.next(); // Object {value: 5, done: false}
bar.next(); // Object {value: 6, done: false}
bar.next(); // Object {value: 7, done: false}
// ...
```

Generators will open possibilities for synchronicity as we can call a generator's next method after some asynchronous event has occurred.

Asynchronous functions – async and await

Asynchronous functions are a TypeScript feature that is scheduled to arrive with the upcoming TypeScript releases. An asynchronous function is a function that is expected to be invoked in a synchronous operation. Developers can use the `await` keyword to wait for the function results without blocking the normal execution of the program.

Asynchronous functions will be implemented using promises when targeting ES6, and promise fallbacks when targeting ES3 and ES5.

Using asynchronous functions generally helps to increase the readability of a piece of code when compared with the use of promises; but technically we can achieve the same features using both promises and synchronous code.

Let's take a sneak-peek at this upcoming feature:

```
var p: Promise<number> = /* ... */;

async function fn(): Promise<number> {
  var i = await p;
  return 1 + i;
}
```

The preceding code snippet declares a promise named `p`. This promise is the piece of code that will wait to be executed. While waiting, the program execution will not be blocked because we will wait from an asynchronous function named `fn`. As we can see, the `fn` function is preceded by the `async` keyword, which is used to indicate to the compiler that it is an asynchronous function.

Inside the function, the `await` keyword is used to suspend execution until `p` is settled. As we can see, the syntax is much more minimalistic and cleaner than it would be if we used the promises API (then and catch methods and callbacks).

> Refer to the TypeScript roadmap to learn more about the stages of development of this feature.

Summary

In this chapter, we saw how to work with functions in depth. We started with a quick recap of some basic concepts and then moved to some lesser known function features and use cases.

Once we saw how to work with functions, we focused on the usage of callbacks, promises, and generators to take advantage of the asynchronous programming capabilities of Typescript.

In the next chapter, we will look at how to work with classes, interfaces, and other object-oriented programming features of the TypeScript programming language.

4
Object-Oriented Programming with TypeScript

In the previous chapter, we explored the use of functions and some asynchronous techniques. In this chapter, we will see how to group our functions in reusable components, such as classes or modules. This chapter is divided into two main sections. The first part will cover the following topics:

- SOLID principles
- Classes
- Association, aggregation, and composition
- Inheritance
- Mixins
- Generic classes
- Generic constraints
- Interfaces

In the second part, we will focus on the declaration and use of namespaces and external modules. The second part will cover the following topics:

- Namespaces (internal modules)
- External modules
- **Asynchronous module definition** (AMD)
- CommonJS modules
- ES6 modules
- Browserify and **universal module definition** (UMD)
- Circular dependencies

SOLID principles

In the early days of software development, developers used to write code with procedural programing languages. In procedural programming languages, the programs follow a top-to-bottom approach and the logic is wrapped with functions.

New styles of computer programming, such as modular programming or structured programming, emerged when developers realized that procedural computer programs could not provide them with the desired level of abstraction, maintainability, and reusability.

The development community created a series of recommended practices and design patterns to improve the level of abstraction and reusability of procedural programming languages, but some of these guidelines required a certain level of expertise. In order to facilitate adherence to these guidelines, a new style of computer programming known as **object-oriented programming (OOP)** was created.

Developers quickly noticed some common OOP mistakes and came up with five rules that every OOP developer should follow to create a system that is easy to maintain and extend over time. These five rules are known as the SOLID principles. SOLID is an acronym introduced by Michael Feathers, which stands for the following principles:

- **Single responsibility principle (SRP)**: This principle states that a software component (function, class, or module) should focus on one unique task (have only one responsibility).

- **Open/closed principle (OCP)**: This principle states that software entities should be designed with application growth (new code) in mind (should be open to extension), but the application growth should require the fewer possible number of changes to the existing code (be closed for modification).

- **Liskov substitution principle (LSP)**: This principle states that we should be able to replace a class in a program with another class as long as both classes implement the same interface. After replacing the class, no other changes should be required, and the program should continue to work as it did originally.

- **Interface segregation principle (ISP)**: This principle states that we should split interfaces that are very large (general-purpose interfaces) into smaller and more specific ones (many client-specific interfaces) so that clients will only need to know about the methods that are of interest to them.

- **Dependency inversion principle (DIP)**: This principle states that entities should depend on abstractions (interfaces) as opposed to depending on concretion (classes).

In this chapter, we will see how to write TypeScript code that adheres to these principles so that our applications are easy to maintain and extend over time.

Classes

We should already be familiar with the basics about TypeScript classes, as we have declared some of them in previous chapters. So we will now look at some details and OOP concepts through examples. Let's start by declaring a simple class:

```
class Person {
  public name : string;
  public surname : string;
  public email : string;
  constructor(name : string, surname : string, email : string){
    this.email = email;
    this.name = name;
    this.surname = surname;
  }
  greet() {
    alert("Hi!");
  }
}

var me : Person = new Person("Remo", "Jansen",
"remo.jansen@wolksoftware.com");
```

We use classes to represent the type of an object or entity. A **class** is composed of a name, attributes, and methods. The class in the preceding example is named `Person` and contains three attributes or properties (`name`, `surname`, and `email`) and two methods (`constructor` and `greet`). Class attributes are used to describe the object's characteristics, while class methods are used to describe its behavior.

A **constructor** is a special method used by the new keyword to create instances (also known as objects) of our class. We have declared a variable named me, which holds an instance of the `Person` class. The new keyword uses the `Person` class's constructor to return an object whose type is `Person`.

A class should adhere to the single responsibility principle (SRP). The `Person` class in the preceding example represents a person, including all their characteristics (attributes) and behaviors (methods). Now let's add some `email` as validation logic:

```
class Person {
  public name : string;
  public surname : string;
```

```typescript
  public email : string;
  constructor(name : string, surname : string, email : string) {
    this.surname = surname;
    this.name = name;
    if(this.validateEmail(email)) {
      this.email = email;
    }
    else {
      throw new Error("Invalid email!");
    }
  }
  validateEmail() {
    var re = /\S+@\S+\.\S+/;
    return re.test(this.email);
  }
  greet() {
    alert("Hi! I'm " + this.name + ". You can reach me at " +
    this.email);
  }
}
```

When an object doesn't follow the SRP and it knows too much (has too many properties) or does too much (has too many methods), we say that the object is a God object. The Person class here is a God object because we have added a method named validateEmail that is not really related to the Person class's behavior.

Deciding which attributes and methods should or should not be part of a class is a relatively subjective decision. If we spend some time analyzing our options, we should be able to find a way to improve the design of our classes.

We can refactor the Person class by declaring an Email class, responsible for e-mail validation, and use it as an attribute in the Person class:

```typescript
class Email {
  public email : string;
  constructor(email : string){
    if(this.validateEmail(email)) {
      this.email = email;
    }
    else {
      throw new Error("Invalid email!");
    }
  }
  validateEmail(email : string) {
    var re = /\S+@\S+\.\S+/;
```

```
    return re.test(email);
  }
}
```

Now that we have an `Email` class, we can remove the responsibility of validating the emails from the `Person` class and update its `email` attribute to use the type `Email` instead of string:

```
class Person {
  public name : string;
  public surname : string;
  public email : Email;
  constructor(name : string, surname : string, email : Email){
    this.email = email;
    this.name = name;
    this.surname = surname;
  }
  greet() {
    alert("Hi!");
  }
}
```

Making sure that a class has a single responsibility makes it easier to see what it does and how we can extend/improve it. We can further improve our `Person` and `Email` classes by increasing the level of abstraction of our classes. For example, when we use the `Email` class, we don't really need to be aware of the existence of the `validateEmail` method; so this method could be invisible from outside the `Email` class. As a result, the `Email` class would be much simpler to understand.

When we increase the level of abstraction of an object, we can say that we are encapsulating the object's data and behavior. Encapsulation is also known as information hiding. For example, the `Email` class allows us to use emails without having to worry about e-mail validation because the class will deal with it for us. We can make this clearer by using access modifiers (`public` or `private`) to flag as private all the class attributes and methods that we want to abstract from the use of the `Email` class:

```
class Email {
  private email : string;
  constructor(email : string){
    if(this.validateEmail(email)) {
      this.email = email;
    }
    else {
      throw new Error("Invalid email!");
    }
```

```
    }
    private validateEmail(email : string) {
      var re = /\S+@\S+\.\S+/;
      return re.test(email);
    }
    get():string {
      return this.email;
    }
  }
```

We can then simply use the `Email` class without needing to explicitly perform any kind of validation:

```
var email = new Email("remo.jansen@wolksoftware.com");
```

Interfaces

The feature that we will miss the most when developing large-scale web applications with JavaScript is probably interfaces. We have seen that following the SOLID principles can help us to improve the quality of our code, and writing good code is a must when working on a large project. The problem is that if we attempt to follow the SOLID principles with JavaScript, we will soon realize that without interfaces, we will never be able to write SOLID OOP code. Fortunately for us, TypeScript features interfaces.

Traditionally, in OOP, we say that a class can extend another class and implement one or more interfaces. An interface can implement one or more interfaces and cannot extend another class or interface. Wikipedia's definition of interfaces in OOP is as follows:

> *In object-oriented languages, the term interface is often used to define an abstract type that contains no data or code, but defines behaviors as method signatures.*

Implementing an interface can be understood as signing a contract. The interface is a contract, and when we sign it (implement it), we must follow its rules. The interface rules are the signatures of the methods and properties, and we must implement them.

We will see many examples of interfaces later in this chapter.

In TypeScript, interfaces don't strictly follow this definition. The two main differences are that in TypeScript:

- An interface can extend another interface or class
- An interface can define data and behaviors as opposed to only behaviors

Association, aggregation, and composition

In OOP, classes can have some kind of relationship with each other. Now, we will take a look at the three different types of relationships between classes.

Association

We call **association** those relationships whose objects have an independent lifecycle and where there is no ownership between the objects. Let's take an example of a teacher and student. Multiple students can associate with a single teacher, and a single student can associate with multiple teachers, but both have their own lifecycles (both can be create and delete independently); so when a teacher leaves the school, we don't need to delete any students, and when a student leaves the school, we don't need to delete any teachers.

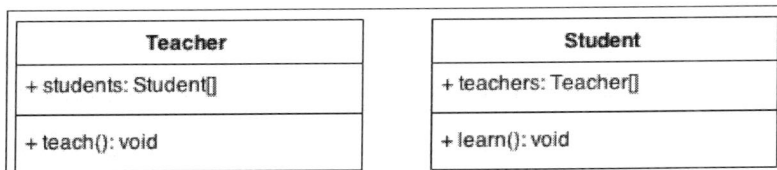

Teacher
+ students: Student[]
+ teach(): void

Student
+ teachers: Teacher[]
+ learn(): void

Aggregation

We call **aggregation** those relationships whose objects have an independent lifecycle, but there is ownership, and child objects cannot belong to another parent object. Let's take an example of a cell phone and a cell phone battery. A single battery can belong to a phone, but if the phone stops working, and we delete it from our database, the phone battery will not be deleted because it may still be functional. So in aggregation, while there is ownership, objects have their own lifecycle.

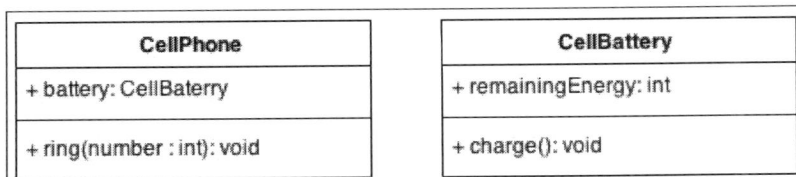

CellPhone
+ battery: CellBaterry
+ ring(number : int): void

CellBattery
+ remainingEnergy: int
+ charge(): void

Composition

We use the term **composition** to refer to relationships whose objects don't have an independent lifecycle, and if the parent object is deleted, all child objects will also be deleted.

Let's take an example of the relationship between questions and answers. Single questions can have multiple answers, and answers cannot belong to multiple questions. If we delete questions, answers will automatically be deleted.

Objects with a dependent life cycle (answers, in the example) are known as **weak entities**.

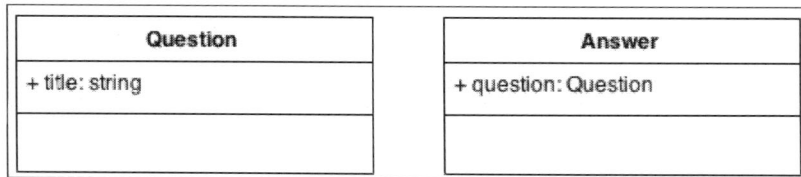

Question	Answer
+ title: string	+ question: Question

Sometimes, it can be a complicated process to decide if we should use association, aggregation, or composition. This difficulty is caused in part because aggregation and composition are subsets of association, meaning they are specific cases of association.

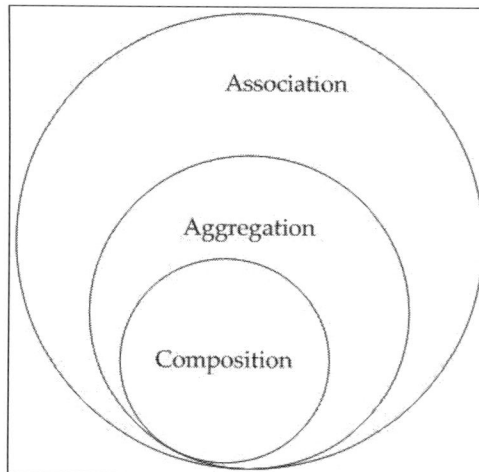

Inheritance

One of the most fundamental object-oriented programming features is its capability to extend existing classes. This feature is known as inheritance and allows us to create a new class (child class) that inherits all the properties and methods from an existing class (parent class). Child classes can include additional properties and methods not available in the parent class. Let's return to our previously declared `Person` class. We will use the `Person` class as the parent class of a child class named `Teacher`:

```
class Person {
  public name : string;
  public surname : string;
  public email : Email;
  constructor(name : string, surname : string, email : Email){
    this.name = name;
    this.surname = surname;
    this.email = email;
  }
  greet() {
    alert("Hi!");
  }
}
```

> This example is included in the companion source code.

Once we have a parent class in place, we can extend it by using the reserved keyword `extends`. In the following example, we declare a class called `Teacher`, which extends the previously defined `Person` class. This means that `Teacher` will inherit all the attributes and methods from its parent class:

```
class Teacher extends Person {
  teach() {
    alert("Welcome to class!");
  }
}
```

Note that we have also added a new method named `teach` to the class `Teacher`. If we create instances of the `Person` and `Teacher` classes, we will be able to see that both instances share the same attributes and methods with the exception of the `teach` method, which is only available for the instance of the `Teacher` class:

```
var teacher = new Teacher("remo", "jansen", new
Email("remo.jansen@wolksoftware.com"));
```

```
var me = new Person("remo", "jansen", new
Email("remo.jansen@wolksoftware.com"));

me.greet();
teacher.greet();
me.teach(); // Error : Property 'teach' does not exist on type
'Person'
teacher.teach();
```

Sometimes, we will need a child class to provide a specific implementation of a method that is already provided by its parent class. We can use the reserved keyword super for this purpose. Imagine that we want to add a new attribute to list the teacher's subjects, and we want to be able to initialize this attribute through the teacher constructor. We will use the super keyword to explicitly reference the parent class constructor inside the child class constructor. We can also use the super keyword when we want to extend an existing method, such as greet. This OOP language feature that allows a subclass or child class to provide a specific implementation of a method that is already provided by its parent classes is known as **method overriding**.

```
class Teacher extends Person {
  public subjects : string[];
  constructor(name : string, surname : string, email : Email, subjects
: string[]){
    super(name, surname, email);
    this.subjects = subjects;
  }
  greet() {
    super.greet();
    alert("I teach " + this.subjects);
  }
  teach() {
    alert("Welcome to Maths class!");
  }
}

var teacher = new Teacher("remo", "jansen", new
Email("remo.jansen@wolksoftware.com"), ["math", "physics"]);
```

We can declare a new class that inherits from a class that is already inheriting from another. In the following code snippet, we declare a class called `SchoolPrincipal` that extends the `Teacher` class, which extends the `Person` class:

```
class SchoolPrincipal extends Teacher {
  manageTeachers() {
    alert("We need to help students to get better results!");
  }
}
```

If we create an instance of the `SchoolPrincipal` class, we will be able to access all the properties and methods from its parent classes (`SchoolPrincipal`, `Teacher`, and `Person`):

```
var principal = new SchoolPrincipal("remo", "jansen", new
Email("remo.jansen@wolksoftware.com"), ["math", "physics"]);
principal.greet();
principal.teach();
principal.manageTeachers();
```

It is not recommended to have too many levels in the inheritance tree. A class situated too deeply in the inheritance tree will be relatively complex to develop, test, and maintain. Unfortunately, we don't have a specific rule that we can follow when we are unsure whether we should increase the **depth of inheritance tree (DIT)**.

We should use inheritance in such a way that it helps us to reduce the complexity of our application and not the opposite. We should try to keep the DIT between 0 and 4 because a value greater than 4 would compromise encapsulation and increase complexity.

Mixins

Sometimes, we will find scenarios in which it would be a good idea to declare a class that inherits from two or more classes simultaneously (known as **multiple inheritance**).

Let's take a look at an example. We will not add any code to the methods in this example because we want to avoid the possibility of getting distracted by it; we should focus on the inheritance tree:

```
class Animal {
  eat() {
    // ...
  }
}
```

We started by declaring a class named `Animal`, which only has one method named `eat`. Now, let's declare two new classes:

```
class Mammal extends Animal {
  breathe() {
    // ...
  }
}

class WingedAnimal extends Animal {
  fly(){
    // ...
  }
}
```

We have declared two new classes named `WingedAnimal` and `Mammal`. Both classes inherit from the `Animal` class.

Now that we have our classes ready, we are going to try to implement a class named `Bat`. Bats are mammals and have wings—creating a new class named `Bat`, which will extend both the `Mammal` and `WingedAnimal` classes, seems logical. However, if we attempt to do so, we will encounter a compilation error:

```
// Error: Classes can only extend a single class.
class Bat extends WingedAnimal, Mammal {
  // ...
}
```

This error is thrown because TypeScript doesn't support multiple inheritance. This means that a class can only extend one class. The designers of programming languages such as C# or TypeScript decided to not support multiple inheritance because it can potentially increase the complexity of applications.

Sometimes, a class inheritance diagram can take a diamond-like shape (as seen in the following figure). This kind of class inheritance diagram can potentially lead us to design issue known as the **diamond problem**.

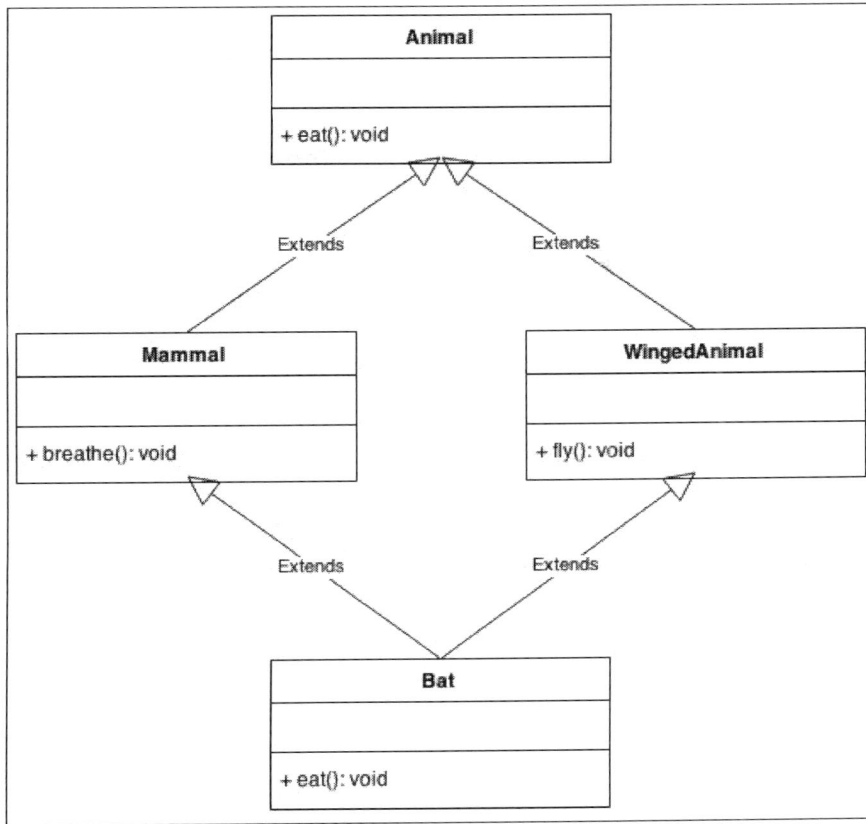

We will not face any problems if we call a method that is exclusive to only one of the classes in the inheritance tree:

```
var bat = new Bat();
bat.fly();
bat.eat();
bat.breathe();
```

The diamond problem takes place when we try to invoke one of the `Bat` class's parent's methods, and it is unclear or ambiguous which of the parent's implementations of that method should be invoked. If we add a method named `move` to both the `Mammal` and the `WingedAnimal` class and try to invoke it from an instance of `Bat`, we will get an ambiguous call error.

Now that we know why multiple inheritance can be potentially dangerous, we will introduce a feature known as **mixin**. Mixins are alternatives to multiple inheritance, but this feature has some limitations.

Let's return to the `Bat` class example to showcase the usage of mixins:

```
class Mammal {
  breathe() : string {
    return "I'm alive!";
  }
}

class WingedAnimal {
  fly() : string{
    return "I can fly!";
  }
}
```

[🖊️ This example is included in the companion source code.]

The two classes presented in the preceding example are not much different from the previous example; we have added some logic to the `breathe` and `fly` methods, so we can have some output to help us to understand this demonstration. Also, note that the classes no longer extend the `Animal` class:

```
class Bat implements Mammal, WingedAnimal {
  breathe : () => string;
  fly : () => string;
}
```

The `Bat` class has some important additions. We have used the reserved keyword `implements` (as opposed to `extends`) to indicate that `Bat` will implement the functionality declared in both the `Mammal` and `WingedAnimal` classes. We have also added the signature of each of the methods that the `Bat` class will implement.

We need to copy the following function somewhere in our code to be able to apply mixins:

```
function applyMixins(derivedCtor: any, baseCtors: any[]) {
  baseCtors.forEach(baseCtor => {
    Object.getOwnPropertyNames(baseCtor.prototype).forEach(name =>
    {
        if (name !== 'constructor') {
          derivedCtor.prototype[name] = baseCtor.prototype[name];
        }
    });
  });
}
```

> The preceding function is a well-known pattern and can be found in many books and online references, including the official TypeScript handbook.

This function will iterate each property of the parent classes (contained in an array named `baseCtors`) and copy the implementation to a child class (`derivedCtor`).

We only need to declare this function once in our application. Once we have done it, we can use it as follows:

```
applyMixins(Bat, [Mammal, WingedAnimal]);
```

The child class (`Bat`) will then contain the implementation of each property and method of the two parent classes (`WingedAnimal` and `Mammal`):

```
var bat = new Bat();
bat.breathe(); // I'm alive!
bat.fly();     // I can fly!
```

As we said at the beginning of this section, mixins have some limitations. The first limitation is that we can only inherit the properties and methods from one level in the inheritance tree. Now we can understand why we removed the `Animal` class prior to applying the mixin. The second limitation is that, if two or more of the parent classes contain a method with the same name, the method that is going to be inherited will be taken from the last class passed in the `baseCtors` array to the `applyMixins` function. We will now see an example that presents both these limitations.

In order to show the first limitation, we will declare the `Animal` class:

```
class Animal {
  eat() : string {
    return "Delicious!";
  }
}
```

We will then declare the `Mammal` and `WingedAnimal` classes, but this time, they will extend the Animal class:

```
class Mammal extends Animal {
  breathe() : string {
    return "I'm alive!";
  }
  move() : string {
    return "I can move like a mammal!";
  }
}
```

```
class WingedAnimal extends Animal {
  fly() : string{
    return "I can fly!";
  }
  move() : string {
    return "I can move like a bird!";
  }
}
```

We will then declare a `Bat` class but we will name it `Bat1`. This class will implement both the `Mammal` and `WindgedAnimal` classes:

```
class Bat1 implements Mammal, WingedAnimal {
  eat : () => string;
  breathe : () => string;
  fly : () => string;
  move : () => string;
}
```

We are ready to invoke the `applyMixins` function. Notice how we pass `Mammal` before `WingedAnimal` in the array:

```
applyMixins(Bat1, [Mammal, WingedAnimal]);
```

We can now create an instance of `Bat1`, and we will be able to observe that the `eat` method has not been inherited from the `Animal` class due to the first limitation:

```
var bat1 = new Bat();
bat1.eat();       // Error: not a function
```

Each of the parent class's methods has been inherited without issues:

```
bat1.breathe(); // I'm alive!
bat1.fly();     // I can fly!"
```

Except the `move` method because according to the second limitation, only the implementation of the last parent class passed to the `applyMixins` method will be implemented. In this case, the implementation is inherited from the `WingedAnimal` class:

```
bat1.move();      // I can move like a bird
```

To finalize, we will see the effect of switching the order of the parent classes when invoking the `applyMixins` method:

```
class Bat2 implements WingedAnimal, Mammal {
  eat : () => string;
  breathe : () => string;
```

```
    fly : () => string;
    move : () => string;
}
```

Notice how we have passed `WingedAnimal` before `Mammal` in the array:

```
applyMixins(Bat2, [WingedAnimal, Mammal]);
var bat2 = new Bat2();
bat2.eat();      // Error: not a function
bat2.breathe(); // I'm alive!
bat2.fly();      // I can fly!
bat2.move()      // I can move like a mammal
```

Generic classes

In the previous chapter, we saw how to work with generic functions. We will now take a look at how to work with generic classes.

Just like with generic functions, generic classes can help us to avoid the duplication of code. Let's take a look at an example:

```
class User {
  public name : string;
  public password : string;
}
```

> This example is included in the companion source code.

We have declared a `User` class, which contains two properties: `name` and `password`. We will now declare a class named `NotGenericUserRepository` without using generics. This class takes a URL via its constructor and has a method named `getAsync`. The `getAsync` method will request a list of users stored in a JSON file using AJAX:

```
class NotGenericUserRepository {
  private _url : string;
  constructor(url : string) {
    this._url = url;
  }
  public getAsync() {
    return Q.Promise((resolve : (users : User[]) => void, reject)
    => {
      $.ajax({
        url: this._url,
```

```
        type: "GET",
        dataType: "json",
        success: (data) => {
          var users = <User[]>data.items;
          resolve(users);
        },
        error: (e) => {
          reject(e);
        }
      });
    });
  }
}
```

Once we have finished declaring the `NotGenericUserRepository` user repository, we can create an instance and invoke the `getAsync` method:

```
var notGenericUserRepository = new NotGenericUserRepository("./demos/
shared/users.json");
notGenericUserRepository.getAsync()
  .then(function(users : User[]){
    console.log('notGenericUserRepository => ', users);
  });
```

If we also need to request another list of entities different from `User`, we could end up duplicating a lot of code. Imagine that we also need to request a list of conference talks. We could create an entity named `Talk` and an almost identical repository class:

```
class Talk {
  public title : string;
  public description : string;
  public language : string;
  public url : string;
  public year : string;
}

class NotGenericTalkRepository {
  private _url : string;
  constructor(url : string) {
    this._url = url;
  }
  public getAsync() {
    return Q.Promise((resolve : (talks : Talk[]) => void, reject)
    => {
      $.ajax({
```

```
      url: this._url,
      type: "GET",
      dataType: "json",
      success: (data) => {
        var users talks = <Talk[]>data.items;
        resolve(userstalks);
      },
      error: (e) => {
        reject(e);
      }
    });
  });
  }
}
```

If the number of entities grows, we will continue to repeatedly duplicate code. We may think that we could use the any type to avoid this problem, but then we would be losing the security provided by the checking type performed by TypeScript at compilation time. A much better solution is to create a Generic repository:

```
class GenericRepository<T> {
  private _url : string;
  constructor(url : string){
    this._url = url;
  }
  public getAsync() {
    return Q.Promise((resolve : (entities : T[]) => void, reject) => {
      $.ajax({
        url: this._url,
        type: "GET",
        dataType: "json",
        success: (data) => {
          var list = <T[]>data.items;
          resolve(list);
        },
        error: (e) => {
          reject(e);
        }
      });
    });
  }
}
```

The repository code is identical to `NotGenericUserRepository`, except for the entity type. We have removed the hardcoded reference to the `User` and `Talk` entities and replaced them with the generic type `T`. We can now declare as many repositories as we wish without duplicating a single line of code:

```
var userRepository = new GenericRepository<User>("./demos/shared/
users.json");
userRepository.getAsync()
  .then((users : User[]) => {
    console.log('userRepository => ', users);
  });

var talkRepository = new GenericRepository<Talk>("./demos/shared/
talks.json");
talkRepository.getAsync()
  .then((talks : Talk[]) => {
    console.log('talkRepository => ', talks);
  });
```

Generic constraints

Sometimes, we might need to restrict the use of a generic class. Take the generic repository from the previous section as an example. We have a new requirement: we need to add some changes to validate the entities loaded via AJAX, and we will return only the valid entities.

One possible solution is to use the `typeof` operator to identify the type of the generic type parameter `T` within a generic class or function:

```
// ...
success: (data) => {
  var list : T[];
  var items = <T[]>data.items;
  for(var i = 0; i < items.length; i++){
    if(items[i] instanceof User) {
      // validate user
    }
    if(items[i] instanceof Talk) {
      // validate talk
    }
  }
  resolve(list);
}
// ...
```

The problem is that we will have to modify our `GenericRepository` class to add extra logic with each new entity. We will not add the validation rules into the `GenericRepository` repository class because a generic class should not be aware of the type used as the generic type.

A better solution is to add a method named `isValid` to the entities, which will return true if the entity is valid:

```
// ...
success: (data) => {
  var list : T[];
  var items = <T[]>data.items;
  for(var i = 0; i < items.length; i++){
    if(items[i].isValid()) { // error
      // ...
    }
  }
  resolve(list);
}
// ...
```

The second approach follows the second SOLID principle, the open/close principle, as we can create new entities and the generic repository will continue to work (open for extension), but no additional changes to it will be required (closed for modification). The only problem with this approach is that, if we attempt to invoke an entity's `isValid` method inside the generic repository, we will get a compilation error.

The error is thrown because we are allowed to use the generic repository with any type, but not all types have a method named `isValid`. Fortunately, this issue can easily be resolved by using a generic constraint. Constraints will restrict the types that we are allowed to use as the generic type parameter `T`. We are going to declare a constraint, so only types that implement an interface named `ValidatableInterface` can be used with the generic method.

Let's start by declaring an interface:

```
interface ValidatableInterface {
  isValid() : boolean;
}
```

[This example is included in the companion source code.]

Now we can proceed to implement the interface. In this case, we must implement the isValid method:

```
class User implements ValidatableInterface {
  public name : string;
  public password : string;
  public isValid() : boolean {
    // user validation...
    return true;
  }
}

class Talk implements ValidatableInterface {
  public title : string;
  public description : string;
  public language : string;
  public url : string;
  public year : string;
  public isValid() : boolean {
    // talk validation...
    return true;
  }
}
```

Now, let's declare a generic repository and add a type constraint so only types derived from ValidatableInterface will be accepted as the generic type parameter T:

```
class GenericRepositoryWithConstraint<T extends
ValidatableInterface> {
  private _url : string;
  constructor(url : string){
    this._url = url;
  }
  public getAsync() {
    return Q.Promise((resolve : (talks : T[]) => void, reject) =>
    {
      $.ajax({
        url: this._url,
        type: "GET",
        dataType: "json",
        success: (data) => {
          var items = <T[]>data.items;
          for(var i = 0; i < items.length; i++) {
```

```
            if(items[i].isValid()) {
                list.push(items[i]);
            }
        }
        resolve(list);
    },
    error: (e) => {
        reject(e);
    }
    });
    });
    }
}
```

> Even though we have used an interface, we used the extends
> keyword and not the implements keyword to declare the
> constraint in the preceding example. There is no special reason for
> that. This is just the way the TypeScript constraint syntax works.

We can then create as many repositories as we want:

```
var userRepository = new
    GenericRepositoryWithConstraint<User>("./users.json");

userRepository.getAsync()
    .then(function(users : User[]){
        console.log(users);
    });

var talkRepository = new
    GenericRepositoryWithConstraint<Talk>("./talks.json");

talkRepository.getAsync()
    .then(function(talks : Talk[]){
        console.log(talks);
    });
```

If we attempt to use a class that doesn't implement the ValidatableInterface of
the generic type parameter T, we will get a compilation error.

Multiple types in generic type constraints

We can only refer to one type when declaring a generic type constraint. Let's imagine that we need a generic class to be constrained, so it only allows types that implement the following two interfaces:

```
interface IMyInterface {
  doSomething();
};
interface IMySecondInterface {
  doSomethingElse();
};
```

We may think that we can define the required generic constraint as follows:

```
class Example<T extends IMyInterface, IMySecondInterface> {
  private genericProperty : T;
  useT() {
    this.genericProperty.doSomething();
    this.genericProperty.doSomethingElse(); // error
  }
}
```

However, this code snippet will throw a compilation error. We cannot specify multiple types when declaring a generic type constraint. However, we can work around this issue by transforming IMyInterface, IMySecondInterface in super-interfaces:

```
interface IChildInterface extends IMyInterface, IMySecondInterface {

}
```

IMyInterface and IMySecondInterface are now super-interfaces because they are the parent interfaces of the IChildInterface interface. We can then declare the constraint using the IChildInterface interface:

```
class Example<T extends IChildInterface> {
  private genericProperty : T;
  useT() {
    this.genericProperty.doSomething();
    this.genericProperty.doSomethingElse();
  }
}
```

The new operator in generic types

To create a new object within generic code, we need to indicate that the generic type T has a constructor function. This means that instead of using `type:T`, we should use `type: { new(): T;}` as follows:

```
function factoryNotWorking<T>(): T {
    return new T(); // compile error could not find symbol T
}

function factory<T>(): T {
  var type: { new(): T ;};
  return new type();
}

var myClass: MyClass = factory<MyClass>();
```

Applying the SOLID principles

As we have previously mentioned, interfaces are fundamental features when it comes to following the SOLID principles, and we have already put the first two SOLID principles into practice.

We have already discussed the single responsibility principle. Now, we will see real examples of the three remaining principles.

The Liskov substitution principle

The `Liskov substitution principle` (LSP) states, *Subtypes must be substitutable for their base types*. Let's take a look at an example to understand what this means.

We will declare a class named `PersistanceService`, the responsibility of which is to persist some object into some sort of storage. We will start by declaring the following interface:

```
interface PersistanceServiceInterface {
  save(entity : any) : number;
}
```

After declaring the `PersistanceServiceInterface` interface, we can implement it. We will use cookies as the storage for the application's data:

```
class CookiePersistanceService implements PersistanceServiceInterface{
  save(entity : any) : number {
    var id =  Math.floor((Math.random() * 100) + 1);
    // Cookie persistance logic...
    return id;
  }
}
```

We will continue by declaring a class named `FavouritesController`, which has a dependency on `PersistanceServiceInterface`:

```
class FavouritesController {
  private _persistanceService : PersistanceServiceInterface;
  constructor(persistanceService : PersistanceServiceInterface) {
    this._persistanceService = persistanceService;
  }
  public saveAsFavourite(articleId : number) {
    return this._persistanceService.save(articleId);
  }
}
```

We can finally create an instance of `FavouritesController` and pass an instance of `CookiePersitanceService` via its constructor:

```
var favController = new FavouritesController(new
CookiePersistanceService());
```

The LSP allows us to replace a dependency with another implementation as long as both implementations are based in the same base type; so, if we decide to stop using cookies as storage and use the HTML5 local storage API instead, we can declare a new implementation:

```
class LocalStoragePersistanceService implements
PersistanceServiceInterface{
  save(entity : any) : number {
    var id =  Math.floor((Math.random() * 100) + 1);
    // Local storage persistance logic...
    return id;
  }
}
```

We can then replace it without having to add any changes to the `FavouritesController` controller class.

```
var favController = new FavouritesController(new
LocalStoragePersistanceService());
```

The interface segregation principle

Interfaces are used to declare how two or more software components cooperate and exchange information with each other. This declaration is known as **application programming interface (API)**. In the previous example, our interface was PersistanceServiceInterface, and it was implemented by the classes LocalStoragePersitanceService and CookiePersitanceService. The interface was consumed by the FavouritesController class; so we say that this class is a client of the PersistanceServiceInterface's API.

The **interface segregation principle (ISP)** states that no client should be forced to depend on methods it does not use. To adhere to the ISP, we need to keep in mind that when we declare the API (how two or more software components cooperate and exchange information with each other) of our application's components, the declaration of many client-specific interfaces is better than the declaration of one general-purpose interface. Let's take a look at an example.

If we design an API to control all the elements in a vehicle (engine, radio, heating, navigation, lights…), we could have one general-purpose interface, which allows us to control every single element of the vehicle:

```
interface VehicleInterface {
  getSpeed() : number;
  getVehicleType: string;
  isTaxPayed() : boolean;
  isLightsOn() : boolean;
  isLightsOff() : boolean;
  startEngine() : void;
  acelerate() : number;
  stopEngine() : void;
  startRadio() : void;
  playCd : void;
  stopRadio() : void;
}
```

> This example is included in the companion source code.

If a class has a dependency (client) in the VehicleInterface interface but it only wants to use the radio methods, we will be facing a violation of the ISP because, as we have already seen, no client should be forced to depend on methods it does not use.

The solution is to split the `VehicleInterface` interface into many client-specific interfaces so that our class can adhere to the ISP by depending only on the `RadioInterface` interface:

```typescript
interface VehicleInterface {
  getSpeed() : number;
  getVehicleType: string;
  isTaxPayed() : boolean;
  isLightsOn() : boolean;
}

interface LightsInterface {
  isLightsOn() : boolean;
  isLightsOff() : boolean;
}

interface RadioInterface {
  startRadio() : void;
  playCd : void;
  stopRadio() : void;
}

interface EngineInterface {
  startEngine() : void;
  acelerate() : number;
  stopEngine() : void;
}
```

The dependency inversion principle

The **dependency inversion (DI)** principle states, *Depend upon abstractions. Do not depend upon concretions.* In the previous section, we implemented `FavouritesController` and we were able to replace an implementation of `PersistanceServiceInterface` with another without having to perform any additional change to `FavouritesController`. This was possible because we followed the DI principle, as `FavouritesController` has a dependency upon `PersistanceServiceInterface` (abstractions) rather than `LocalStoragePersitanceService` or `CookiePersitanceService` (concretions).

> Depending on your background, you may wonder if there are any **Inversion of Control (IoC)** containers available for TypeScript. We can indeed find some IoC containers available online. However, because Typescript's runtime doesn't support reflection or interfaces, they can arguably be considered pseudo IoC containers rather than real IoC containers.
>
> If you want to learn more about inversion of control, I highly recommend the article, Inversion of Control Containers and the Dependency Injection pattern, by Martin Fowler, available at `http://martinfowler.com/articles/injection.html`.

Namespaces

TypeScript features namespaces (previously known as internal modules). Namespaces are mainly used to organize our code.

If we are working on a large application, as the code base grows we will need to introduce some kind of organization scheme to avoid naming collisions and make our code easier to follow and understand.

We can use namespaces to encapsulate interfaces, classes, and objects that are somehow related. For example, we could wrap all our application models inside an internal module named model:

```
namespace app {
  export class UserModel {
    // ...
  }
}
```

When we declare a namespace, all its entities are private by default. We can use the `export` keyword to declare what parts of our namespace we wish to make public.

We are allowed to nest a namespace inside another. Let's create a file named `models.ts` and add the following code snippet to it:

```
namespace app {
  export namespace models {
    export class UserModel {
      // ...
    }
```

```
      export class TalkModel {
        // ...
      }
    }
  }
}
```

In the preceding example, we have declared a namespace named app, and inside it, we have declared a public namespace named models, which contains two public classes: UserModel and TalkModel. We can then call the namespace from another TypeScript file by indicating the full namespace name:

```
var user = new app.models.UserModel();
var talk = new app.models.TalkModel();
```

If an internal module becomes too big, it can be divided into multiple files to increase its maintainability. If we take the preceding example, we could add more contents to the internal module named app by referencing it in another file.

Let's create a new file named validation.ts and add the following code to it:

```
namespace app {
  export namespace validation {
    export class UserValidator{
      // ...
    }

    export class TalkValidator {
      // ...
    }
  }
}
```

Let's create a file named main.ts and add the following code to it:

```
var user = new app.models.UserModel();
var talk = new app.models.TalkModel();
var userValidator = new app.validation.UserValidator();
var talkValidator = new app.validation.TalkValidator();
```

Even though the namespaces' models and validation are in two different files, we are able to access them from a third file.

Namespace can contain periods. For example, instead of nesting the namespaces (validation and models) inside the app module, we could have used periods in the validation and model internal module names:

```
namespace app.validation {
```

```
  // ...
}
namespace app.models {
  // ...
}
```

The `import` keyword can be used within an internal module to provide an alias for another module:

```
import TalkValidatorAlias = app.validation.TalkValidator;
var talkValidator = new TalkValidatorAlias();
```

Once we have finished declaring our namespaces, we can decide if we want to compile each one into JavaScript or if we prefer to concatenate all the files into one single file.

We can use the `--out` flag to compile all the input files into a single JavaScript output file:

```
tsc --out output.js input.ts
```

The compiler will automatically order the output file based on the reference tags present in the files. We can then import our files or file using an HTML `<script>` tag.

Modules

TypeScript also has the concept of external modules or just modules. The main difference between using modules (instead of namespaces) is that after declaring all our modules, we will not import them using an HTML `<script>` tag and we will be able to use a module loader instead.

A **module loader** is a tool that allows us to have better control over the module loading process. This allows us to perform tasks such as loading files asynchronously or combining multiple modules into a single highly optimized file with ease.

Using the `<script>` tag is not recommended because when a web browser finds a `<script>` tag, it downloads the file using asynchronous requests. We should attempt to load as many files as possible using asynchronous requests because doing so will significantly improve the network performance of a web application.

> We will discover more about network performance in *Chapter 6, Application Performance*.

The JavaScript versions prior to ECMAScript 6 (ES6) don't include native module support. Developers were forced to develop their own module loaders. The open source community tried to come up with improved solutions over the years. As a result, today there are several module loaders available, and each one uses a different module definition syntax. The most popular ones are as follows:

- **RequireJS**: RequireJS uses a syntax known as asynchronous module definition (AMD)

- **Browserify**: Browserify uses a syntax known as CommonJS.

- **SystemJS**: SystemJS is a universal module loader, which means that it supports all the available module syntaxes (ES6, CommonJS, AMD, and UMD).

> Node.js applications also use the CommonJS syntax.

Fortunately, TypeScript allows us to choose which kind of module definition syntax (ES6, CommonJS, AMD, SystemJS, or UMD) we want to use at runtime.

We can indicate our preference by using the `--module` flag when compiling:

```
tsc --module commonjs main.ts  // use CommonJS
tsc --module amd main.ts       // use AMD
tsc --module umd main.ts       // use UMD
tsc --module system main.ts    // use SytemJS
```

While we can select four different module definition syntaxes at runtime. However, only two are available at design time:

- External module syntax (The default module syntax in the TypeScript versions prior to 1.5)

- ES6 module syntax (The recommended external module syntax in TypeScript 1.5 or higher)

It is important to understand that we can use one kind of module definition syntax at design time (ES6, CommonJS, AMD, SystemJS, or UMD) and another at runtime (external modules or ES6).

Since the release of TypeScript 1.5, it is recommended you use the ECMAScript 6 module definition syntax because it is based on standards, and in the future, we will be able to use this syntax at both design time and runtime.

We will now take a look at each of the available module definition syntaxes.

ES6 modules – runtime and design time

TypeScript 1.5 introduces support for the ES6 module syntax. Let's define an external module using it:

```
class UserModel {
  // ...
}
export { UserModel };
```

We have defined an external module. We don't need to use the `namespace` keyword, but we must continue to use the `export` keyword. We used the `export` keyword at the bottom of the module, but it is also possible to use it just before the `class` keyword like we did in the internal module example:

```
export class UserModel {
  // ...
}
```

We can also export an entity using an alias:

```
class UserModel {
  // ...
}
export { UserModel as User }; // UserModel exported as User
```

An export declaration exports all meanings of a name:

```
interface UserModel {
  // ...
}

class UserModel {
  // ...
}
export { UserModel }; // Exports both interface and function
```

To import a module, we must use the `import` keyword as follows:

```
import { UserModel } from "./models";
```

The `import` keyword creates a variable for each imported component. In the preceding code snippet, a new variable named `UserModel` is declared and its value contains a reference to the `UserModel` class, which was declared and exported in the `models.ts` file.

We can use the export keyword to import multiple entities from one module:

```
class UserValidator {
  // ...
}

class TalkValidator {
  // ...
}

export { UserValidator, TalkValidator };
```

Furthermore, we can use the `import` keyword to import multiple entities from a single module as follows:

```
import { UserValidator, TalkValidator } from "./validation.ts"
```

> Throughout the rest of this book, we will use the ES6 syntax at design-time and the CommonJS syntax at runtime.

External modules – design time only

Before TypeScript 1.5, modules were declared using a kind of module syntax known as external module syntax. This kind of syntax was used at design time (TypeScript code). However, once compiled into JavaScript, it was transformed and executed (runtime) into AMD, CommonJS, UMD, or SystemJS modules.

We should try to avoid using this syntax and use the new ES6 syntax instead. However, we will take a quick look at the external module syntax because we may have to work on old applications or outdated documentation.

We can import a module using the `import` keyword:

```
import User = require("./user_class");
```

The preceding code snippet declares a new variable named `User`. The `User` variable takes the exported content of the `user_class` module as its value.

To export a module, we need to use the `export` keyword. We can apply the `export` keyword directly to a class or interface:

```
export class User {
  // ...
}
```

We can also use the `export` keyword on its own by assigning to it the value that we desire to export:

```
class User {
 // ...
}
export = User;
```

External modules can be compiled into any of the available module definition syntaxes (AMD, CommonJS, SystemJS, or UMD).

AMD modules – runtime only

If we compile the initial external module into an AMD module (using the flag `--compile amd`), we will generate the following AMD module:

```
define(["require", "exports"], function (require, exports) {
    var UserModel = (function () {
        function UserModel() {
        }
        return UserModel;
    })();
    return UserModel;
});
```

The define function takes an array as its first argument. This array contains a list of the names of the module dependencies. The second argument is a callback that will be invoked once all the module dependencies have been loaded. The callback takes each of the module dependencies as its parameters and contains all the logic from our TypeScript component. Notice how the return type of the callback matches the components that we declared as public by using the `export` keyword. AMD modules can then be loaded using the RequireJS module loader.

> We will not discuss AMD and RequireJS further in this book, but if you want to learn more about them, you can do so by visiting http://requirejs.org/docs/start.html.

CommonJS modules – runtime only

We begin by compiling our external module into a CommonJS module (using the flag `--compile commonjs`). We will compile the following code snippet:

```
class User {
 // ...
}
export = User;
```

As a result, the following CommonJS module is generated:

```
var UserModel = (function () {
    function UserModel() {
      //...
    }
    return UserModel;
})();
module.exports = UserModel;
```

As we can see in the preceding code snippet, the CommonJS module definition syntax is almost identical to the deprecated TypeScript (1.4 or prior) external module syntax.

The preceding CommonJS module can be loaded by a Node.js application without any additional changes using the `import` keyword and the `require` function:

```
import UserModel = require('./UserModel');
var user = new UserModel();
```

However, if we attempt to use the `require` function in a web browser, an exception will be thrown because the `require` function is undefined. We can easily solve this problem by using Browserify.

All that we need to follow is three simple steps:

1. Install Browserify using npm:

   npm install -g browserify

2. Use Browserify to bundle all your CommonJS modules into a JavaScript file that you can import using an HTML `<script>` tag. We can do this by executing the following command:

   browserify main.js -o bundle.js

   In the preceding command, `main.js` is the file that contains the root module within our application's dependency tree. The `bundle.js` file is the output file that we will be able to import using a HTML script tag.

3. Import the `bundle.js` file using a HTML `<script>` tag.

> If you need more information about Browserify, visit the official documentation at `https://github.com/substack/node-browserify#usage`.

UMD modules – runtime only

If we want to release a JavaScript library or framework, we will need to compile our TypeScript application into both CommonJS and AMD modules. Our library should also allow developers to load it directly in a web browser using a HTML script tag.

The web development community has developed the following code snippet to help us to achieve **universal module definition (UMD)** support:

```
(function (root, factory) {
  if (typeof exports === 'object') {
    // CommonJS
    module.exports = factory(require('b'));
  } else if (typeof define === 'function' && define.amd) {
    // AMD
    define(['b'], function (b) {
      return (root.returnExportsGlobal = factory(b));
    });
  } else {
    // Global Variables
    root.returnExportsGlobal = factory(root.b);
  }
}(this, function (b) {
  // Your actual module
  return {};
}));
```

This code snippet is great, but we want to avoid manually adding it to every single module in our application. Fortunately, there are a few options available to achieve UMD support with ease.

The first option is to use the flag `--compile umd` to generate one UMD module for each module in our application. The second option is to create one single UMD module that will contain all the modules in the application using a module loader known as Browserify.

[
Refer to the official Browserify project website at
`http://browserify.org/` to learn more about Browserify.
Refer to the `Browserify-standalone` option to learn more
about the generation of one unique optimized file.
]

SystemJS modules – runtime only

While UMD gives you a way to output a single module that works in both AMD
and CommonJS, SystemJS will allow you to use ES6 modules closer to their native
semantics without requiring an ES6-compatible browser engine.

SytemJS is used by Angular 2.0, which is the upcoming version of a popular web
application development framework.

[
Refer to the official SytemJS project website at `https://github.com/`
`systemjs/systemjs` to learn more about SystemJS.

There is a free list of common module mistakes available online at
`http://www.typescriptlang.org/Handbook#modules-`
`pitfalls-of-modules`.
]

Circular dependencies

A circular dependency is an issue that we can encounter when working with
multiple components and dependencies. Sometimes, it is possible to reach a
point in which one component (A) has a dependency on a second component (B),
which depends on the first component (A). In the following graph, each node is a
component, and we can observe that the nodes **circular1.ts** and **circular2.ts** have
a circular dependency. The node named `doesNotDependOnAnything.ts` doesn't
have dependencies and the node named `onlyDependsOnOtherStuff.ts` has a
dependency on `circular1.ts` but doesn't have circular dependencies..

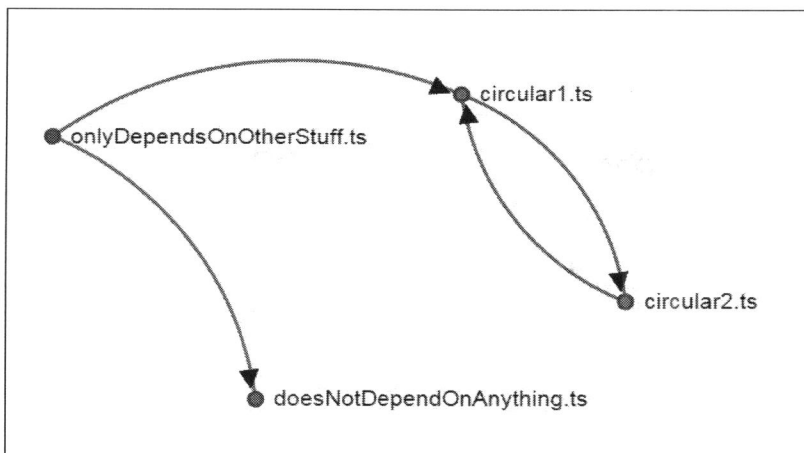

The circular dependencies don't need to necessarily involve just two components. We can encounter scenarios in which a component depends on another component, which depends on other components, and some of the components in the dependency tree end up pointing to one of their parent components in the tree.

Identifying a circular dependency is very time consuming. Fortunately, Atom includes a command-line tool that will generate a dependency tree graph for us like the preceding one. In order to access the Atom command line, we need to navigate to **View** (in the top menu) and then to **Toggle Command Palette**.

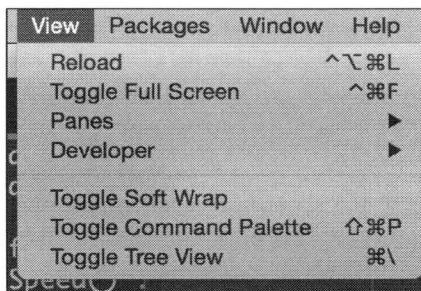

After opening the **Toggle Command Palette**, we need to type **TypeScript: Dependency View** to display the graph:

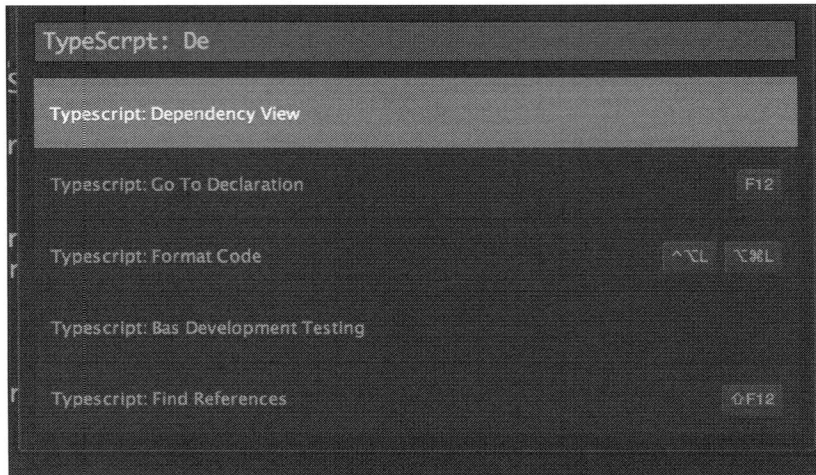

> If you want to learn more about dependency graphs, you can visit its official documentation at `https://github.com/TypeStrong/atom-typescript/blob/master/docs/dependency-view.md`.

Summary

In this chapter, we saw how to work with classes, interfaces, and modules in depth. We were able to reduce the complexity of our application by using techniques such as encapsulation and inheritance.

We were also able to create external modules and manage our application dependencies using tools such as RequireJS or Browserify.

In the next chapter, we will discuss the TypeScript runtime.

5
Runtime

After completing this book, you will probably be eager to start a new project to put into practice all your new knowledge. As the new project grows and you develop more complex features, you might encounter some runtime issues.

We should be able to resolve design-time issues with ease because in the previous chapter, we looked at the main TypeScript features.

However, we have not learned much about the TypeScript runtime. The good news is that, depending on your background, you may already know a lot about it, as the TypeScript runtime is the JavaScript runtime. TypeScript is only used at design time; the TypeScript code is then compiled into JavaScript and finally executed. The JavaScript runtime is in charge of the execution. Is important to understand that we never execute TypeScript code and we always execute JavaScript code. For this reason, when we refer to the TypeScript runtime, we will, in fact, be talking about the JavaScript runtime.

When we compile our TypeScript code, we will generate JavaScript code, which will be executed on the server side (with Node.js) or on the client side (in a web browser). It is then that we may encounter some challenging runtime issues.

In this chapter, we will cover the following topics:

- The environment
- The event loop
- The `this` operator
- Prototypes
- Closures

Let's start by learning about the environment.

The environment

The runtime environment is one of the first things that we must consider before we can start developing a TypeScript application. Once we have compiled our TypeScript code, it can be executed in many different JavaScript engines. While the majority of those engines will be web browsers, such as Chrome, Internet Explorer, or Firefox, we might also want to be able to run our code on the server side or in a desktop application in environments such as Node.js or RingoJS.

It is important to keep in mind that there are some variables and objects available at runtime that are environment-specific. For example, we could create a library and access the document.layers variable. While document is part of the W3C **Document Object Model (DOM)** standard, the layers property is only available in Internet Explorer and is not part of the W3C DOM standard.

The W3C defines the DOM as follows:

> *The Document Object Model is a platform- and language-neutral interface that will allow programs and scripts to dynamically access and update the content, structure and style of documents. The document can be further processed and the results of that processing can be incorporated back into the presented page.*

In a similar manner, we can also access a set of objects known as the **Browser Object Model (BOM)** from a web browser runtime environment. The BOM consists of the objects navigator, history, screen, location, and document, which are properties of the window object.

You need to realize that the DOM is part of the web browsers but not part of JavaScript. If we want to run our application in a web browser, we will be able to access the DOM and BOM. However, in environments like Node.js or RingoJS, they will not be available, since they are standalone JavaScript environments completely independent of a web browser. We can also find other objects on the server-side environments (such as process.stdin in Node.js) that will not be available if we attempt to execute our code in a web browser.

As if this wasn't enough work, we also need to keep in mind the existence of multiple versions of these JavaScript environments. We will have to support multiple browsers and multiple versions of Node.js. The recommended practice when dealing with this problem is to add logic that looks for the availability of features rather than the availability of a particular environment or version.

> A really good library is available that can help us to implement feature detection when developing for web browsers. The library is called **Modernizr** and can be downloaded at http://modernizr.com/.

The runtime

The TypeScript runtime (JavaScript) has a concurrency model based on an **event loop**. This model is quite different to the models in other languages such as C or Java. Before we focus on the event loop itself, you must understand some runtime concepts.

What follows is a visual representation of some important runtime concepts: heap, stack, queue, and frame:

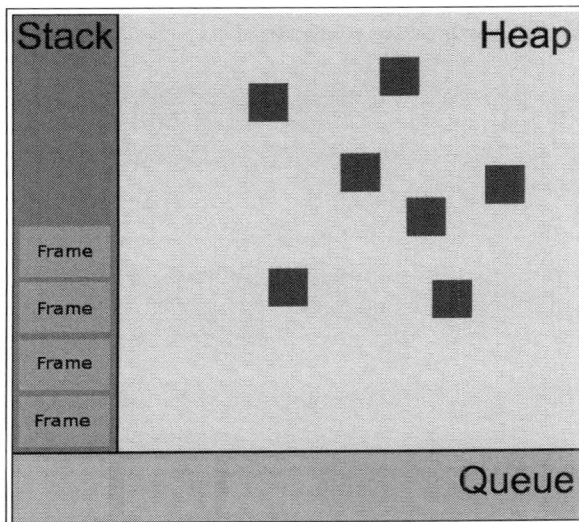

We will now look at the role of each of these runtime concepts.

Frames

A frame is a sequential unit of work. In the preceding diagram, the frames are represented by the blocks inside the stack.

When a function is called in JavaScript, the runtime creates a frame in the stack. The frame holds that particular function's arguments and local variables. When the function returns, the frame is popped out of the stack. Let's take a look at an example:

```
function foo(b){
  var a = 12;
  return a+b+35;
}

function bar(x){
```

```
    var m = 4;
    return foo(m*x);
}
```

After declaring the `foo` and `bar` functions, we invoke the `bar` function:

```
bar(21);
```

When `bar` is executed, the runtime will create a new frame containing the arguments of `bar` and all the local variables. The frame (represented as a square in the preceding diagram) is then added to the top of the stack.

Internally, `bar` invokes `foo`. When `foo` is invoked, a new frame is created and allocated in the top of the stack. When the execution of `foo` is finished (`foo` has returned), the top frame is removed from the stack. When the execution of `bar` is also complete, it is removed from the stack as well.

Now, let's imagine what would happen if the `foo` function invoked the `bar` function. We would create a never-ending function call loop. With each function call, a new frame would be added to the stack, and eventually, there would be no more space in the stack, and an error would be thrown. Most developers are familiar with this error, known as a stack overflow error.

Stack

The stack contains the sequential steps (frames) that a message needs to execute. A stack is a data structure that represents a simple **Last In First Out (LIFO)** collection of objects. Therefore, when a frame is added to the stack, it is always added to the top of the stack.

Since the stack is a LIFO collection, the event loop processes the frames stored in it from top to bottom. The dependencies of a frame are added to the top of it in the stack to ensure that all the dependencies of each of the frames are met.

Queue

The queue contains a list of messages waiting to be processed. Each message is associated with a function. When the stack is empty, a message is taken out of the queue and processed. The processing consists of calling the associated function and adding the frames to the stack. The message processing ends when the stack becomes empty again.

In the previous runtime diagram, the blocks inside the queue represent the messages.

Heap

The heap is a memory container that is not aware of the order of the items stored in it. The heap contains all the variables and objects currently in use. It may also contain frames that are currently out of scope but have not yet been removed from memory by the garbage collector.

The event loop

Concurrency is the ability for two or more operations to be executed simultaneously. The runtime execution takes place on one single thread, which means that we cannot achieve real concurrency.

The event loop follows a run-to-completion approach, which means that it will process a message from beginning to end before any other message is processed.

> As we discussed in *Chapter 3, Working with Functions*, we can use the `yield` keyword and generators to pause the execution of a function.

Every time a function is invoked, a new message is added to the queue. If the stack is empty, the function is processed (the frames are added to the stack).

When all the frames have been added to the stack, the stack is cleared from top to bottom. At the end of the process, the stack is empty and the next message is processed.

> Web workers can performance background tasks in a different thread. They have their own queue, heap, and stack.

One of the advantages of the event loop is that the execution order is quite predictable and easy to follow. Another important advantage of the event loop approach is that it features non-blocking I/O. This means that when the application is waiting for an input and output (I/O) operation to finish, it can still process other things, such as user input.

A disadvantage of this approach is that if a message takes too long to complete, the application becomes unresponsive. Good practice is to make message processing short, and if possible, split one message function into several messages functions.

The this operator

In JavaScript, the `this` operator behaves a little differently than other languages. The value of the `this` operator is often determined by the way a function is invoked. Its value cannot be set by assignment during execution, and it may be different each time a function is invoked.

> The `this` operator also has some differences when using the strict and nonstrict modes. To learn more about the strict mode, refer to https://developer.mozilla.org/en-US/docs/Web/JavaScript/Reference/Strict_mode.

The this operator in the global context

In the global context, the `this` operator will always point to the global object. In a web browser, the `window` object is the global object:

```
console.log(this === window); // true
this.a = 37;
console.log(window.a); // 37
console.log(this.document === document === window. document); // true
```

The this operator in a function context

The value of `this` inside a function depends on how the function is invoked. If we simply invoke a function in the nonstrict mode, the value of `this` within the function will point to the global object:

```
function f1(){
  return this;
}
f1() === window; // true
```

However, if we invoke a function in the strict mode, the value of `this` within the function's body will point to `undefined`:

```
console.log(this); // global (window)

function f2(){
  "use strict";
  return this; // undefined
}
console.log(f2()); // undefined
console.log(this); // window
```

However, the value of the `this` operator inside a function invoked as an instance method points to the instance. In other words, the value of the `this` operator within a function that is part of a class points to that class:

```
var p = {
  age: 37,
  getAge: function() {
    return this.age; // this points to the class instance (p)
  }
};
console.log(p.getAge()); // 37
```

In the preceding example, we have used object literal notation to define an object named p, but the same applies when declaring objects using prototypes:

```
function Person() {}
Person.prototype.age = 37;
Person .prototype.getAge = function () {
  return this.age;
}
var p = new Person();
p.age;     // 37
p.getAge(); // 37
```

When a function is used as a constructor (with the `new` keyword), the `this` operator points to the object being constructed:

```
function Person() { // function used as a constructor
  this.age = 37;
}
var p = new Person();
console.log(p.age); // logs 37
```

The call, apply, and bind methods

All the functions inherit the `call`, `apply`, and `bind` methods from `Function.prototype`. We can use these methods to set the value of the `this` operator when it is used inside the body of a function.

The `call` and `apply` methods are almost identical; both methods allow us to invoke a function and set the value of the `this` operator within the function. The main difference between `call` and `apply` is that while `apply` lets us invoke the function with arguments as an array and `call` requires the function parameters to be listed explicitly.

> A useful mnemonic is *A (apply) for array and C (call) for comma.*

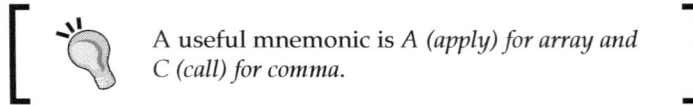

Let's take a look at an example. We will start by declaring a class named `Person`. This class has two properties (`name` and `surname`) and one method (`greet`). The `greet` method uses the `this` operator to access the `name` and `surname` instance properties:

```
class Person {
  public name : string;
  public surname : string;

  constructor(name : string, surname : string) {
    this.name = name;
    this.surname = surname;
  }

  public greet(city : string, country : string) {
    // we use the this operator to access name and surname
    var msg = `Hi, my name is ${this.name} ${this.surname}. `;
    msg += `I'm from ${city} (${country}).`;
    console.log(msg);
  }
}
```

After declaring the `Person` class, we will create an instance:

```
var person = new Person("remo", "jansen");
```

If we invoke the `greet` method, it will work as expected:

```
person.greet.("Seville", "Spain");
// Hi, my name is remo jansen. I'm from Seville (Spain).
```

Alternatively, we can invoke the method using the `call` and `apply` functions. We have supplied the `person` object as the first parameter of both functions because we want the `this` operator (inside the `greet` method) to take `person` as its value:

```
person.greet.call(person, "seville", "spain");
person.greet.apply(person, ["seville", "spain"]);
```

If we provide a different value to be used as the value of `this`, we will not be able to access the `name` and `surname` properties within the `greet` function:

```
person.greet.call(null, "seville", "spain");
person.greet.apply(null, ["seville", "spain"]);
// Hi, my name is undefined.I'm from seville spain.
```

The two preceding examples may seem useless because the first one invoked the function directly and the second one caused an unexpected behavior. The `apply` and `call` methods make sense only when we want the `this` operator to take a different value when a function is invoked:

```
var valueOfThis = { name : "anakin", surname : "skywalker" };
person.greet.call(valueOfThis, "mos espa", "tatooine");
person.greet.apply(valueOfThis, ["mos espa", "tatooine"]);
// Hi, my name is anakin skywalker. I'm from mos espa tatooine.
```

The `bind` method can be used to set the value of the `this` operator (within a function) regardless of how it is invoked.

When we invoke a function's `bind` method, it returns a new function with the same body and scope as the original function, but the `this` operator (within the body function) is permanently bound to the first argument of `bind`, regardless of how the function is invoked.

Let's take a look at an example. We will start by creating an instance of the `Person` class that we declared in the previous example:

```
var person = new Person("remo", "jansen");
```

Then, we can use `bind` to set the `greet` function to be a new function with the same scope and body:

```
var greet = person.greet.bind(person);
```

If we try to invoke the `greet` function using `bind` and `apply`, just like we did in the previous example, we will be able to observe that this time the `this` operator will always point to the object instance independent of how the function is invoked:

```
greet.call(person, "seville", "spain");
greet.apply(person, ["seville", "spain"]);
// Hi, my name is remo jansen. I'm from seville spain.

greet.call(null, "seville", "spain");
greet.apply(null, ["seville", "spain"]);
// Hi, my name is remo jansen. I'm from seville spain.

var valueOfThis = { name: "anakin", surname: "skywalker" };
greet.call(valueOfThis, "mos espa", "tatooine");
greet.apply(valueOfThis, ["mos espa", "tatooine"]);
// Hi, my name is remo jansen. I'm from mos espa tatooine.
```

> Using the `apply`, `call`, and `bind` functions is not recommended unless you really know what you are doing, because they can lead to complex runtime issues for other developers.

Once we bind an object to a function with `bind`, we cannot override it:

```
var valueOfThis = { name: "anakin", surname: "skywalker" };
var greet = person.greet.bind(valueOfThis);
greet.call(valueOfThis, "mos espa", "tatooine");
greet.apply(valueOfThis, ["mos espa", "tatooine"]);
// Hi, my name is remo jansen. I'm from mos espa tatooine.
```

> The use of the `bind`, `apply`, and `call` methods is often discouraged because it can lead to confusion. Modifying the default behavior of the `this` operator can lead to really unexpected results. Remember to use these methods only when strictly necessary and to document your code properly to reduce the risk caused by potential maintainability issues.

Prototypes

When we compile a TypeScript program, all classes and objects become JavaScript objects. Sometimes, we will encounter our application behaving unexpectedly at runtime, and we will not be able to identify and understand the root cause of this behavior without a good understanding of how inheritance works in JavaScript. This understanding will allow us to have much better control over our application at runtime.

The runtime inheritance system uses a prototypal inheritance model. In a prototypal inheritance model, objects inherit from objects, and there are no classes available. However, we can use prototypes to simulate classes. Let's see how it works.

At runtime, almost every JavaScript object has an internal property called prototype. The value of the prototype attribute is an object, which contains some attributes (data) and methods (behavior).

In TypeScript, we can use a class-based inheritance system:

```
class Person {
  public name : string;
  public surname : string;
  public age : number = 0;
  constructor(name : string, surname : string){
    this.name = name;
```

```
      this.surname = surname;
  }
  greet() {
    var msg =`Hi! my name is ${this.name} ${this.surname}`;
    msg += `I'm ${this.age}`;
  }
}
```

We have defined a class named `Person`. At runtime, this class is declared using prototypes instead of classes:

```
var Person = (function () {
    function Person(name, surname) {
        this.age = 0;
        this.name = name;
        this.surname = surname;
    }
    Person.prototype.greet = function () {
        var msg = "Hi! my name is " + this.name +
                " " + this.surname;
        msg += "I'm " + this.age;
    };
    return Person;
})();
```

The TypeScript compiler wraps the object definition (we will not refer it as the class definition because technically, it is not a class) with an **immediately invoked function expression (IIFE)**. Inside the IIFE, we can find a function named `Person`. If we examine the function and compare it to the TypeScript class, we will notice that it takes the same parameters, like the constructor in the TypeScript class. This function is used to create new instances of the `Person` class.

After the constructor, we can see the definition of the `greet` method. As you can see, the prototype attribute is used to attach the `greet` method to the `Person` class.

Instance properties versus class properties

As JavaScript is a dynamic programming language, we can add properties and methods to an instance of an object at runtime; and they don't need to be part of the object (class) itself. Let's take a look at an example:

```
function Person(name, surname) {
        // instance properties
        this.name = name;
```

```
        this.surname = surname;
    }
    var me = new Person("remo", "jansen");
    me.email = "remo.jansen@wolksoftware.com";
```

Here, we defined a constructor function for an object named `Person`, which takes two variables (`name` and `surname`) as arguments. Then, we have created an instance of the `Person` object and added a new property named `email` to it. We can use a `for...in` statement to check the properties of `me` at runtime:

```
for(var property in me) {
  console.log("property: " + property + ", value: '" +
  me[property] + "'");
}
// property: name, value: 'remo'
// property: surname, value: 'jansen'
// property: email, value: 'remo.jansen@wolksoftware.com'
// property: greet, value: 'function (city, country) {
//          var msg = "Hi, my name is " + this.name + " " +
//this.surname;
//          msg += "\nI'm from " + city + " " + country;
//          console.log(msg);
//      }'
```

All these properties are **instance properties** because they hold a value for each new instance. If, for example, we create a new instance of `Person`, both instances will hold their own values:

```
var hero = new Person("John", "117");
hero.name; // "John"
me.name;   // "remo"
```

We have defined these instance properties using the `this` operator, because in the class constructor, the `this` operator points to the object's prototype. This explains why we can alternatively define instance properties through the object's prototype:

```
Person.prototype.name = name;    // instance property
Person.prototype.name = surname; // instance property
```

We can also declare class properties and methods. The main difference is that the value of class properties and methods is shared between all the instances of an object. Class properties and methods are sometimes called static properties and methods.

Class properties are often used to store static values:

```
function MathHelper() {
  /* ... */
}

// class property
MathHelper.PI = 3.14159265359;
```

Class methods are also often used as utility functions that perform calculations upon supplied parameters and return a result:

```
function MathHelper() { /* ... */ }

// class method
MathHelper.areaOfCircle = function(radius) {
  return radius * radius * this.PI;
}

// class property
MathHelper.PI = 3.14159265359;
```

In the preceding example, we have accessed a class attribute (PI) from a class method (areaOfCircle). We can access class properties from instance methods, but we cannot access instance properties or methods from class properties or methods. We can demonstrate this by declaring PI as an instance property instead of a class property:

```
function MathHelper() {
  // instance property
  this.PI = 3.14159265359;
}
```

If we then attempt to access PI from a class method, it will be undefined:

```
// class method
MathHelper.areaOfCircle = function(radius) {
  return radius * radius * this.PI;  // this.PI is undefined
}

MathHelper.areaOfCircle(5); // NaN
```

We are not supposed to access class methods or properties from instance methods, but there is a way to do it. We can achieve it using the prototype's constructor property. We can also demonstrate this as follows:

```
function MathHelper () { /* ... */ }

// class property
MathHelper.PI = 3.14159265359;

// instance method
MathHelper.prototype.areaOfCircle = function(radius) {
    return radius * radius * this.constructor.PI;
}

var math = new MathHelper ();
console.log(MathHelper.areaOfCircle(5)); // 78.53981633975
```

We can access PI (the class property) from areaOfCircle (the instance method) using the prototype's constructor property because this property returns a reference to the object's constructor.

Inside areaOfCircle, the this operator returns a reference to the object's prototype:

```
this === MathHelper.prototype    //true
```

We may deduce that this.constructor is equal to MathHelper.prototype. constructor and, therefore, MathHelper.prototype.constructor is equal to MathHelper.

Prototypal inheritance

You might be wondering how the extends keyword works. Let's create a new TypeScript class, which inherits from the Person class, to help you understand it:

```
class SuperHero extends Person {
  public superpower : string;
  constructor(name : string, surname : string, superpower :
  string){
     super(name, surname);
     this.superpower = superpower;
  }
  userSuperPower() {
  return `I'm using my ${this.superpower}`
  }
}
```

The preceding class is named `SuperHero` and extends the `Person` class. It has one extra attribute (`superpower`) and method (`useSuperPower`). If we compile the code, we will notice the following piece of code:

```
var __extends = this.__extends || function (d, b) {
    for (var p in b) if (b.hasOwnProperty(p)) d[p] = b[p];
    function __() { this.constructor = d; }
    __.prototype = b.prototype;
    d.prototype = new __();
};
```

This piece of code is generated by TypeScript. Even though it is a really small piece of code, it showcases almost every concept contained in this chapter, and understanding it can be quite challenging. We might need to examine it multiple times to understand it, but the effort is worth it. Let's take a look at the function.

Before the function expression is evaluated for the first time, the `this` operator points to the global object, which does not contain a method named `__extends`. This means that the `__extends` variable is undefined at this point:

```
console.log(this.__extends); // undefined
```

When the function expression is evaluated for the first time, the value of the function expression (an anonymous function) is assigned to the `__extends` property in the global scope:

```
console.log(this.__extends); // extends(n, e, t);
```

TypeScript generates the function expression once for each TypeScript file containing the extends keyword. However, the function expression is only evaluated once (when the `__extends` variable is undefined). This behavior is implemented in the first line of code:

```
var __extends = this.__extends || function (d, b) { // ...
```

The first time this line of code is executed, the function expression is evaluated. The value of the function expression is an anonymous function, which is assigned to the `__extends` variable in the global scope. As we are in the global scope, `var __extends` and `this.__extends` refer to the same variable at this point.

When a new file is executed, the `__extends` variable is already available in the global scope and the function expression is not evaluated. This means that the value of the function expression is only assigned to the `__extends` variable once.

As you already know, the value of the function expression is an anonymous function. Let's now focus on it:

```
function (d, b) {
    for (var p in b) if (b.hasOwnProperty(p)) d[p] = b[p];
    function __() { this.constructor = d; }
    __.prototype = b.prototype;
    d.prototype = new __();
}
```

This function takes two arguments named d and b. When we invoke it, we should pass a derived object constructor (d) and a base object constructor (b).

The first line inside the anonymous function iterates each class property and method from the base class and creates their copy in the derived class:

```
for (var p in b) if (b.hasOwnProperty(p)) d[p] = b[p];
```

> When we use a for...in statement to iterate an instance of an object, it will iterate the object's instance properties. However, if we use a for...in statement to iterate the properties of an object's constructor, the statement will iterate its class properties. In the preceding example, the for...in statement is used to inherit the object's class properties and methods. To inherit the instance properties, we will copy the object's prototype.

The second line declares a new constructor function named __, and inside it, the this operator is used to access its prototype:

```
function __() { this.constructor = d; }
```

The prototype contains a special property named constructor, which returns a reference to the object's constructor. The function named __ and this.constructor are pointing to the same variable at this point. The value of the derived object constructor (d) is then assigned to the __ constructor.

In the third line, the value of the prototype object from the base object constructor is assigned to the prototype of the __ object constructor:

```
__.prototype = b.prototype;
```

In the last line, a new __() is invoked, and the result is assigned to the derived class (d) prototype. By performing all these steps, we have achieved all that we need to invoke the following:

```
var instance = new d():
```

Upon doing so, we will get an object that contains all the properties from both the derived class (d) and the base class (b). Furthermore, the instance of operator will work as we would expect:

```
var superHero = new SuperHero();
console.log(superHero instanceof Person);    // true
console.log(superHero instanceof SuperHero); // true
```

We can see the function in action by examining the runtime code that defines the `SuperHero` class:

```
var SuperHero = (function (_super) {
    __extends(SuperHero, _super);
    function SuperHero(name, surname, superpower) {
        _super.call(this, name, surname);
        this.superpower = superpower;
    }
    SuperHero.prototype.userSuperPower = function () {
        return "I'm using my " + superpower;
    };
    return SuperHero;
})(Person);
```

We can see an IIFE here again. This time, the IIFE takes the `Person` object constructor as the argument. Inside the function, we will refer to this argument using the name `_super`. Inside the IIFE, the `__extends` function is invoked and the `SuperHero` (derived class) and `_super` (base class) arguments are passed to it.

In the next line, we can find the declaration of the `SuperHero` object constructor and the `useSuperPower` function. We can use `SuperHero` as an argument of `__extend` before it is declared, because functions declarations are hoisted to the top of the scope.

> Function expressions are not hoisted. When we assign a function to a variable in a function expression, the variable is hoisted, but its value (the function itself) is not hoisted.

Inside the `SuperHero` constructor, the base class (`Person`) constructor is invoked using the `call` method:

```
_super.call(this, name, surname);
```

As we discussed previously in this chapter, we can use `call` to set the value of the `this` operator in a function context. In this case, we are passing the `this` operator, which points to the instance of `SuperHero` being created:

```
function Person(name, surname) {
    // this points to the instance of SuperHero being created
    this.name = name;
    this.surname = surname;
}
```

The prototype chain

When we try to access a property or method of an object, the runtime will search for that property or method in the object's own properties and methods. If it is not found, the runtime will continue searching through the object's inherited properties by navigating the entire inheritance tree. As a derived object is linked to its base object through the prototype property, we refer to this inheritance tree as the prototype chain.

Let's take a look at an example. We will declare two simple TypeScript classes named `Base` and `Derived`:

```
class Base {
  public method1(){ return 1; };
  public method2(){ return 2; };
}

class Derived extends Base {
  public method2(){ return 3; };
  public method3(){ return 4; };
}
```

Now, we will examine the JavaScript code generated by TypeScript:

```
var Base = (function () {
    function Base() {
    }
    Base.prototype.method1 = function () { return 1; };
    ;
    Base.prototype.method2 = function () { return 2; };
    ;
    return Base;
})();
```

```
var Derived = (function (_super) {
    __extends(Derived, _super);
    function Derived() {
        _super.apply(this, arguments);
    }
    Derived.prototype.method2 = function () { return 3; };
    ;
    Derived.prototype.method3 = function () { return 4; };
    ;
    return Derived;
})(Base);
```

We can then create an instance of the `Derived` class:

```
var derived = new Derived();
```

If we try to access the method named `method1`, the runtime will find it in the instance's own properties:

```
console.log(derived.method1()); // 1
```

The instance also has its own property named `method2` (with value 2), but there is also an inherited property named `method2` (with value 3). The object's own property (`method2` with value 3) prevents access to the prototype property (`method2` with value 2). This is known as **property shadowing**:

```
console.log(derived.method2()); // 3
```

The instance does not have its own property named `method3`, but it has a property named `method3` in its prototype:

```
console.log(derived.method3()); // 4
```

Both the instance and the objects in the prototype chain (the `Base` class) don't have a property named `method4`:

```
console.log(derived.method4()); // error
```

Accessing the prototype of an object

Prototypes can be accessed in three different ways:

- `Person.prototype`: We can access the prototype of a function directly using the prototype attribute
- `Person.getPrototypeOf(person)`: We want this function to access the prototype of an instance of an object we can use the `getPrototypeOf` function

- `person.__proto__`: This is a property that exposes the internal prototype of the object through which it is accessed

> The use of __proto__ is controversial and has been discouraged by many. It was never originally included in the ECMAScript language spec, but modern browsers decided to implement it anyway. Today, the __proto__ property has been standardized in the ECMAScript 6 language specification and will be supported in the future, but it is still a slow operation that should be avoided if performance is a concern.

The new operator

We can use the `new` operator to generate an instance of `Person`:

```
var person = new Person("remo", "jansen");
```

The runtime does not follow a class-based inheritance model. When we use the `new` operator, the runtime creates a `new` object that inherits from the `Person` class prototype.

We may conclude that the behavior of the new operator at runtime (JavaScript) is not really different from the `extends` keyword at design time (TypeScript).

Closures

Closures are one of the most powerful features available at runtime, but they are also one of the most misunderstood. The Mozilla developer network defines closures as follows:

> *"Closures are functions that refer to independent (free) variables. In other words, the function defined in the closure 'remembers' the environment in which it was created."*

We understand **independent (free) variables** as variables that persist beyond the lexical scope from which they were created. Let's take a look at an example:

```
function makeArmy() {
  var shooters = []
  for(var i = 0; i < 10; i++) {
    var shooter = function() { // a shooter is a function
      alert(i) // which should alert it's number
    }
```

```
      shooters.push(shooter)
    }
    return shooters;
}
```

We have declared a function named makeArmy. Inside the function, we have created an array of functions named shooters. Each function in the shooters array will alert a number, the value of which was set from the variable i inside a for statement. We will now invoke the makeArmy function:

```
var army = makeArmy();
```

The army variable should now contain the array of functions shooters. However, we will notice a problem if we execute the following piece of code:

```
army[0](); // 10 (expected 0)
army[5](); // 10 (expected 5)
```

The preceding code snippet does not work as expected because we made one of the most common mistakes related to closures. When we declared the shooter function inside the makeArmy function, we created a closure without knowing it.

The reason for this is that the functions assigned to shooter are closures; they consist of the function definition and the captured environment from the makeArmy function's scope. Ten closures have been created, but each one shares the same single environment. By the time the shooter functions are executed, the loop has run its course and the i variable (shared by all the closures) has been left pointing to the last entry (10).

One solution in this case is to use more closures:

```
function makeArmy() {
  var shooters = []
  for(var i = 0; i < 10; i++) {
    (function(i){
      var shooter = function() {
        alert(i);
      }
      shooters.push(shooter)
    })(i);
  }
  return shooters;
}

var army = makeArmy();
army[0](); // 0
army[5](); // 5
```

This works as expected. Rather than the shooter functions sharing a single environment, the immediately invoked function creates a new environment for each one, in which i refers to the corresponding value.

Static variables with closures

In the previous section, we saw that when a variable is declared in a closure context it can be shared between multiple instances of a class, or in other words, the variable behaves as a static variable.

We will now see how we can create variables and methods that behave like static variables. Let's start by declaring a TypeScript class named Counter:

```
class Counter {
  private static _COUNTER = 0;
  constructor() {}
  private _changeBy(val) {
    Counter._COUNTER += val;
  }
  public increment() {
    this._changeBy(1);
  }
  public decrement() {
    this._changeBy(-1);
  }
  public value() {
    return Counter._COUNTER;
  }
}
```

The preceding class contains a static member named _COUNTER. The TypeScript compiler transforms it into the following resulting code:

```
var Counter = (function () {
    function Counter() {
    }
    Counter.prototype._changeBy = function (val) {
        Counter._COUNTER += val;
    };
    Counter.prototype.increment = function () {
        this._changeBy(1);
    };
    Counter.prototype.decrement = function () {
        this._changeBy(-1);
    };
```

```
    Counter.prototype.value = function () {
        return Counter._COUNTER;
    };
    Counter._COUNTER = 0;
    return Counter;
}) ();
```

As you can observe, the static variable is declared by the TypeScript compiler as a class property (as opposed to an instance property). The compiler uses a class property because class properties are shared across all instances of a class.

Alternatively, we could write some JavaScript (remember that all valid JavaScript is valid TypeScript) code to emulate static properties using closures:

```
var Counter = (function() {
    // closure context
    var _COUNTER = 0;

    function changeBy(val) {
        _COUNTER += val;
    }

    function Counter() {};

    Counter.prototype.increment = function() {
      changeBy(1);
    };
    Counter.prototype.decrement = function() {
      changeBy(-1);
    };
    Counter.prototype.value = function() {
      return _COUNTER;
    };
    return Counter;
}) ();
```

The preceding code snippet declares a class named Counter. The class has some methods used to increment, decrement, and read the variable named _COUNTER. The _COUNTER variable itself is not part of the object prototype.

The Counter constructor function is part of a closure. As a result, all the instances of the Counter class will share the same closure context, which means that the context (the variable counter and the function changeBy) will behave as a singleton.

> The singleton pattern requires an object to be declared as a static variable to avoid the need to create its instance whenever it is required. The object instance is, therefore, shared by all the components in the application. The singleton pattern is frequently used in scenarios where it is not beneficial, which introduces unnecessary restrictions in situations where a unique instance of a class is not actually required, and introduces global states into an application.

So, you now know that it is possible to use closures to emulate static variables:

```
var counter1 = new Counter();
var counter2 = new Counter();
console.log(counter1.value()); // 0
console.log(counter2.value()); // 0
counter1.increment();
counter1.increment();
console.log(counter1.value()); // 2
console.log(counter2.value()); // 2 (expected 0)
counter1.decrement();
console.log(counter1.value()); // 1
console.log(counter2.value()); // 1 (expected 0)
```

Private members with closures

We have seen that the closure function can access variables that persist beyond the lexical scope from which they were created. These variables are not part of the function prototype or body, but they are part of the closure function context.

As there is no way to directly access the context of a closure function, the context variables and methods can be used to emulate private members. The main advantage of using closures to emulate private members (instead of the TypeScript private access modifier) is that closures will prevent access to private members at runtime.

TypeScript avoids emulating private properties at runtime. The TypeScript compiler will throw an error at compilation time if we attempt to access a private member.

However, TypeScript avoids the use of closures to emulate private members to improve the application performance. If we add or remove an access modifier to or from one of our classes, the resulting JavaScript code will not change at all. This means that private members of a class become public members at runtime.

However, it is possible to use closures to emulate private properties at runtime. Just like when we emulated a static variable using closures, we can only achieve this kind of advanced control over the behavior of closures by writing pure JavaScript. Let's take a look at an example:

```
function makeCounter() {

    // closure context
    var _COUNTER = 0;
    function changeBy(val) {
        _COUNTER += val;
    }

    function Counter() {};

    Counter.prototype.increment = function() {
      changeBy(1);
    };
    Counter.prototype.decrement = function() {
      changeBy(-1);
    };
    Counter.prototype.value = function() {
      return _COUNTER;
    };
    return new Counter();
};
```

The preceding class is almost identical to the class that we previously declared to demonstrate how to emulate static variables at runtime using closures.

This time, a new closure context is created every time we invoke the makeCounter function, so each new instance of Counter will remember an independent context (counter and changeBy):

```
var counter1 = makeCounter();
var counter2 = makeCounter();
console.log(counter1.value()); // 0
console.log(counter2.value()); // 0
counter1.increment();
counter1.increment();
console.log(counter1.value()); // 2
console.log(counter2.value()); // 0 (expected 0)
counter1.decrement();
console.log(counter1.value()); // 1
console.log(counter2.value()); // 0 (expected 0)
```

Since the context cannot be accessed directly, we can say that the variable `counter` and the `changeBy` function are private members:

```
console.log(counter1.counter); // undefined
counter1.changeBy(2); // changeBy is not a function
console.log(counter1.value()); // 1
```

Summary

In this chapter, we discovered how to understand the runtime, which allows us not only to resolve runtime issues with ease but also to be able to write better TypeScript code. A deep understanding of closures and prototypes will allow you to develop some complex features that it would have not been possible to develop without this knowledge.

In the next chapter, we will focus on performance, memory management, and exception handling.

6

Application Performance

In this chapter, we will take a look at how can we manage available resources in an efficient manner to achieve great performance. You will understand the different types of resource, performance factors, performance profiling and automation.

The chapter begins by introducing some core performance concepts, such as latency or bandwidth, and continues by showcasing how to measure and monitor performance as part of the automated build process.

As we discussed in previous chapters, we can use TypeScript to generate JavaScript code that can be executed in many different environments (web browsers, Node. js, mobile devices, and so on). In this chapter, we will explore performance optimization, which is mainly applicable to the development of web applications. The following topics will be covered in this chapter:

- Performance and resources
- Aspects of performance
- Memory profiling
- Network Profiling
- CPU and GPU profiling
- Performance testing
- Performance recommendations
- Performance automation

Prerequisites

Before we get started, we need to install Google Chrome because we will use its developer tools to perform web performance analysis.

Performance and resources

Before we get our hands dirty doing some performance analysis, monitoring, and automation, we must first spend some time understanding some core concepts and aspects about performance.

A good application is one that has a set of desirable characteristics, which includes functionality, reliability, usability, reusability, efficiency, maintainability, and portability. Over the course of this book so far, we have understood a lot about maintainability and reusability. In this chapter, we will focus on performance, which is closely related to reliability and maintainability.

The term performance refers to the amount of useful work accomplished compared to the time and resources used. A resource is a physical (CPU, RAM, GPU, HDD, and so on) or virtual (CPU times, RAM regions, files, and so on) component with limited availability. As the availability of a resource is limited, each resource is shared between processes. When a process finishes using a resource, it must release the resource before any other process can use it. Managing available resources in an efficient manner will help to reduce the time other processes spend waiting for the resources to become available.

When we work on a web application, we need to keep in mind that the following resources will have limited availability:

- **Central Processing Unit** (CPU): This carries out the instructions of a computer program by performing the basic arithmetic, logical, control, and input/output (I/O) operations specified by the instructions.

- **Graphics Processor Unit (GPU)**: This is a specialized processor is used in the manipulation and alteration of memory to accelerate the creation of images in a frame buffer intended for output to a display. The GPU is used when we create applications that use the WebGL API or when we use some CSS3 animations.

- **Random Access Memory (RAM)**: This allows data items to be read and written in approximately the same amount of time regardless of the order in which data items are accessed. When we declare a variable, it will be stored in RAM memory; when the variable is out of the scope, it will be removed from RAM by the garbage collector.

- **Hard Disk Drive (HDD)** and **Solid State Drive (SSD)**: Both of these are data storage devices used to store and retrieve information. When developing client-side web applications, we will not have to worry about these resources really often because these applications don't usually extensively use persistent data storage. However, we should keep in mind that, whenever we store an object in a persistent manner (cookies, local storage, IndexedDB, and so on), the performance of our application will be affected by the availability of the HDD or SSD.

- **Network throughput**: This determines how much actual data can be sent per unit of time across a network. The network throughput is determined by factors such as the network latency or bandwidth (we will discuss more about these factors later in this chapter).

> All the resources presented in the preceding list are also limited when working on a Node.js application or a hybrid application. However, it is not really common to extensively use the GPU while working on a Node.js application, but it is a possible scenario.

Performance metrics

As performance is influenced by the availability of multiple types of physical and virtual device, we can find a few different performance metrics (factors to measure performance). Some popular performance metrics include availability, response time, processing speed, latency, bandwidth, and scalability. These measurement mechanisms are usually directly related to one of the general resources (CPU, network throughput, and so on) that were mentioned in the previous section. We will now look at each of these performance metrics in detail.

Availability

The availability of a system is related to its performance, because if the system is not available at some stage, we will perceive it as bad performance. The availability can be improved by improving the reliability, maintainability, and testability of the system. If the system is easy to test and maintain, it will be easy to increase its reliability.

The response time

The response time is the amount of time that it takes to respond to a request for a service. A service here does not refer to a web service; a service can be any unit of work. The response time can be divided into three parts:

- **Wait time**: This is the amount of time that the requests will spend waiting for other requests that took place earlier to be completed.

- **Service time**: This is the amount of time that it takes for the service (unit of work) to be completed.

- **Transmission time**: Once the unit of work has been completed, the response will be sent back to the requestor. The time that it takes for the response to be transmitted is known as the transmission time.

Processing speed

Processing speed (also known as clock rate) refers to the frequency at which a processing unit (CPU or GPU) runs. An application contains many units of work. Each unit of work is composed of instructions for the processor; usually, the processors can perform an instruction in each clock tick. Since a few clock ticks are required for an operation to be completed, the higher the clock rate (processing speed), the more instructions will be completed.

Latency

Latency is a term we can apply to many elements in a system; but when working on web applications, we will use this term to refer to network latency. Network latency indicates any kind of delay that occurs in data communication over the network.

High latency creates bottlenecks in the communication bandwidth. The impact of latency on network bandwidth can be temporary or persistent, based on the root cause of the delays. High latency can be caused by problems in the medium (cables or wireless signals), problems with routers and gateways, and anti-virus, among other things.

Bandwidth

Just like in the case of latency, whenever we mention bandwidth in this chapter, we will be referring to the network bandwidth. The bandwidth, or data transfer rate, is the amount of data that can be carried from one point to another in a given time. The network bandwidth is usually expressed in bits per second.

Network performance can be affected by many factors. Some of these factors can degrade the network throughput. For example, a high packet loss, latency, and jitter will reduce the network throughput, while a high bandwidth will increase it.

Scalability

Scalability is the ability of a system to handle a growing amount of work. A system with good scalability will be able to pass some performance tests, such as spike or stress testing.

We will discover more about performance tests (such as spike and stress) later in this chapter.

Performance analysis

Performance analysis (also known as performance profiling) is the observation and study of resource usage by an application. We will perform profiling in order to identify performance issues in our applications. A different performance profiling process will be carried out for each type of resource using specific tools. We will now take a look at how we can use Google Chrome's developer tools to perform network profiling.

Network performance analysis

We are going to start by analyzing network performance. Not so long ago, in order to be able to analyze the network performance of an application, we would have had to write a small network logging application ourselves. Today, things are much easier thanks to the arrival of the performance timing API (`http://www.w3.org/TR/resource-timing/`). The performance timing API allows us to access detailed network timing data for each loaded resource.

The following diagram illustrates the network timing data points that the API provides:

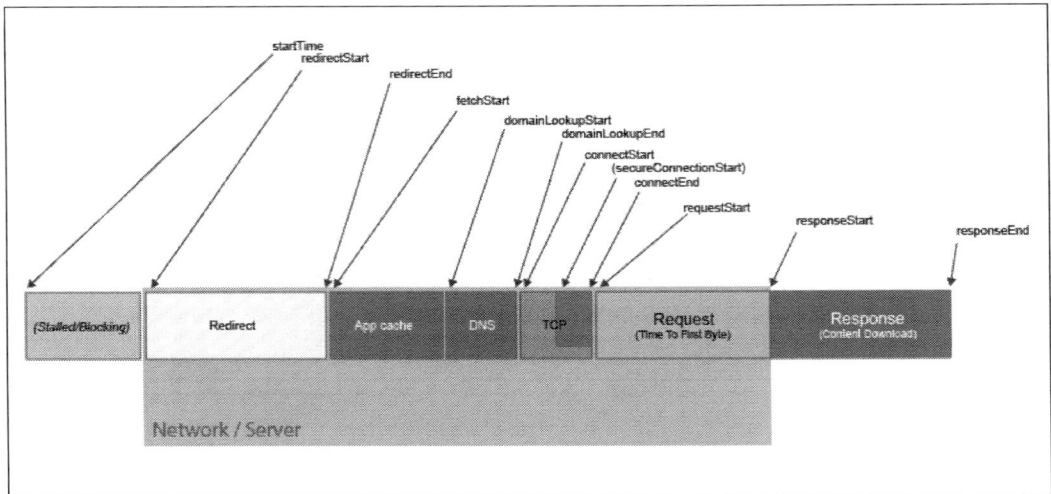

We can access the performance timing API via the global object:

```
window.performance
```

The performance attribute in the global object has some properties (`memory`, `navigation`, and `timing`) and methods (`clearMarks`, `clearMeasures`, and `getEntries`). We can use the `getEntries` function to get an array that contains the taming data points of each request:

```
window.performance.getEntries()
```

Each entity in the array is an instance of `PerformanceResourceTiming`, which contains the following information:

```
{
    connectEnd: 1354.525000002468
    connectStart: 1354.525000002468
    domainLookupEnd: 1354.525000002468
    domainLookupStart: 1354.525000002468
    duration: 179.89400000078604
    entryType: "resource"
    fetchStart: 1354.525000002468
    initiatorType: "link"
    name: "https://developer.chrome.com/static/css/out/site.css"
    redirectEnd: 0
    redirectStart: 0
    requestStart: 1380.8379999827594
```

```
    responseEnd: 1534.419000003254
    responseStart: 1533.6550000065472
    secureConnectionStart: 0
    startTime: 1354.525000002468
}
```

Unfortunately, the timing data points in the preceding format may not be really useful, but there are tools that can help us to analyze them with ease. The first of these tools is a browser extension called **performance-bookmarklet**. This extension is open source and is available for Chrome and Firefox. The extension download links can be found at `https://github.com/micmro/performance-bookmarklet`.

In the following screenshot, you can see one of the graphs generated by the extension. The graphs display the performance typing API information in a much better way, allowing us to spot performance issues with ease:

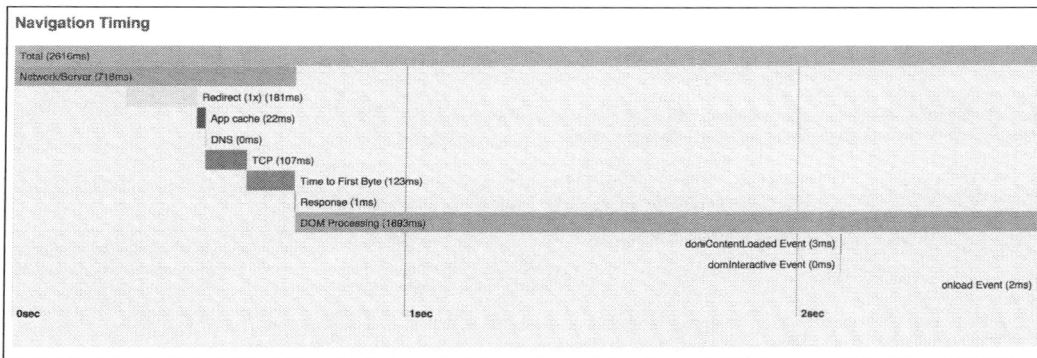

Alternatively, you can use the network panel in the Chrome developer tools to perform network performance profiling. To access the network panel, navigate to **View**, **Developer**, and then **Developer Tools**:

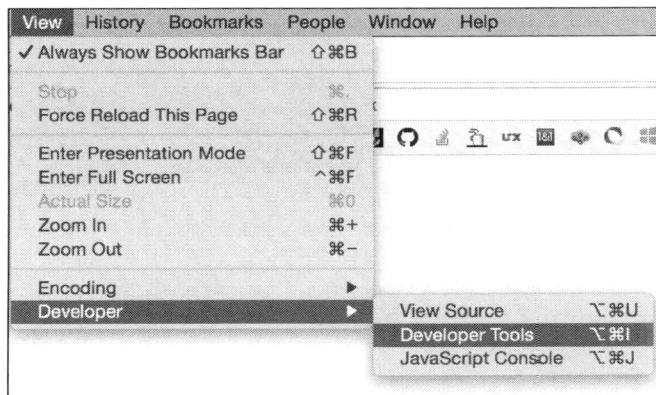

> Windows users can access the developer tools by pressing the *F12* key. OS X users can access it using the *Alt + Cmd + I* shortcut.

Once the developer tools are visible, you can access the **Network** tab by clicking on it:

Clicking on the **Network** tab will lead you to a screen similar to the one seen here:

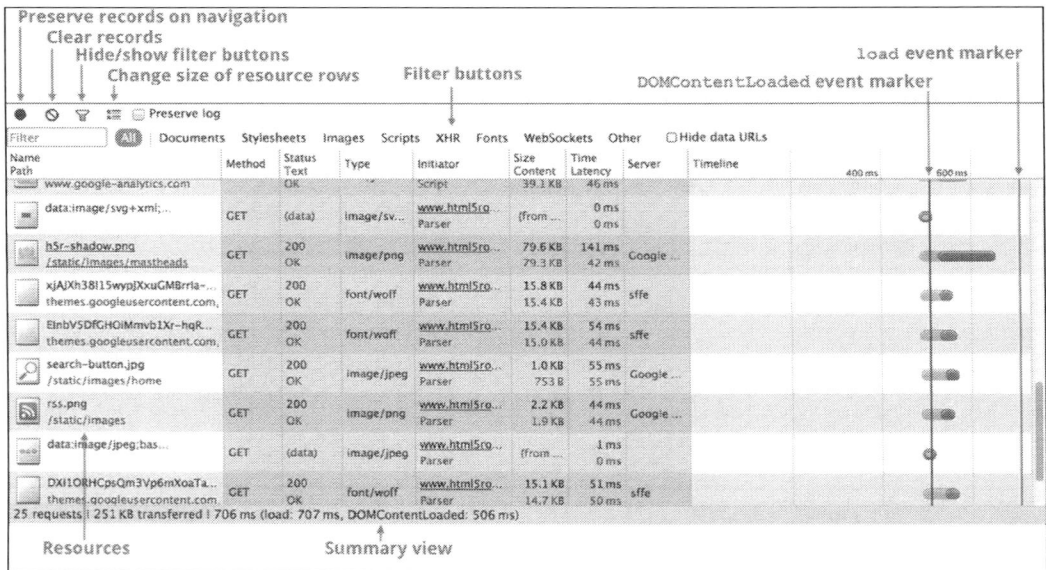

As you can observe, the information is presented in a table in which each file loaded is displayed as a row. On the right-hand side, you can see that one of the columns is the timeline. The timeline displays the performance timing API in a similar way to the way that the performance-bookmarklet extension did.

Two important elements in the timeline are the red and blue lines. These lines let us know when the DOMContentLoaded event is triggered (the blue line), following which the load event is triggered (the red line):

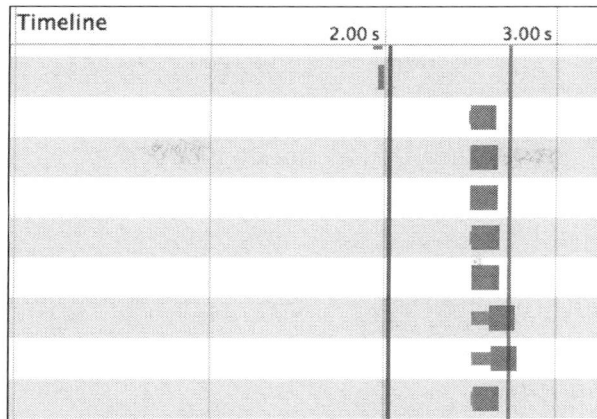

These two events are important because we can examine which requests were completed when the event was fired to get an idea of which contents were available for the user when they took place:

- The DOMContentLoaded event is fired when the engine has completed parsing of the main document
- The load event is fired when all the page's resources have been loaded

If you hover over one of the cells of the timing column, you will be able to see each of the performance timing API data points:

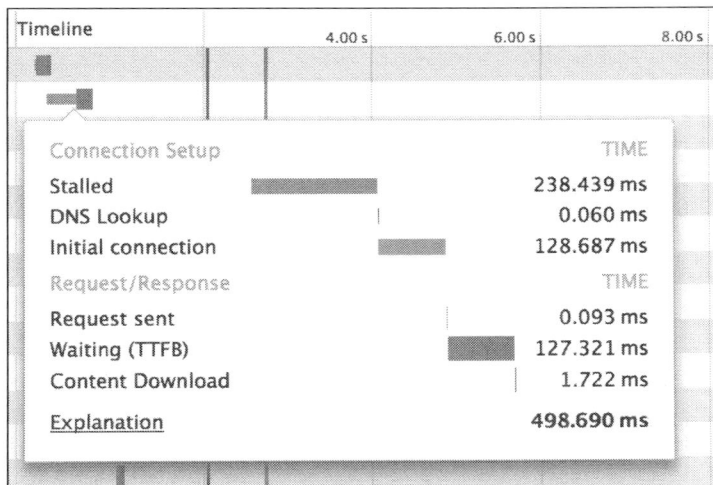

Connection Setup		TIME
Stalled		238.439 ms
DNS Lookup		0.060 ms
Initial connection		128.687 ms
Request/Response		TIME
Request sent		0.093 ms
Waiting (TTFB)		127.321 ms
Content Download		1.722 ms
Explanation		498.690 ms

It is interesting to know that this developer tool actually reads this information using the performance timing API. Let's understand the meaning of each of the data points:

Performance timing API data point	Description
Stalled/Blocking	This is the time the request spent waiting before it could be sent; there is a maximum number of open TCP connections for an origin. When the limit is reached, some requests will display blocking time rather than stalled time.
Proxy Negotiation	This is the time spent negotiating a connection with a proxy server.
DNS Lookup	This is the time spent resolving a DNS address; resolving a DNS requires a full round-trip to the DNS server for each domain in the page.
Initial Connection / Connecting	This is the time it took to establish a connection.
SSL	This is the time spent establishing an SSL connection.
Request Sent / Sending	This is the time spent issuing the network request, typically a fraction of a millisecond.
Waiting (TTFB)	This is the time spent waiting for the initial byte to be received—the time to first byte (TTFB). The TTFB can be used to find out the latency of a round-trip to the server in addition to the time spent waiting for the server to deliver the response.
Content Download / Downloading	This is the time taken for the response data to be received.

Network performance and user experience

Now that you know how we can analyze network performance, it is time to identify the performance goals we should aim for. Numerous studies have proved that it is really important to keep loading times as low as possible. The Akamai study, published in September 2009, interviewed 1,048 online shoppers and found the following:

- 47 percent of people expect a web page to load in two seconds or less
- 40 percent will abandon a web page if it takes more than three seconds to load
- 52 percent of online shoppers claim that quick page loads are important for their loyalty to a site
- 14 percent will start shopping at a different site if page loads are slow; 23 percent will stop shopping or even walk away from their computer
- 64 percent of shoppers who are dissatisfied with their site visit will go somewhere else to shop next time

[📝 You can read the full Akamai study at `http://www.akamai.com/html/about/press/releases/2009/press_091409.html`.]

From the preceding study conclusions, we should assume that network performance matters. Our first priority should be to try to improve the loading speed.

If we try to improve the performance of a site to make sure that it loads in less than two seconds, we might make a common mistake: trying to get the `onLoad` event to be triggered in under two seconds.

While triggering the `onLoad` event as early as possible will probably improve the network performance of an application, it doesn't mean that the user experience will be equally improved. The `onLoad` event is insufficient to determine performance. We can demonstrate this by comparing the loading performance of the Twitter and Amazon websites. As you can see in the following screenshot, users have the opportunity to engage with Amazon much sooner than with Twitter. Even though the `onLoad` event is the same on both sites, the user experience is drastically different:

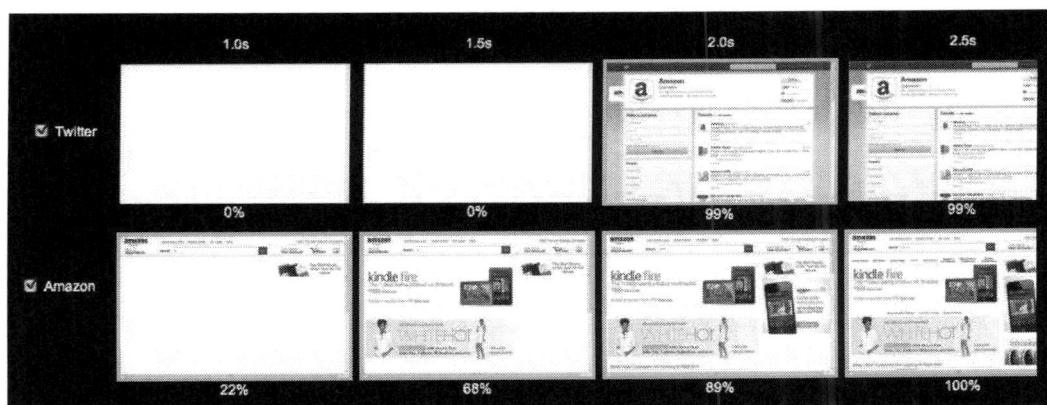

This example demonstrates that to improve the user experience, we must try to reduce the loading times, but we must also try to load the web contents in such a way that the user engagement can begin as early as possible. To achieve this, we should load all the secondary content in an asynchronous manner.

[📝 Refer to *Chapter 3, Working with Functions* to learn more about asynchronous programming with TypeScript.]

Network performance best practices and rules

Another easy way to analyze the performance of a web application is by using a best-practices tool for network performance, such as the Google PageSpeed Insights application or the Yahoo YSlow application.

Google PageSpeed Insights can be used online or as a Google Chrome extension. To try this tool, you can visit the online version at `https://developers.google.com/speed/pagespeed/insights/` and insert the URL of the web application that you want to analyze. In just a few seconds, you will get a report like the one in the following screenshot:

The report contains some effective recommendations that will help us to improve the network performance and overall user experience of our web applications. Google PageSpeed Insights uses the following rules to rate the speed of a web application:

- Avoid landing page redirects
- Enable compression

- Improve server response time

- Leverage browser caching

- Minify resources

- Optimize images

- Optimize CSS Delivery

- Prioritize visible content

- Remove render-blocking JavaScript

- Use asynchronous scripts

When you use this tool, if you click on the score of each rules, you can see recommendations and details that will help you to understand what is wrong and what you need to do to increase the score achieved for one particular rule.

On the other hand, Yahoo YSlow is available as a browser extension, a Node.js module, and a PhantomJS plugin, among others. We can find the right version for our needs at `http://yslow.org/`. When we run YSlow, it will generate a report that will provide us with a general score and a detailed score of the website, like the one in the following screenshot:

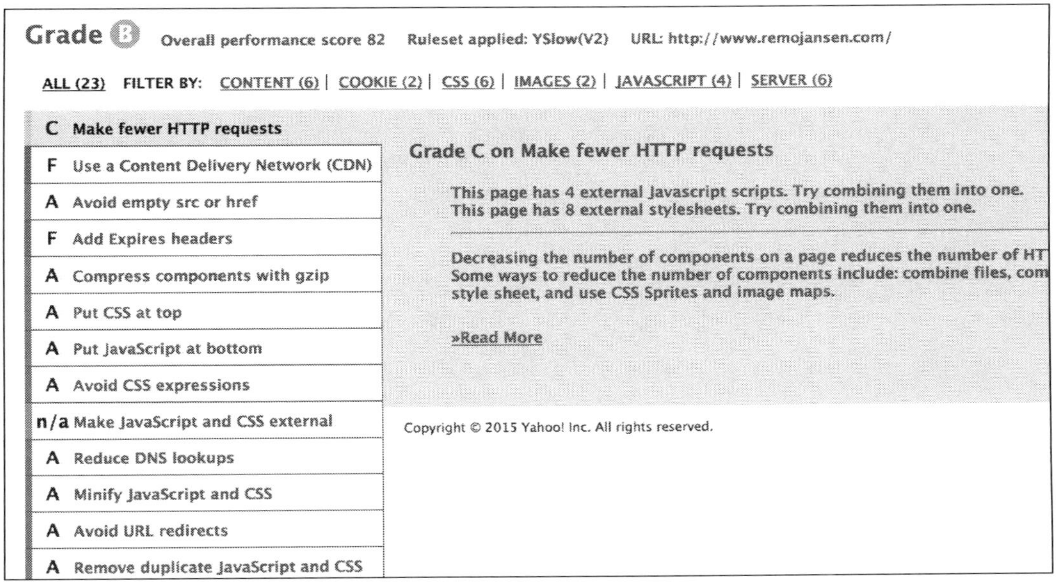

YSlow uses the following set of rules to rate the speed of a web application:

- Minimize HTTP requests
- Use a content delivery network
- Avoid empty `src` or `href`
- Add an expires or a cache-control header
- Gzip components
- Put stylesheets at the top
- Put scripts at the bottom
- Avoid CSS expressions
- Make JavaScript and CSS external
- Reduce DNS lookups
- Minify JavaScript and CSS
- Avoid redirects
- Remove duplicate scripts
- Configure ETags
- Make AJAX cacheable
- Use GET for AJAX requests
- Reduce the number of DOM elements
- Prevent 404 errors
- Reduce cookie size
- Use cookie-free domains for components
- Avoid filters
- Do not scale images in HTML
- Make `favicon.ico` small and cacheable

Just like before, when you use this tool, if you click on each of the rules scored you can see recommendations and details that will help you to understand what is wrong and what you need to do to increase the score achieved for one particular rule.

> If you want to learn more about network performance optimization, please take a look at the book *High Performance Browser Networking* by *Ilya Grigorik*.

GPU performance analysis

The rendering of some elements in web applications is accelerated by the use of the GPU. The GPU is specialized in the processing of graphics-related instructions and can, therefore, deliver much better performance than the CPU when it comes to graphics. For example, CSS3 animations in modern web browsers are accelerated by the GPU, while the CPU performs JavaScript animations. In the past, the only way to achieve some animations was via JavaScript. But today, we should avoid using them when possible and use CSS3 instead because it will help us to achieve great web performance.

In recent years, access to the GPU has been added to browsers via the WebGL API. This API allows web developers to create 3D games and other highly visual applications by using the power of the GPU.

Frames per second (FPS)

We will not go into much detail about the performance of 3D applications because it is a really extensive field and we could write an entire book talking about it. However, we will mention an important concept that can be applied to any kind of web application: **frames per second** (FPS) or frame rate. When a web application is displayed on screen, it is done at a number of images (frames) per second. A low frame rate can be detrimental to the overall user experience when perceived by the users. A lot of research has been carried out on this topic, and 60 frames per second seems to be the optimum frame rate for a great user experience.

Whenever we develop a web application, we should take a look at the frame rate and try to prevent it from dropping below 40 FPS. This is especially important during animations and user actions.

An open source library called `stats.js` can help us to see the frame rate while developing a web application. This library can be downloaded from GitHub at `https://github.com/mrdoob/stats.js/`. We need to download the library and load it in a web page. We can then load the following code snippet by adding a new file or just execute it in the developer console:

```
var stats = new Stats();
stats.setMode(1); // 0: fps, 1: ms

// position of the frame rate counter (align top-left)
stats.domElement.style.position = 'absolute';
stats.domElement.style.left = '0px';
stats.domElement.style.top = '0px';
```

```
document.body.appendChild( stats.domElement );

var update = function () {
    stats.begin();
    // monitored code goes here
    stats.end();
    requestAnimationFrame( update );
};
requestAnimationFrame( update );
```

If everything goes well, we will be able to see the frame rate counter in the top-left corner of the screen. Clicking on it will switch from the FPS view to the millisecond (MS) view:

- The FPS view displays the frames rendered in the last second. The higher this number is, the better.

- The MS view displays the milliseconds needed to render a frame. The lower this number is, the better.

> Some advanced WebGL applications may require an in-depth performance analysis. For such cases, Chrome provides the Trace Event Profiling Tool. If you wish to learn more about this tool, visit the official page at https://www.chromium.org/developers/how-tos/trace-event-profiling-tool.

CPU performance analysis

To analyze the usage of the processing time, we will take a look at the execution path of our application. We will examine each of the functions invoked and how long it takes to complete their execution. We can access all this information by opening the Chrome developer tools' **Profiles** tab:

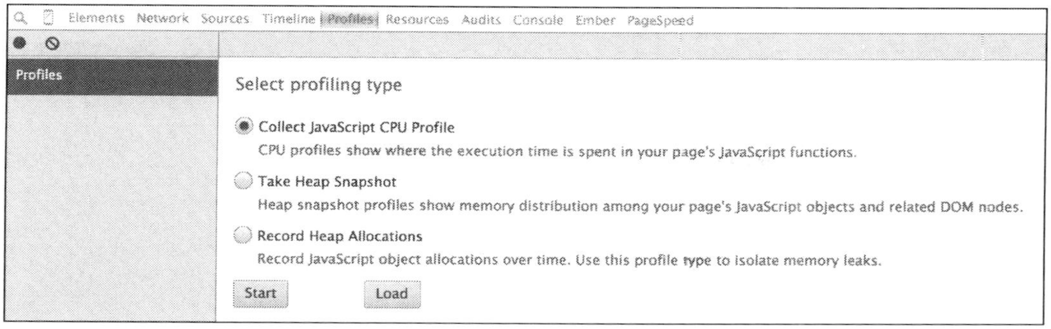

In this tab, we can select **Collect JavaScript CPU Profile** and then click on the **Start** button to start recording the CPU usage. Being able to select when we want to start and stop recording the CPU usage helps us select the specific functions that we want to analyze. If, for example, we want to analyze a function named `foo`, all we need to do is start recording the CPU usage, invoke the `foo` function and stop recording. A timeline like the one in the following screenshot will then be displayed:

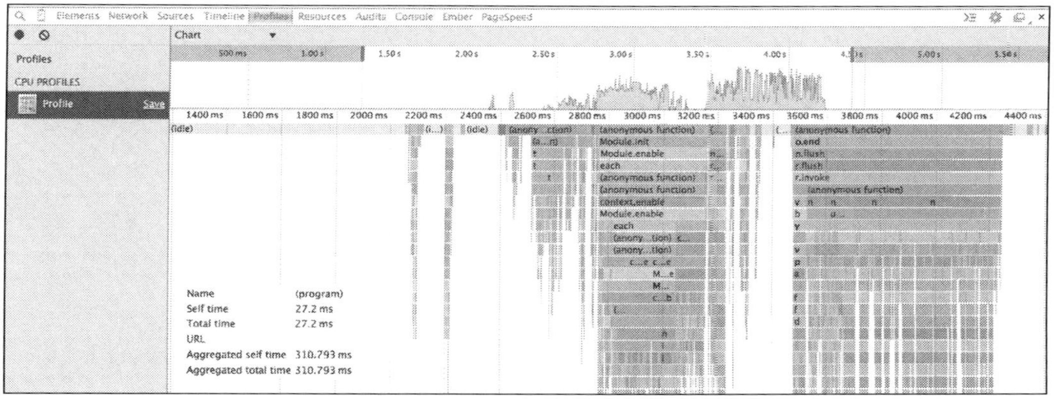

The timeline displays (horizontally) the functions invoked in the chronological order. If the function invokes other functions, the function's call-stack is displayed vertically. When we hover over one of these functions, we will be able to see its details in the bottom-left corner of the timeline:

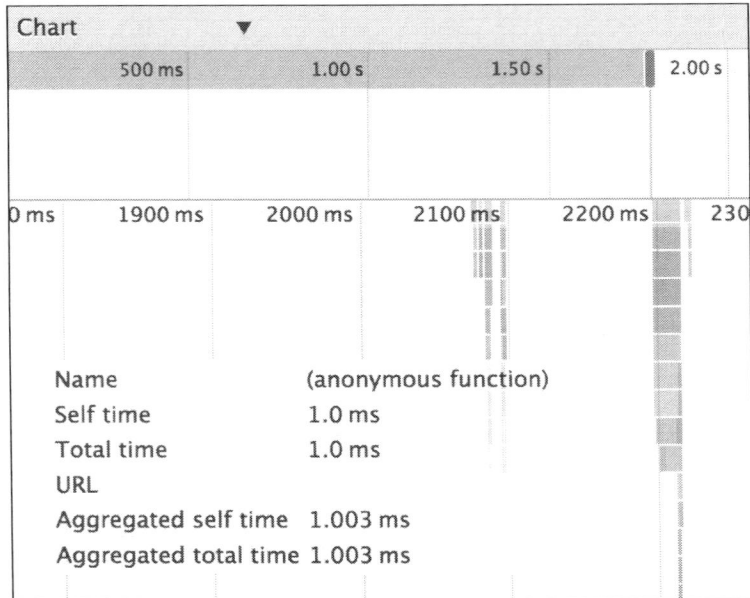

The details include the following information:

- **Name**: The name of the function.
- **Self time**: The time spent on the completion of the current invocation of the function. We will take into account the time spent in the execution of the statements within the function, not including any functions that it called.
- **Total time**: The total time spent on the completion of the current invocation of the function. We will take into account the time spent in the execution of the statements within the function, including functions that it called.
- **Aggregated self time**: The time for all invocations of the function across the recording, not including functions called by this function.
- **Aggregated total time**: The time for all invocations of the function across the recording, including functions called by this function.

As we saw in the previous chapter, all the JavaScript code is executed in one single thread at runtime. For this reason, when a function is executed, no other function will be executed. Sometimes, the execution of a function takes too long to be completed, and the application becomes unresponsive. We can use the CPU profile report to identify which functions are consuming too much processing time. Once we have identified these functions, we can refactor and then to try to improve the application responsiveness. Some common improvements include using an asynchronous execution flow when possible and reducing the size of the functions.

Memory performance analysis

When we declare a variable, it is allocated in the RAM. Some time after the variable is out of the scope, it is cleared from memory by the garbage collector. Sometimes, we can generate a scenario in which a variable never goes out of scope. If the variable never goes out of scope, it will never be cleared from memory. This can eventually lead to some serious memory leaking issues. A **memory leak** is the continuous loss of available memory.

When dealing with memory leaks, we can take advantage of the Google Chrome developer tools to identify the root cause of the problem with ease.

The first thing that we might wonder is whether our application has memory leaks or not. We can find out by visiting the timeline tab and clicking on the top-left icon to start recording the resource usage. Once we stop recording, a timeline graph like the one in the following screenshot will be displayed:

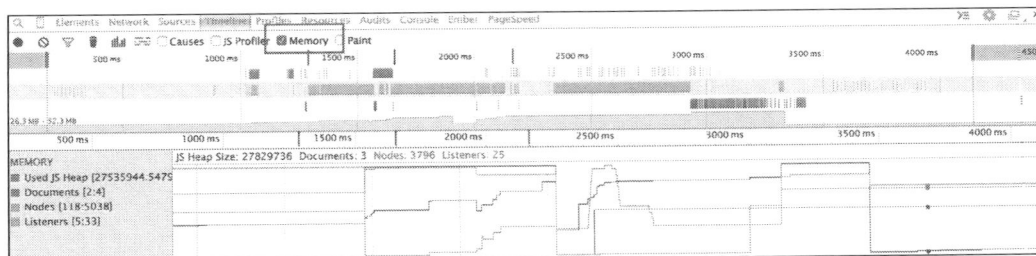

In the timeline, we can select **Memory** to see the memory usage (**Used JS Heap**) over time (the blue line in the image). In the preceding example, we can see a notable drop towards the end of the line. This is a good sign because it indicates that the majority of the used memory has been cleared when the page has finished loading.

The memory leaks can also take place after loading; in that case, we can use the application for a while and observe how the memory usage varies in the graph to identify the cause of the leak.

An alternative way to detect memory leaks is by observing the memory allocations. We can access this information by recording the heap allocations in the **Profiles** tab:

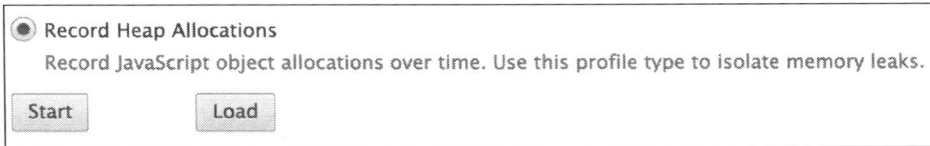

The report will be displayed after we have recorded some usage of the resources. We can do this by clicking on the **Start** and **Stop** buttons. The memory allocation report will display a timeline like the one in the following screenshot. Each of the blue lines is a memory allocation that took place during the recorded period. The height of the line represents the amount of memory used. As you can see, the memory is almost cleared completely around the eighth second:

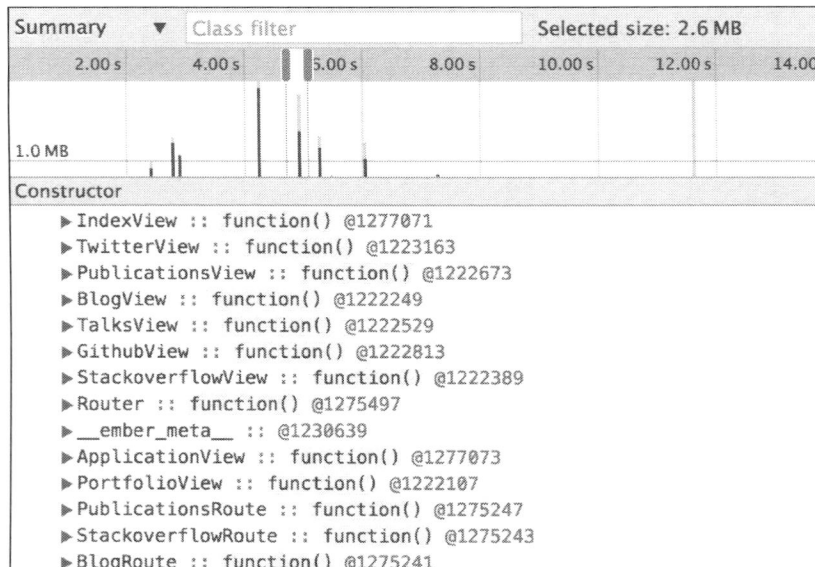

If we click on one of the blue lines, we will be able to navigate through all the variables that were stored in memory when the allocation took place and examine their values. It is also possible to take a memory snapshot at any given point from the **Profiles** tab:

This feature is particularly useful when we are debugging and we want to see the memory usage at a particular breakpoint. The memory snapshot works like the details view in the previously explained allocations view:

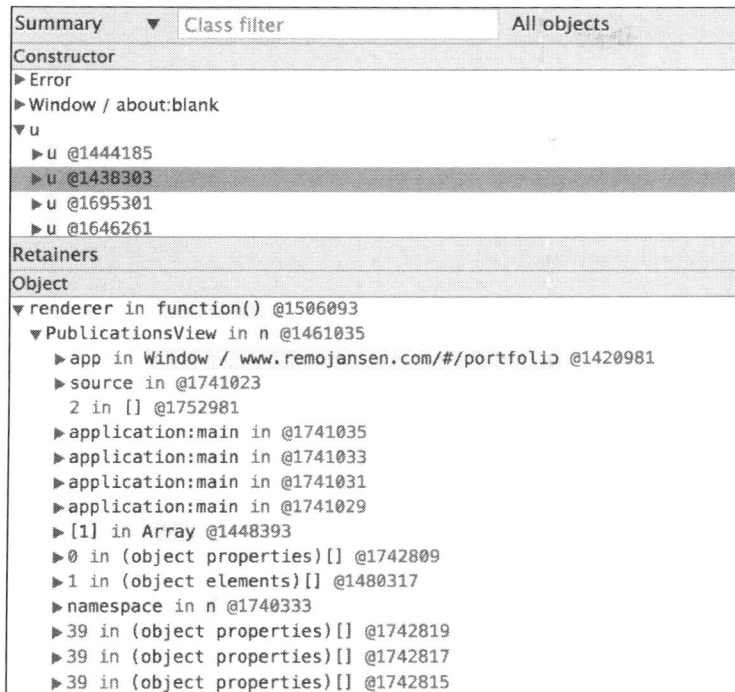

```
Summary      ▼  Class filter                    All objects
Constructor
▶ Error
▶ Window / about:blank
▼ u
   ▶ u @1444185
   ▶ u @1438303
   ▶ u @1695301
   ▶ u @1646261
Retainers
Object
▼ renderer in function() @1506093
   ▼ PublicationsView in n @1461035
      ▶ app in Window / www.remojansen.com/#/portfolio @1420981
      ▶ source in @1741023
        2 in [] @1752981
      ▶ application:main in @1741035
      ▶ application:main in @1741033
      ▶ application:main in @1741031
      ▶ application:main in @1741029
      ▶ [1] in Array @1448393
      ▶ 0 in (object properties)[] @1742809
      ▶ 1 in (object elements)[] @1480317
      ▶ namespace in n @1740333
      ▶ 39 in (object properties)[] @1742819
      ▶ 39 in (object properties)[] @1742817
      ▶ 39 in (object properties)[] @1742815
```

As you can see in the preceding screenshot, the memory snapshot allows us to navigate through all the variables that were stored in memory when the snapshot was taken and examine their values.

The garbage collector

Programing languages with a low level of abstraction have low-level memory management mechanisms. On the other hand, in languages with a higher level of abstraction, such as C# or JavaScript, the memory is automatically allocated and freed by a process known as the garbage collector.

The JavaScript garbage collector does a great job when it comes to memory management, but it doesn't mean that we don't need to care about memory management.

Independent of which programming language we are working with, the memory life cycle pretty much follows the same pattern:

- Allocate the memory you need
- Use the memory (read/write)
- Release the allocated memory when it is not needed any more

The garbage collector will try to release the allocated memory when is not needed any more using a variation of an algorithm known as the **mark-and-sweep algorithm**. The garbage collector performs periodical scans to identify objects that are out of the scope and can be freed from the memory. The scan is divided in two phases: the first one is known as **mark** because the garbage collector will flag or mark the items that can be freed from the memory. During the second phase, known as **sweep**, the garbage collector will free the memory consumed by the items marked in the previous phase.

The garbage collector is usually able to identify when an item can be cleared from the memory; but we, as developers, must try to ensure that objects get out of scope when we don't need them any more. If a variable never gets out of the scope, it will be allocated in memory forever, potentially leading to a severe memory leak issue.

The number of references pointing to an item in memory will prevent it from being freed from memory. For this reason, most cases of memory leaks can be fixed by ensuring that there are no permanent references to variables. Here are a few rules that can help us to prevent potential memory leak issues:

- Remember to clear intervals when you don't need them any more.
- Remember to clear event listeners when you don't need them any more.
- Remember that when you create a closure, the inner function will remember the context in which it was declared. This means that there will be some extra items allocated in memory.
- Remember that when using object composition, if circular references are created, you can end up having some variables that will never be cleared from memory.

Performance automation

In this section we will understand how we can automate many of the performance optimization tasks, from concatenation and compression of contents to the automation of the performance monitoring and performance testing processes.

Performance optimization automation

After analyzing the performance of our application, we will start working on some performance optimizations. Many of these optimizations involve the concatenation and compression of some of the application's components. The problem with compressed components is that they are more complicated to debug and maintain. We will also have to create a new version of the concatenated and compressed contents every time one of the original components (not concatenated and not compressed) changes. As these include many highly repetitive tasks, we can use the task runner Gulp to perform many of these tasks for us. We can find online plugins that will allow us to concatenate and compress components, optimize images, generate a cache manifest, and perform many other performance optimization tasks.

> If you would like to learn more about Gulp, refer to *Chapter 2, Automating Your Development Workflow*.

Performance monitoring automation

We have seen that we can automate many of the performance optimization tasks using the Gulp task runner. In a similar way, we can also automate the performance monitoring process.

In order to monitor the performance of an existing application, we will need to collect some data that will allow us to compare the application performance over time. Depending on how we collect the data, we can identify three different types of performance monitoring:

- **Real user monitoring (RUM)**: This is a type of solution used to capture performance data from real user visits. The collection of data is performed by a small JavaScript code snippet loaded in the browser. This type of solution can help us to collect data and discover performance trends and patterns.

- **Simulated browsers**: This type of solution is used to capture performance data from simulated browsers. This is the most economic option, but it is limited because simulated browsers cannot offer as accurate a representation of the real user experience.

- **Real-browser monitoring**: This is used to capture the performance data of real browsers. This information provides a more accurate representation of the real user experience, as the data is collected using exactly what a user would see if they visited the site with the given environment (browser, geographic location, and network throughput).

In *Chapter 2, Automating Your Development Workflow*, we saw how to configure a Gulp task that used the Karma test runner to execute a test suite in a headless browser known as **PhantomJS**.

PhantomJS is a simulated browser that can be configured to generate **HTTP Archive (HAR)** files. A HAR file uses a common format for recording HTTP tracing information. This file contains a variety of information, but for our purposes, it has a record of each object being loaded by a browser.

There are multiple scripts available online that showcase how to collect the data and reformat it using the PhantomJS API. One of the examples, `netsniff.js`, exports the network traffic in HAR format. The `netsniff.js` file (and other examples) can be found at `https://github.com/ariya/mjs/tree/master/examples`.

Once we have generated the HAR files, we can use another application to see the collected performance information on a visual timeline. This application is called HAR viewer, and it can be found at `https://github.com/janodvarko/harviewer`.

Alternatively, we could write a custom script or Gulp task to read the HAR files and break the automated build if the application performance doesn't meet our needs.

It is also possible to configure PhantomJS to run the YSlow performance analysis report and integrate it with the automated build. To learn more about PhantomJS and performance monitoring, refer to the official documentation at `http://phantomjs.org/network-monitoring.html`.

> If you are considering using RUM, take a look at the New Relic solutions at `http://newrelic.com/`, or Google Analytics at `http://www.google.com/analytics/`.

Performance testing automation

Another way to improve the performance of an application is to write automated performance tests. These tests can be used to guarantee that the system meets a set of performance goals. There are multiple types of performance testing, but some of the most common ones include the following:

- **Load testing**: This is the most basic form of performance testing. We can use a load test to understand the behavior of the system under a specific expected load (number of concurrent users, number of transactions, and duration). There are multiple types of load testing:

- Stress testing: This is normally used to understand the maximum capacity limits of an application. This kind of test determines if an application is able to handle an extreme load by using an extreme load for an extended period of time.

  Stress testing is not really useful when working on a client-side application. However, it can be really helpful when working on a Node.js application, since Node.js applications can have many simultaneous users.

- Soak testing: This is also known as endurance testing. This kind of test is similar to the stress test, but instead of using an extreme load, it uses the expected load for an extended period of time. It is a common practice to collect memory usage data during this kind of test to detect potential memory leaks. This kind of test helps us to detect if the performance
  suffers some kind of degradation after an extended period of time.

- Spike testing: This is also similar to the stress test, but instead of using an extreme time load during an extended time period, it uses sudden intervals of extreme and expected load. This kind of test helps us to determine if an application is able to handle dramatic changes in load.

- Configuration testing: This is used to determine the effects of configuration changes on the performance and behavior of an application. A common example would be experimenting with different methods of load balancing.

> This kind of test can also be automated by using tools such as JMeter (http://jmeter.apache.org) or Locust (http://locust.io).

Exception handling

Understanding how to use the available resources in an efficient manner will help us to create better applications. In a similar manner, understanding how to handle runtime errors will help us to improve the overall quality of our applications. Exception handling in TypeScript involves three main language elements.

The Error class

When a runtime error takes place, an instance of the Error class is thrown:

```
throw new Error();
```

We can create custom errors in a couple of different ways. The easiest way to achieve it is by passing a string as argument to the `Error` class constructor:

```
Throw new Error("My basic custom error");
```

If we need more customizable and advanced control over custom exceptions, we can use inheritance to achieve it:

```
module CustomException {
    export declare class Error {
        public name: string;
        public message: string;
        public stack: string;
        constructor(message?: string);
    }

    export class Exception extends Error {

        constructor(public message: string) {
            super(message);
            this.name = 'Exception';
            this.message = message;
            this.stack = (<any>new Error()).stack;
        }
        toString() {
            return this.name + ': ' + this.message;
        }
    }
}
```

In the preceding code snippet, we have declared a class named `Error`. This class is available at runtime but is not declared by TypeScript, so we will have to do it ourselves. Then, we have created an `Exception` class, which inherits from the `Error` class.

Finally, we can create `customError` by inheriting from our `Exception` class:

```
class CustomError extends CustomException.Exception {
  // ...
}
```

The try...catch statements and throw statements

A `catch` clause contains statements that specify what to do if an exception is thrown in the `try` block. We should perform some operations in the `try` block, and if they fail, the program execution flow will move from the `try` block to the `catch` block.

Additionally, there is an optional block known as `finally`, which is executed after both the `try` and `catch` (if there was an exception in `catch`) blocks:

```
try {
    // code that we want to work
    throw new Error("Oops!");
}
catch (e){
    // code executed if expected to work fails
    console.log(e);
}
finally {
    // code executed always after try or try and catch (when
    errors)
    console.log("finally!");
}
```

It is also important to mention that in the majority of programming languages, including TypeScript, throwing and catching exceptions is an expensive operation in terms of resource consumption. We should use these statements if we need them, but sometimes it is necessary to avoid them because they can potentially negatively affect the performance of our applications. Therefore, we should keep in mind that it is a good idea to avoid the use of `try...catch` and `throw` statements in performance-critical functions and loops.

Summary

In this chapter, we saw what performance is and how the availability of resources can influence it. We also looked at how to use some tools to analyze the way a TypeScript application uses available resources. These tools allow us to spot some possible issues, such as a low frame rate, memory leaks, and high loading times. We have also discovered that we can automate many kinds of performance optimization task, as well as the performance monitoring and testing processes.

In the following chapter, we will see how we can automate the testing process of our TypeScript applications to achieve great application maintainability and reliability.

7
Application Testing

In this chapter, we are going to take a look at how to write unit tests for TypeScript applications. We will see how to use tools and frameworks to facilitate the testing process of our applications.

The contents of this chapter cover the following topics:

- Setting up a test infrastructure
- Testing planning and methodologies
- How to work with Mocha, Chai, and Sinon.JS
- How to work with test assertions, specs, and suites
- Test spies
- Test stubs
- Testing on multiple environments
- How to work with Karma and PhantomJS
- End-to-end testing
- Generating test coverage reports

We will get started by installing some necessary third-party software dependencies.

Software testing glossary

Across this chapter, we will use some concepts that may not be familiar to those readers without previous software testing experience. Let's take a quick look at some of the most popular testing concepts before we get started.

Assertions

An **assertion** is a condition that must be tested to confirm that a certain piece of code behaves as expected or, in other words, to confirm conformance to a requirement.

Let's imagine that we are working as part of one of the Google Chrome development team and we have to implement the JavaScript `Math` object. If we are working on the `pow` method, the requirement could be something like the following:

"The Math.pow(base, exponent) function should return the base (the base number) to the exponent (the exponent used to raise the base power – that is, base ^ exponent)."

With this information, we could create the following implementation:

```
class Math1 {
  public static pow(base: number, exponent: number) {
    var result = base;
    for(var i = 1; i < exponent; i++){
      result = result * base;
    }
    return result;
  }
}
```

To ensure that the method is correctly implemented, we must test it conforms with the requirement. If we analyze the requirements closely, we should identify at least two necessary assertions.

The function should return the base to the exponent:

```
var actual = Math1.pow(3,5);
var expected = 243;
var asertion1 = (Math1.pow(base1, exponent1) === expected1);
```

The exponent is not used as the base (or the base is not used as the exponent):

```
var actual = Math1.pow(5,3);
var expected = 125;
var asertion2 = (Math1.pow(base2, exponent2) === expected2);
```

If both assertions are valid, then our code adheres to the requirements, and we know that it will work as expected:

```
var isValidCode = (asertion1 && asertion2);
console.log(isValidCode);
```

Specs

Spec is a term used by software development engineers to refer to test specifications. A test specification (not to be confused with a test plan) is a detailed list of all the scenarios that should be tested, how they should be tested, and so on. We will see later in this chapter how we can use a testing framework to define a test spec.

Test cases

A **test case** is a set of conditions used to determine whether one of the features of an application is working as it was originally established to work. We might wonder what the difference between a test assertion and a test case is. While a test assertion is a single condition, a test case is a set of conditions. We will see later in this chapter how we can use a testing framework to define test cases.

Suites

A **suite** is a collection of test cases. While a test case should focus on only one test scenario, a test suite can contain test cases for many test scenarios.

Spies

Spies are a feature provided by some testing frameworks. They allow us to wrap a method and record its usage (input, output, number of times invoked). When we wrap a function with a spy, the underlying method's functionality does not change.

Dummies

A **dummy** object is an object that is passed around during the execution of a test but is never actually used.

Stubs

A **stub** is a feature provided by some testing frameworks. Stubs also allow us to wrap a method to observe its usage. Unlike spies, when we wrap a function with a stub, the underlying method's functionality is replaced with a new behavior.

Mocks

Mocks are often confused with stubs. Martin Fowler once wrote the following in an article titled Mocks Aren't Stubs:

> *In particular I see them often (mocks) confused with stubs - a common helper to testing environments. I understand this confusion - I saw them as similar for a while too, but conversations with the mock developers have steadily allowed a little mock understanding to penetrate my tortoiseshell cranium. This difference is actually two separate differences. On the one hand there is a difference in how test results are verified: a distinction between state verification and behavior verification. On the other hand is a whole different philosophy to the way testing and design play together, which I term here as the classical and mockist styles of Test Driven Development.*

Both mocks and stubs provide some sort of input to the test case; but, despite their similarities, the flow of information from each is very different:

- Stubs provide input for the application under test so that the test can be performed on something else
- Mocks provide input to the test to decide whether the test should pass or fail

The difference between mocks and stubs will become clearer as we move towards the end of this chapter.

Test coverage

The term test coverage refers to a unit of measurement, which is used to illustrate the number of portions of code in an application that have been tested via automated tests. Test coverage can be obtained by automatically generating test coverage reports. Towards the end of the chapter, we will see how to create such reports using a tool called Istanbul (`http://gotwarlost.github.io/istanbul/`).

Prerequisites

Throughout this chapter, we will use some third-party tools, including some frameworks and automation tools. We will start by looking at each tool in detail. Before we get started, we need to use npm to create a `package.json` file in the folder that we are going to use to implement the examples in this chapter.

Let's create a new folder named app and run the `npm init` command inside it to generate a new `package.json` file:

```
npm init
```

> Refer to *Chapter 2, Automating Your Development Workflow*
> for additional help on npm.

Gulp

We will use the Gulp task runner to run some tasks necessary to execute our tests.
We can install Gulp using npm:

```
npm install gulp -g
```

> If you are not familiar with task runners and continuous
> integration build servers, take a look at *Chapter 2, Automating
> Your Development Workflow*.

Karma

Karma is a test runner. We will use Karma to automatically execute our tests. This
is useful because sometimes the execution of the test will not be started by one of
the members of our software development team. Instead, it will be triggered by a
continuous integration build server (usually via a task runner).

Karma can be used with multiple testing frameworks, thanks to the installation of
plugins. Let's install Karma using the following command:

```
npm install --save-dev karma
```

We will also install another Karma plugin that facilitates the creation of test
coverage reports:

```
npm install --save-dev karma-coverage
```

Istanbul

Istanbul is a tool that identifies which lines of our application are processed during
the execution of the automated test. It can generate reports known as test coverage
reports. These reports can help us to get an idea of the level of testing of a project
because they show which lines of code were not executed and a percentage value
that represents the fraction of the application that has been tested. It is recommended
that a test coverage value of at least 75 percent of the overall application should be
achieved, while many open source projects target a test coverage of 100 percent.

Mocha

Mocha is a popular JavaScript testing library that facilitates the creation of test suites, test cases, and test specs. Mocha can be used to test TypeScript in the frontend and backend, identify performance issues, and generate different types of test reports, among many other features.

Let's install Mocha and the Karma-Mocha plugin using the following command:

```
npm install --save-dev mocha karma-mocha
```

Chai

Chai is a test assertion library that supports **test-driven development** (TDD) and **behavior-driven development** (BDD) test styles.

[We will see more about TDD and BDD later in this chapter.]

The main goal of Chai is to reduce the amount of work necessary to create a test assertion and make the test more readable.

We can install Chai and the Karma-Chai plugin using the following command:

```
npm install --save-dev chai karma-chai
```

Sinon.JS

Sinon.JS is an isolation framework that provides us with a set of APIs (test spies, stubs, and mocks) that can help us to test a component in isolation. Testing isolated software components is difficult because there is a high level of coupling between the components. A mocking library such as Sinon.JS can help us isolate the components in order to test individual features.

We can install Sinon.JS and the Karma-Sinon plugin using the following command:

```
npm install --save-dev sinon karma-sinon
```

Type definitions

To be able to work with third-party libraries in JavaScript with a good support, we need to import the type definitions of each library. We will use the tsd package manager to install the necessary type definitions:

```
tsd install mocha --save
```

```
tsd install chai --save
tsd install sinon --save
tsd install jquery - -save
```

> Refer to *Chapter 2, Automating Your Development Workflow* for additional help on tsd.

PhantomJS

PhantomJS is a headless browser. We can use PhantomJS to run our tests in a browser without having to actually open a browser. Being able to do this is useful for a few reasons; the main one is that PhantomJS can be executed via a command interface, and it is really easy to integrate with task runners and continuous integration servers. The second reason is that not having to open a browser potentially reduces the time required to complete the execution of the tests suites.

We need to install the Karma plugin that will run the test in PhantomJS:

```
npm install --save-dev phantomjs
npm install --save-dev karma-phantomjs-launcher
```

Selenium and Nightwatch.js

Selenium is a test runner but it was especially designed to run a particular type of test known as an **end-to-end** (E2E) test.

> We will learn more about E2E testing later on this chapter, so we don't need to worry too much about this topic for now.

Though we will see how to use selenium towards the end of the chapter, we can install it now. We will not work with Selenium directly because we are going to use another tool (known as Nightwatch.js) for E2E testing, which will automatically run Selenium for us.

Nightwatch.js is an automated testing framework, written in Node.js for web applications and websites, which uses the Selenium WebDriver API. It is a complete browser automation (end-to-end) solution.

We can install Nightwatch.js and Selenium by executing the following commands:

```
npm install --save-dev gulp-nightwatch
npm install selenium-standalone -g
selenium-standalone install
```

> The Selenium standalone requires the Java binaries to be installed in the development environment and accessible through the $PATH variable. Refer to the official Java documentation at https://www.java.com/en/download/help/index_installing.xml to learn more about the Java installation.

Testing planning and methodologies

When it comes to software development, we usually have many choices. Every time we have to develop a new application, we can choose the type of database, the architecture, and frameworks that we will use. Not all our choices are about technologies. For example, we can also choose a software development methodology such as extreme programming or scrum. When it comes to testing, there are two major styles or methodologies: test-driven development (TDD) and behavior-driven development (BDD).

Test-driven development

Test-driven development is a testing methodology that focuses on encouraging developers to write tests before they write application code. Usually, the process of writing code in TDD consists of the following basic steps:

1. Write a test that fails.
2. Run the test and ensure that it fails (there is no code at this point so it should fail).
3. Write the code to make the test pass.
4. Run the test and ensure that it passes.
5. Run all the other tests to ensure that no other parts of the application break.
6. Repeat the process.

The difference between using TDD or not is really a mindset. Many developers don't like writing tests, so chances are that' if we leave their implementation as the last task in the development process, the tests will not implemented or the application will just be partially tested.

TDD is recommended because it effectively helps you and your team to increase the test coverage of your applications and, therefore, significantly reduce the number of potential issues.

Behavior-driven development (BDD)

Behavior-driven development appeared after TDD with the mission of being a refined version of TDD. BDD focuses on the way tests are described (specs) and states that the tests should focus on the application requirements and not the test requirements. Ideally, this will encourage developers to think less about the tests themselves and more about the application as a whole.

> The original article in which the BDD principles were introduced for the first time by *Dan North* is available online at http://dannorth.net/introducing-bdd/.

As we have already seen, Mocha and Chai provide APIs for the TDD and BDD approaches. Later in this chapter, we will further explore these two approaches.

Recommending one of these methodologies is not trivial because TDD and BDD are both really good testing methodologies. However, BDD was developed after TDD with the objective to improve it, so we can argue that BDD has some additional advantages over TDD. In BDD, the description of a test focuses on what the application should do and not what the test code is testing. This can help the developers to identify tests that reflect the behavior desired by the customer. BDD tests are then used to document the requirements of a system in a way that can be understood and validated by both the developer and the customer. On the other hand, TDD tests cannot be understood with ease by the customer.

Tests plans and test types

The term test plan is sometimes incorrectly used to refer to a test specification. While tests specifications define the scenarios that will be tested and how they will be tested, the test plan is a collection of all the test specs for a given area.

It is recommended to create an actual planning document because a test plan can involve many processes, documents, and practices. One of the main goals of a test plan is to identify and define what kind of test is adequate for a particular component or set of components in an application.

Following are the most commonly used test types:

- **Unit tests**: These are used to test an isolated component. If the component is not isolated—or in other words, the component has some dependencies—we will have to use some tools and practices such as mocks or dependency injection to try to isolate it as much as we can during the test.

  If it is not possible to manipulate the component dependencies, we will use spies to facilitate the creation of the unit tests.

  Our main goal should be to achieve the total isolation of a component when it is tested. A unit test should also be fast, and we should try to avoid input/output, network usage, and any other operation that could potentially affect the speed of the test.

- **Partial integration tests and full integration tests**: These are used to test a set of components (partial integration test) or the entire application as a whole (full integration test). In integration, we will normally use known test data to feed the backend with information that will be displayed in the frontend. We will then assert that the displayed information is correct.

- **Regression tests**: These tests are used to verify that an issue has been fixed. If we are using TDD or BDD, whenever we encounter an issue we should create a unit test that reproduces the issue, and then change the code. By doing this, we will be able to run attempts to reproduce past issues and ensure that everything is still working.

- **Performance / Load tests**: These tests verify if the application meets our performance expectations. We can use performance tests to verify that our application will be able to handle many concurrent users or activity spikes. To learn more about this type of test, take a look at the previous chapter: *Chapter 6, Application Performance*.

- **End-to-end (E2E) tests**: These tests are not really different from full integration tests. The main difference is that in an E2E testing session, we will try to emulate an environment almost identical to the real user environment. We will use Nightwatch.js and Selenium for this purpose.

- **User acceptance tests (UAT)**: These are used so that the system meets all the requirements of the end user.

Setting up a test infrastructure

As we saw previously in this chapter when we talked about unit tests, usually, testing requires being able to isolate the individual software component of our applications.

In order to be able to isolate the components of our application, we will need to adhere to some principles (such as the dependency inversion principle) that will help us to increase the level of decoupling between the components.

We will now configure a testing environment using Gulp and Karma and write some automated test using Mocha and Chai. By the end of this chapter, we will know how writing unit tests can help us to increase the level of decoupling and isolation between the components of an application, and how they can lead us to the development of great applications, especially when it comes to maintainability and reliability.

Let's get started by creating the folder structure of a new application. We will create two folders inside the app folder that we created at the beginning of this chapter.

Let's name the first folder `source` and the second folder `test`. Here, we can see how our directory tree should look by the end of the chapter:

```
├──app
    ├── gulpfile.js
    ├── index.html
    ├── karma.conf.js
    ├── nightwatch.json
    ├── package.json
    ├── source
    │   ├── calculator_widget.ts
    │   ├── demos.ts
    │   ├── interfaces.d.ts
    │   ├── math_demo.ts
    ├── style
    │   └── demo.css
    ├── test
    │   ├── bdd.test.ts
    │   ├── e2e.test.ts
    │   ├── tdd.test.ts
    ├── tsd.json
    └── typings
```

We are going to develop a really small application to be able to write a unit test. We are going to write a unit test and an end-to-end test.

> The source code of the entire demo can be found in the companion code samples.

Once we have completed our application, we will be able to open it in a browser, where we should see a form like the one in the following screenshot. This form allows us to find the result of a number (base) to the power of another (exponent).

Test Application

Base	Exponent	Result	
2	8	256	Submit

Building the application with Gulp

We will get started by creating a new `gulpfile.js` file as we did in *Chapter 2, Automating Your Development Workflow*. The first thing that we are going to do is import all the necessary node modules:

```
var gulp         = require("gulp"),
    browserify   = require("browserify"),
    source       = require("vinyl-source-stream"),
    buffer       = require("vinyl-buffer"),
    run          = require("gulp-run"),
    nightwatch   = require('gulp-nightwatch'),
    tslint       = require("gulp-tslint"),
    tsc          = require("gulp-typescript"),
    browserSync  = require('browser-sync'),
    karma        = require("karma").server,
    uglify       = require("gulp-uglify"),
    docco        = require("gulp-docco"),
    runSequence  = require("run-sequence"),
    header       = require("gulp-header"),
    pkg          = require(__dirname + "/package.json");
```

> Remember that we need to install all necessary packages by using the npm package manager. We can take a look at the `package.json` file to see all the dependencies and their respective versions.

The second thing that we are going to do is to create some tasks to compile our TypeScript code. Here, we should notice that we are going compile the application code into the /build/source folder and the application tests into the /build/test folder:

```
var tsProject = tsc.createProject({
  removeComments : false,
  noImplicitAny : false,
  target : "ES5",
  module : "commonjs",
  declarationFiles : false
});


gulp.task("build-source", function() {
  return gulp.src(__dirname + "/source/*.ts")
             .pipe(tsc(tsProject))
             .pipe(gulp.dest(__dirname + "/build/source/"));
});
```

The previous Gulp task compiles the TypeScript files under the source folder into JavaScript files that will be stored in inside the build/source folder. We should be able to run the task by executing the following command:

`gulp build-source`

> The preceding command will fail if no source files are available. You can copy project source files from the companion source code or continue reading this chapter and create the files as we progress.

We will also declare a second task to compile our unit tests, but the output will be stored under the build/test folder:

```
var tsTestProject = tsc.createProject({
  removeComments : false,
  noImplicitAny : false,
  target : "ES5",
  module : "commonjs",
  declarationFiles : false
});


gulp.task("build-test", function() {
  return gulp.src(__dirname + "/test/*.test.ts")
             .pipe(tsc(tsTestProject))
             .pipe(gulp.dest(__dirname + "/build/test/"));
});
```

We should be able to run this new task using Gulp by using the following command:

```
gulp build-test
```

Once the JavaScript is under the build folder, we need to bundle the external modules (as we used { `module : "commonjs"` } in the preceding compiler settings) into bundled libraries that can be executed in a web browser.

Browserify needs a unique entry point for each library. For this reason, we are going to create three tasks—one for each bundled library.

We will create a task to bundle the application itself:

```
gulp.task("bundle-source", function () {
  var b = browserify({
    standalone : 'demos',
    entries: __dirname + "/build/source/demos.js",
    debug: true
  });

  return b.bundle()
    .pipe(source("demos.js"))
    .pipe(buffer())
    .pipe(gulp.dest(__dirname + "/bundled/source/"));
});
```

Just like we did with the previous Gulp tasks, we can invoke the new task by using the following command:

```
gulp bundle-source
```

We will also create another task to bundle all the unit tests in our application into a single bundled suite of tests:

```
gulp.task("bundle-test", function () {

  var b = browserify({
    standalone : 'test',
    entries: __dirname + "/build/test/bdd.test.js",
    debug: true
  });

  return b.bundle()
    .pipe(source("bdd.test.js"))
    .pipe(buffer())
    .pipe(gulp.dest(__dirname + "/bundled/test/"));
});
```

> The companion code has tests using both the TDD and BDD styles in two independent files named `tdd.test.ts` and `bdd.test.ts`. However, in the examples in this chapter, we will only focus on the BDD style.

We can invoke the new task by using the following command:

```
gulp bundle-test
```

Finally, we will create another task to bundle all the E2E tests in the application into a single bundled E2E test suite:

```
gulp.task("bundle-e2e-test", function () {

  var b = browserify({
    standalone : 'test',
    entries: __dirname + "/build/test/e2e.test.js",
    debug: true
  });

  return b.bundle()
    .pipe(source("e2e.test.js"))
    .pipe(buffer())
    .pipe(gulp.dest(__dirname + "/bundled/e2e-test/"));
});
```

We can invoke the new task by using the following command:

```
gulp bundle-e2e-test
```

Running the unit test with Karma

We have already covered the basics of Karma in *Chapter 2, Automating Your Development Workflow*. We are going to create a task to execute Karma:

```
gulp.task("run-unit-test", function(cb) {
  karma.start({
    configFile : __dirname + "/karma.conf.js",
    singleRun: true
  }, cb);
});
```

The Karma task configuration is really simple because the majority of the configuration is located in the `karma.conf.js` file, which is included in the companion code. Let's take a look at the configuration file:

```javascript
module.exports = function (config) {
  'use strict';

  config.set({
    basePath: '',
    frameworks: ['mocha', 'chai', 'sinon'],
    browsers: ['PhantomJS'],
    reporters: ['progress', 'coverage'],
    coverageReporter: {
      type : 'lcov',
      dir : __dirname + '/coverage/'
    },
    plugins : [
      'karma-coverage',
      'karma-mocha',
      'karma-chai',
      'karma-sinon',
      'karma-phantomjs-launcher'
    ],
    preprocessors: {
      '**/bundled/test/bdd.test.js' : 'coverage'
    },
    files : [
      {
        pattern: "/bundled/test/bdd.test.js",
        included: true
      },
      {
        pattern: "/node_modules/jquery/dist/jquery.min.js",
        included: true
      },
      {
        pattern:
        "/node_modules/bootstrap/dist/js/bootstrap.min.js",
        included: true
      }
    ],
```

```
    client : {
      mocha : {
        ui : "bdd"
      }
    },
    port: 9876,
    colors: true,
    autoWatch: false,
    logLevel: config.DEBUG
  });
};
```

If we take a look at the configuration file, we will see that we have configured the path where the tests are located and the browser that we want to use to run the test (PhantomJS). Declaring what browser we want to use is not enough; we also need to install a plugin so Karma can launch that browser.

Since we are going to write test using Mocha, Chai, and Sinon.JS, we have loaded the plugins to integrate Karma with each of these frameworks. There are many other popular testing frameworks, and the majority of them are compatible with Karma via the use of plugins.

Another interesting setting in the preceding configuration file is the client entry. We use it to configure the options of Mocha and indicate that we are going to use a BDD testing style.

When Karma executes the Mocha unit tests, it generates an HTML page internally and adds all the required files indicated in the files field as well as some files indicated by the plugins field. For the preceding example, Karma will generate an HTML page that will contain reference (using the <script> tags) to Mocha, Chai, and Sinon.JS (indicated by the plugins) as well as jQuery, Bootstrap, and the bdd. test.js file (indicated by the files field).

> The companion source code includes the package.json file. We can use this file to run the npm install command and download all the third-party dependencies (including jQuery and Bootstrap).

It is important to understand that only files loaded via the files field will be available during the test execution, and that all the files will be loaded using a script tag. Sometimes, we may encounter issues related to missing files or parsing errors (when a non-JavaScript file is loaded using a script tag). We can have a better control over the file inclusion process using the settings pattern, included, served, and watched:

Settings	Description
pattern	The pattern to use to match files.
included	If autoWatch is true, all files that have set watched to true will be watched for changes.
served	Should the files be served by Karma's webserver?
watched	Should the files be included in the browser using the `<script>` tag? We will use false if we want to load them manually (for example, using RequireJS).

The karma.conf.js file also contains some settings to generate test coverage reports, but we will skip those for now and focus on them towards the end of the chapter.

> Remember that you can find all the details about each field in the karma.conf.js file at http://karma-runner.github. io/0.8/config/configuration-file.html.

Running E2E tests with Selenium and Nightwatch.js

Karma (in combination with Mocha, Chai, and Sinon.JS) is a great tool when it comes to writing and executing unit tests and partial integration tests. However, Karma is not the best tool when it comes to writing E2E tests. For this reason, we will write a collection of E2E tests that will be written and executed using a separate set of tools: Selenium and Nightwatch.js.

To configure Nightwatch.js, we will start by creating a new Gulp task that will be in charge of the execution of the E2E tests. We only need to specify the location of an external configuration file named Nightwatch.js:

```
gulp.task('run-e2e-test', function(){
  return gulp.src('')
    .pipe(nightwatch({
      configFile: __dirname + '/nightwatch.json'
    }));
});
```

> We are going to focus on Nightwatch.js because it is designed to work with the majority of frameworks; but if you are working with AngularJS, I would recommend you to take a look at Protractor. Protractor is a great E2E testing framework that has a high level of integration with AngularJS.

The `nightwatch.js` file contains the entire required configuration necessary to execute our E2E tests. We need to specify the location of the E2E test suites and the basic Selenium configuration.

We need to think that Selenium is more or less like Karma; it is a tool that can execute a unit test in a browser. The main difference is that Selenium allows us to write tests in a way that simulates much better how a real user would behave. It is important to understand that Nightwatch.js is not the tool directly in charge of execution of the test. Nightwatch.js is a framework that helps to write E2E tests and can communicate with Selenium to execute the tests.

In this case, we will tell Nightwatch.js not to run Selenium for us using the `start_process` entry in the `nightwatch.json` configuration file. The `nightwatch.json` file should look as follows:

```json
{
    "src_folders" : ["bundled/e2e-test/"],
    "output_folder" : "reports",
    "selenium" : {
      "start_process" : false
    },
    "test_settings" : {
      "default" : {
        "silent": true,
        "screenshots" : {
          "enabled" : true,
          "path" : "screenshots"
        },
        "desiredCapabilities": {
          "browserName": "chrome",
          "javascriptEnabled" : true,
          "acceptSslCerts" : true
        }
      },
      "phantomjs" : {
        "desiredCapabilities": {
          "browserName": "phantomjs",
          "javascriptEnabled" : true,
```

```
          "acceptSslCerts" : true,
          "phantomjs.binary.path" :
          "./node_modules/phantomjs/bin/phantomjs"
        }
      },
      "chrome" : {
        "desiredCapabilities": {
          "browserName": "chrome",
          "javascriptEnabled": true,
          "acceptSslCerts": true
        }
      }
    }
  }
}
```

We will run Selenium manually using the `selenium-standalone` npm package
(we can check the prerequisites section for installation details):

selenium-standalone start

Besides configuring Selenium, we need to configure which web browsers we are
going to use during the execution of our E2E tests and to run the web application
on a web server.

> If you wish to learn more about all the available Nightwatch.js
> configuration parameters, please visit the official documentation
> at http://nightwatchjs.org/guide#settings-file.

Finally, to be able to run the E2E test, we will also need to run the application itself
on a web server. As we saw in *Chapter 2, Automating Your Development Workflow*, we
can use `browserSync` for that purpose; so we will add a task to deploy `browserSync`:

```
gulp.task('serve', function(cb) {
    browserSync({
        port: 8080,
        server: {
            baseDir: "./"
        }
    });

    gulp.watch([
      "./**/*.js",
      "./**/*.css",
      "./index.html"
    ], browserSync.reload, cb);
});
```

If one test is failing and we don't know what is causing it to fail, we will be able to test it manually by running the application in a web browser.

It is important to run the tasks in the correct order. We need to open a console or terminal and start Selenium:

```
selenium-standalone start
```

Open another console or terminal and run the following commands:

```
gulp build-source
```

```
gulp build-test
```

```
gulp bundle-source
```

```
gulp bundle-e2e-test
```

```
gulp serve
```

Finally, open a third console and run the following command:

```
gulp run-e2e-test
```

Creating test assertions, specs, and suites with Mocha and Chai

Now that the test infrastructure is ready, we will start writing a unit test. We need to remember that we are going to follow the BDD development testing style, which means that we will write the test before we actually write the code.

We will write a web calculator; because we want to keep it simple, we will only implement one of its features. After doing some analysis, we have come up with a design interface that will help us to understand the requirements. We will declare the following interface in the `interfaces.d.ts` file:

```
interface MathInterface {
  PI : number;
  pow( base: number, exponent: number);
}
```

As we can see, the calculator will allow us to calculate the exponent of a number and to get the number `PI`. Now that we know the requirements, we can start writing some unit tests. Let's create a file named `bdd.test.ts` and add the following code:

```
///<reference path="../typings/tsd.d.ts" />
///<reference path="../source/interfaces.d.ts" />
```

```
import { MathDemo } from "../source/math_demo";

var expect = chai.expect;

describe('BDD test example for MathDemo class \n', () => {

  before(function(){ /* invoked once before ALL tests */ });
  after(function(){ /* invoked once after ALL tests */ });
  beforeEach(function(){ /* invoked once before EACH test */ });
  afterEach(function(){ /* invoked once before EACH test */ });

  it('should return the correct numeric value for PI \n', () => {
    var math : MathInterface = new MathDemo();
    expect(math.PI).to.equals(3.14159265359);
    expect(math.PI).to.be.a('number');
  });

  // ...
});
```

In the preceding code snippet, we have imported the necessary type definition files and an external module named `MathDemo`. This external module will declare the `MathDemo` class, which will implement the `MathInterface` that we are about to test.

We can also see a shortcut for `expect`, so we don't need to write `chai.expect` every time we need to invoke expect:

```
var expect = chai.expect;
```

Just below the shortcut we can find the first test suite:

```
describe('BDD test example for MathDemo class \n', () => {
```

Test suites are declared using the `describe()` function and are used to wrap a set of unit tests; and the unit tests themselves are declared using the `it()` function:

```
it('should return the correct numeric value for PI \n', () => {
```

Inside the unit test, we can perform one or more assertions. The Chai assertions provide easily readable code thanks to the usage of a chainable style:

```
expect(math.PI).to.equals(3.14159265359);
expect(math.PI).to.be.a('number');
```

There are cases in which we will notice that we are repeating a certain test initialization logic across multiple unit tests within a test suite. There are some helper functions that we can use to avoid code duplication.

The `before()` function will be invoked before any test in the suite case is executed. The `after()` function will be executed after all the tests in the test suite have been executed:

```
before(function(){ /* invoked once before ALL tests */ });
after(function(){ /* invoked once after ALL tests */ });
```

The `beforeEach()` function is executed once (before the test is executed) for each test in the test suite, while the `afterEach()` function is executed once (after the test is executed) for each test in the test suite:

```
beforeEach(function(){ /* invoked once before EACH test */ });
afterEach(function(){ /* invoked once before EACH test */ });
```

If we run the test at this point, it will fail because the feature being tested (PI) is not implemented. Let's create a file named `math_demo.ts` and add the following code:

```
///<reference path="./interfaces.d.ts" />

class MathDemo implements MathInterface{
  public PI : number;

  constructor() {
    this.PI = 3.14159265359;
  }

  //...
}
export { MathDemo };
```

If we execute the test with Karma, it should pass without errors. It is important to run the tasks in the correct order. To do this, we need to open a console or terminal and run the following commands:

`gulp build-source`

`gulp build-test`

`gulp bundle-source`

`gulp bundle-test`

Finally, we can run the unit tests using the following command:

`gulp run-unit-test`

There was another requirement in the `MathInterface` interface, so we are going to repeat the entire BDD process once more; but this time, we will test a function named pow instead of a property. We will start by adding a new test to the test suite that we have preciously created:

```
it('should return the correct numeric value for pow \n', () => {
    var math : MathInterface = new MathDemo();
    var result = math.pow(3,5);
    var expected = 243;
    expect(result).to.be.a('number');
    expect(result).to.equal(expected);
});
```

As we can see in the previously declared `MathInterface` interface, the function that we are going to test is named pow and takes two numeric arguments. So we have created a test that will create a new instance of `MathDemo` and invoke its pow method, passing the numeric values 3 and 5 as arguments. The expected value of calculating 3*3*3*3*3 is 243; for this reason, we have asserted that the pow() function returns a numeric value and its value is 243.

At this point, the preceding test will fail because the pow method has not been implemented. Let's return to the `math_demo.ts` file and implement the pow method:

```
///<reference path="./interfaces.d.ts" />

class MathDemo implements MathInterface{
  public PI : number;

  constructor() {
    this.PI = 3.14159265359;
  }

  public pow(base: number, exponent: number) {
    var result = base;
    for(var i = 1; i < exponent; i++){
      result = result * base;
    }
    return result;
  }

  // ...
}
    export { MathDemo };
```

If we run the tests again, we will be able to see the number of tests that have been executed, how many of them have failed, and how long it took to finish the execution of all the tests:

```
Executed 2 of 2 SUCCESS (0.007 secs / 0.008 secs)
```

Testing the asynchronous code

In *Chapter 3, Working with Functions*, we learned how to work with a synchronous code; and in *Chapter 6, Application Performance*, we saw that using asynchronous code is one of the golden rules of web application performance. We should aim to write asynchronous code as much as we can, and for this reason, it is important to learn how to test asynchronous code.

Let's write an asynchronous version of the pow function to demonstrate how we can test an asynchronous function. We will start with the requirements:

```
interface MathInterface {
  // ..
  powAsync(base: number, exponent: number, cb : (result : number)
  => void);
}
```

We need to implement a function named powAsync, which takes two numeric values as parameters (just like before) and a callback function. The test for the asynchronous version is almost identical to the test that we wrote for the synchronous function:

```
it('should return the correct numeric value for pow (async) \n',
(done) => {
  var math : MathInterface = new MathDemo();
  math.powAsync(3, 5, function(result) {
    var expected = 243;
    expect(result).to.be.a('number');
    expect(result).to.equal(expected);
    done(); // invoke done() inside your call back or fulfilled
    promises
  });
});
```

The main thing that we need to notice is that, this time, the callback passed to the it method receives an argument named done. The argument is a function that we need to execute to indicate that the test execution is finished.

By default, the `it` method waits for the callback to return, but when testing asynchronous code, the function may return before the test execution is finished:

```
public powAsyncSlow(base: number, exponent: number, cb : (result :
number) => void) {
    var delay = 45; //ms
    setTimeout(() => {
      var result = this.pow(base, exponent);
      cb(result);
    }, delay);
}
```

When testing asynchronous code, Mocha will consider the test as failed (timeout) if it takes more than 2,000 milliseconds to invoke the `done` function. The time limit before a timeout can be configured, as can be warnings for slow functions.

> Mocha recommends that, when a function takes more than 40 milliseconds, we should consider investigating how to improve its performance. If the function execution takes over 100 milliseconds, we must investigate. Execution times of over 2,000 milliseconds are not tolerated by default.

Asserting exceptions

Asserting the types or values of variables is straightforward, as we have been able to explore in the previous examples; but there is one scenario that perhaps is not as intuitive as the previous one. This scenario is testing for an exception.

Let's add a new method to the `MathInterface` interface with the only purpose of illustrating how to test for an exception:

```
interface MathInterface {
  // ...
  bad(foo? : any) : void;
}
```

The `bad` method throws an exception when it is invoked with a non-numeric argument:

```
public bad(foo? : any) {
  if(isNaN(foo)){
    throw new Error("Error!");
  }
  else {
    //...
  }
}
```

In the following test, we can see how we can use Chai's expect API to assert that an exception is thrown:

```
it('should throw an exception when no parameters passed \n', () => {
  var math : MathInterface = new MathDemo();
  var throwsF = function() { math.bad(/* missing args */) };
  expect(throwsF).to.throw(Error);
});
```

> If you wish to learn more about assertions, visit the Chai official documentation available at http://chaijs.com/api/bdd/.

TDD versus BDD with Mocha and Chai

TDD and BDD follow many of the same principles but have some differences in their style. While these two styles provide the same functionality, BDD is considered to be easier to read by many of the members of a software development team (not just developers).

The following table compares the naming and style of suites, tests, and assertions between the TDD and BBD styles:

TDD	BDD
suite	describe
setup	before
teardown	after
suiteSetup	beforeEach
suiteTeardown	afterEach
test	it
assert.equal(math.PI, 3.14159265359);	expect(math.PI).to.equals(3.14159265359);

> In the companion code samples, you will find all the examples in this chapter following both the TDD and BDD styles.

Test spies and stubs with Sinon.JS

We have been working on the `MathDemo` class. We have implemented and tested its features using unit tests and assertions. Now we are going to create a little web widget that will internally use the `MathDemo` class to perform a mathematical operation. We can think of this new class as a graphical user interface for the `MathDemo` class. We need the following HTML:

```
<div id="widget">
  <input type="text" id="base" />
  <input type="text" id="exponent" />
  <input type="text" id="result" />
  <button id="submit" type="submit">Submit</button>
</div>
```

> In the companion code, the HTML code contains more attributes, such as CSS classes; but they been have removed here for clarity.

Let's create a file named `calculator_widget.ts` under the source directory. We are going to store the HTML code in a string variable located in the scope of the web widget. The new class will be called `CalculatorWidget`, and it will implement the `CalculatorWidgetInterface` interface:

```
interface CalculatorWidgetInterface {
  render(id : string);
  onSubmit() : void;
}
```

We should write the unit test before we implement the `CalculatorWidget` class, but this time we will break the BDD rules in an attempt to facilitate the understanding of stubs and spies:

```
///<reference path="./interfaces.d.ts" />
///<reference path="../typings/tsd.d.ts" />

var template = 'HTML...';

class CalculatorWidget implements CalculatorWidgetInterface{

 private _math : MathInterface;
 private $base: JQuery;
 private $exponent: JQuery;
 private $result: JQuery;
 private $btn: JQuery;
```

```
constructor(math : MathInterface) {
  if(math == null) throw new Error("Argument null exception!");
  this._math = math;
}

public render(id : string) {
  $(id).html(template);
  this.$base = $("#base");
  this.$exponent = $("#exponent");
  this.$result = $("#result");
  this.$btn = $("#submit");
  this.$btn.on("click", (e) => {
    this.onSubmit();
  });
}

public onSubmit() {
  var base = parseInt(this.$base.val());
  var exponent = parseInt(this.$exponent.val());

  if(isNaN(base) || isNaN(exponent)) {
    alert("Base and exponent must be a number!");
  }
  else {
    this.$result.val(this._math.pow(base, exponent));
  }
}
}
export { CalculatorWidget };
```

As we can see, we have defined a variable that contains the HTML that we previously examined but it is not displayed for brevity. A new class named `CalculatorWidget` is also defined together with the class constructor. We can observe that the class has two properties: a variable named `_dom` and an implementation of `MathInterface` named `_math`. We are depending on an interface because as we saw in *Chapter 4, Object-Oriented Programming with TypeScript*, it is a good practice (dependency inversion principle) to do so.

Notice that the class constructor takes an implementation of `MathInterface` as its only argument. Passing the dependencies of a component via its constructor is also a good practice and is used to reduce the coupling between components.

The first method in the class is named `render` and takes the ID (string) of an HTML element as its only argument. The ID is used to select the node that matches the ID using a jQuery selector. Once it has been selected, the HTML that we previously examined is inserted into the selected node. We can say that the component is in charge of rendering its own HTML and can be reused easily just by changing its container. This is how web widgets usually work: they are independent components that can be considered as reusable standalone applications within a parent application that is no more than just a collection of web widgets.

After rendering the HTML, the render method creates shortcuts for each component of the widget's form and initializes a click event listener:

```
public render(id : string) {
  $(id).html(template);
  this._dom.$base = $("#base");
  this._dom.$exponent = $("#exponent");
  this._dom.$result = $("#result");
  this._dom.$btn = $("#submit");

  this._dom.$btn.on("click", (e) => {
    this.onSubmit();
  });
}
```

When a user clicks on the button with id equals to submit, an event is triggered, and the event listener invokes the `onSubmit` function that we can find in the following code snippet. This function will read the values for base and exponent using the shortcuts previously declared:

```
public onSubmit() {
  var base = parseInt(this._dom.$base.val());
  var exponent = parseInt(this._dom.$exponent.val());

  if(isNaN(base) || isNaN(exponent)) {
    alert("Base and exponent must be a number!");
  }
  else {
    this._dom.$result.val(this._math.pow(base, exponent));
  }
}
```

If the values of the inputs (base and exponent) are not numeric values, an alert message is displayed to provide the users with error feedback. If the values are numeric, the `pow` method of the `MathDemo` class is invoked, and the result is assigned to the `result` field value via one of the previously created shortcuts.

Writing unit tests can become a complex task when the components being tested are highly coupled with other components. In the previous section, we tried to follow some good practices such as the dependency inversion principle or injecting dependencies via the constructor of the dependent; but sometimes, even when using good practices, we will have to deal with highly coupled code.

Spies, mocks, and stubs can help us to take away some of the pain caused by highly coupled components. These features can also help us to identify the root cause of an issue. If we replace all the dependencies of a component with stubs and a test fail, we will know that the issue is located in the component being tested and not in one of its dependencies.

For example, the `CalculatorWidget` class has a dependency on the `MathDemo` class. If there is an issue in the calculator website, we will not be able to know if the root cause of the issue is located in the `CalculatorWidget` class or the `MathDemo` class. However, if we write some unit tests for the `CalculatorWidget` class in isolation (replacing its `MathDemo` dependency with a stub) and some of the tests fail, we will know for sure that the root cause of the issue is located in the `CalculatorWidget` and not in the `MathDemo` class.

Let's take a look at some test examples.

Spies

We are going to start by taking a look at the use of spies by creating a new test suite. This time we will use the `before()` and `beforeEach()` functions. When the `before()` function is invoked (before any unit test is executed), a new HTML node is created to hold the widget's HTML.

The `beforeEach()` function is used to reset the container before each test. This way, we can ensure that a new widget is created for each test in the test suite. This is a good idea because it will prevent one test from potentially affecting the results of another.

```
describe('BDD test example for CalculatorWidget class \n', () => {

  before(function() {
    $("body").append('<div id="widget"/>');
  });
```

```
beforeEach(function() {
  $("#widget").empty();
});
```

> Usually, testing frameworks (regardless of the language we are working with) won't allow us to control the order in which the unit tests and test suites are executed. The tests can even be executed in parallel by using multiple threads. For this reason, it is important to ensure that the unit tests in our test suites are independent of each other.

Now that the test suite is ready, we can create unit tests for the render() and onSubmit() methods. The test starts by the creation of an instance of MathDemo, which is then passed to CalculatorWidget constructor to create a new instance named calculator.

The render method is then invoked to render the widget inside the HTML node with the ID widget. The HTML node should be available at this stage because it was created by the before() method. After the widget has been rendered, a value is set for the inputs with IDs base and exponent.

The test specification (onSubmit should be invoked when #submit is clicked) should help us understand that we are testing the click event. We are going to use a spy to observe the onSubmit() function; so, when the button with ID submit is clicked, the spy will detect that the onSubmit() function was invoked.

To finish the test, we are going to trigger a click event on the button with ID submit and assert that the onSubmit() function was actually only invoked once:

```
it('onSubmit should be invoked when #submit is clicked', () => {
  var math : MathInterface = new MathDemo();
  var calculator = new CalculatorWidget(math);
  calculator.render("#widget");
  $('#base').val("2");
  $('#exponent').val("3");

  // spy on onSubmit
  var onSubmitSpy = sinon.spy(calculator, "onSubmit");
  $("#submit").trigger("click");

  // assert calculator.onSubmit was invoked when click on #submit
  expect(onSubmitSpy.called).to.equal(true);
  expect(onSubmitSpy.callCount).to.equal(1);
  expect($("#result").val()).to.equal("8");
});
```

Spies will allow us to perform many operations: from checking how many times a function has been invoked to checking if it was invoked using the `new` operator, or if it was invoked with a set of specific parameters.

The last assertion helps us guarantee that `onSubmit()` is setting the correct result in the result input.

> All the possible operations are detailed in the Sinon.JS online documentation found at `http://sinonjs.org/docs/#sinonspy`.

Stubs

It may look like we have already tested the entire application by now, but that is usually never the case. Let's analyze what exactly we have tested so far:

- We have tested the entire `MathDemo` class, and we know that it returns the correct value when `pow` is invoked
- We know that the `CalculatorWidget` class is rendering the HTML correctly
- We know that the `CalculatorWidget` class is setting up some events and reading some values from the HTML inputs as expected

So far, we have created some tests for the `MathDemo` class and the `CalculatorWidget` class, but we have forgotten to test the integration between them.

We have been testing using 2 as base and 3 as exponent, but if we wrongly used the same value as base and exponent, we could have missed one potential issue: maybe the `CalculatorWidget` class is passing the arguments in incorrect order to the `MathDemo` class when the function `pow()` is invoked in the body of the `onSubmit()` function.

> Later on in this chapter, we will see how to generate a kind of report (a test coverage report) that can help us to identify areas of our application that have not been tested.

We can test this scenario by isolating the `CalculatorWidget` class from its dependency on the `MathDemo` class. We can achieve this by using a stub. Let's take a look at the upcoming unit tests to see a stub in action.

At the beginning of the method, a new instance of `MathDemo` is created, and a stub is used against its `pow` method. The stub will replace the `pow` method with a new method. The new method will assert that the parameters received are in the correct order:

```
it('pass the right args to Math.pow', (done) => {
  var math : MathInterface = new MathDemo();

  // replace pow method with a method for testing
  sinon.stub(math, "pow", function(a, b) {
    // assert that CalculatorWidget.onSubmit invokes
    // math.pow with the right arguments
    expect(a).to.equal(2);
    expect(b).to.equal(3);
    done();
  });

  var calculator = new CalculatorWidget(math);
  calculator.render("#widget");
  $('#base').val("2");
  $('#exponent').val("3");

  $("#submit").trigger("click");
});
```

Once the stub is ready, a new instance of the `CalculatorWidget` class is created, but instead of passing a normal instance of `MathDemo` as its only argument, we are injecting the stub. By doing this, we are no longer testing the `MathDemo` class, and we are testing the `CalculatorWidget` class in an isolated environment. This would have been much more complicated without a design that facilitates replacing the class dependencies via a constructor injection.

To finish the test, we render the calculator widget, set the value of the inputs with IDs base and exponent, and trigger a click on the button with ID submit. The event will invoke the `onSubmit` function, which will then invoke the pow method. When the parameters are in the incorrect order, we will be able to be 100 percent sure about the location of the root cause of this issue: the `onSubmit` function.

Creating end-to-end tests with Nightwatch.js

Writing an E2E test with Nightwatch.js is an intuitive process. We should be able to read an E2E test and be able to understand it even if it is the first time that we encounter one.

If we take a look at the following code snippet, we will see that, once we have reached the page, the test will wait 1 second for the body of the page to be visible. The test will then wait 0.1 seconds for some elements to be visible. The elements can be selected using CSS selectors or XPath syntax. If the elements are visible, the setValue method will insert 2 in the text input with base as ID and 3 in the text input with exponent as ID:

```
var test = {
  'Calculator pow e2e test example' : function (client) {
    client
      .url('http://localhost:8080/')
      .waitForElementVisible('body', 1000)
      .assert.waitForElementVisible('TypeScriptTesting', 100)
      .assert.waitForElementVisible('input#base' ,100)
      .assert.waitForElementVisible('input#exponent', 100)
      .setValue('input#base', '2')
      .setValue('input#exponent', '3')
      .click('button#submit')
      .pause(100)
      .assert.value('input#result', '8')
      .end();
  }
};

export = test;
```

The test will then find the submit button and trigger an on-click event. After 0.1 seconds, the test asserts that the correct value has been inserted into the text input with result as ID. We can see each of these steps in the console during the test execution.

We can run the tests using the following command:

```
gulp run-e2e-test
```

> Remember that we must run the tasks to compile and bundle the E2E tests as well as run the application in a web server with BrowserSync and execute Selenium before being able to run E2E tests.

Generating test coverage reports

Earlier in in this chapter, when we configured Karma, we added some settings to generate test coverage reports. Let's take a look at the `karma.conf.js` file to identify test coverage-related configuration:

```javascript
module.exports = function (config) {
  'use strict';

  config.set({
      basePath: '',
      frameworks: ['mocha', 'chai', 'sinon'],
      browsers: ['PhantomJS'],
      reporters: ['progress', 'coverage'],
      coverageReporter: {
        type : 'lcov',
        dir : __dirname + '/coverage/'
      },
      plugins : [
        'karma-coverage',
        'karma-mocha',
        'karma-chai',
        'karma-sinon',
        'karma-phantomjs-launcher'
      ],
      preprocessors: {
        '**/bundled/test/bdd.test.js' : 'coverage'
      },
      files : [
        {
          pattern: "/bundled/test/bdd.test.js",
          included: true
        },
        {
          pattern: "/node_modules/jquery/dist/jquery.min.js",
          included: true
        },
        {
          pattern:
          "/node_modules/bootstrap/dist/js/bootstrap.min.js",
          included: true
        }
      ],
      client : {
        mocha : {
          ui : "bdd"
        }
      },
```

```
        port: 9876,
        colors: true,
        autoWatch: false,
        logLevel: config.DEBUG
    });
};
```

As we can see, we need to set the folder in which the test coverage report will be stored. We also need to add coverage to the reporter's setting and a new entry named `coverageReport` to configure the format of the report.

We cannot forget to install the `karma-coverage` plugin using npm and adding a reference in the `karma.conf.js` under the plugins field. Finally, we need to add coverage to the preprocessor field:

```
npm karma-coverage
```

To generate the report, we just need to execute the Gulp tasks used to run all the unit tests in the application. We can do so by using the following command:

```
gulp run-unit-test
```

Once the execution of the test has been completed, we can open the folder in which we decided to store the coverage reports and open the available `index.html` file in a web browser. The HTML report allows us to navigate to the coverage statistics of a specific file by clicking on the name of one of the source files.

Code coverage report for **test/bdd.test.js**

| Statements: **82.24%** (88 / 107) | Branches: **33.33%** (10 / 30) | Functions: **93.33%** (28 / 30) | Lines: **93.15%** (68 / 73) | Ignored: none |

All files » test/ » bdd.test.js

```
25    1    MathDemo.prototype.powAsyncReallySlow = function (base, exponent, cb) {
26    1        var _this = this;
27    1        var result = base ^ exponent;
28    1        setTimeout(function () {
29    1            var result = _this.pow(base, exponent);
30    1            cb(result);
31        }, 101);
32    };
33    1    MathDemo.prototype.powAsyncTooSlow = function (base, exponent, cb) {
34            var _this = this;
35            var result = base ^ exponent;
36            setTimeout(function () {
37                var result = _this.pow(base, exponent);
38                cb(result);
39        }, 2001);
40    };
41    1    return MathDemo;
42    })();
43    1 module.exports = MathDemo;
44
```

The report can help us to identify with ease the parts of our code that have not been tested (lines are highlighted in red). The test coverage report also calculates the number of lines tested against the number of lines in the application. As we can see in the preceding screenshot, only 82.24 percent of the statements are tested in the example.

> If you would like to learn more about all the tools that we have discussed in this chapter, I highly recommend checking out the book *Backbone.js Testing* written by *Ryan Roemer*.

Summary

In this chapter, we discussed some core testing concepts (including stubs, spies, suites, and more). We also looked at the test-driven development and behavior-driven development approaches and how to work with some of the leading JavaScript testing frameworks, such as Mocha, Chai, Sinon.JS, Karma, Selenium, and Nightwatch.js.

Towards the end of the chapter we explored how to test across multiple devices and how to generate test coverage reports.

In the next chapter, we will look at decorators and the metadata reflection API — two exciting new features introduced by TypeScript 1.5.

8
Decorators

In this chapter, you are going to learn about annotations and decorators—the two new features based on the future ECMAScript 6 specification, but we can use them today with TypeScript 1.5.

You will learn about the following topics:

- Annotations and decorators:
  - Class decorators
  - Method decorators
  - Property decorators
  - Parameter decorators
  - Decorator factory
  - Decorators with parameters
- The reflection metadata API

Prerequisites

The TypeScript features in this chapter require TypeScript 1.5 or higher. We can use Gulp as we have done in previous chapters, but we need to ensure that the latest version of TypeScript is used by the `gulp-typescript` package. Let's start by creating a `package.json` file and installing the required packages:

```
npm init
npm install --save-dev gulp gulp-typescript typescript
npm install --save reflect-metadata
```

Once we have installed the packages, we can create a `gulpfile.js` file and add a new task to compile our code.

The following code snippet shows the required compiler configuration. The compilation target must be ES5 and the `emitDecoratorMetadata` setting must be set as `true`. We also need to specify the package that provides the TypeScript compiler to ensure that the latest version is used:

```
var gulp       = require("gulp"),
    tsc        = require("gulp-typescript"),
    typescript = require("typescript");

var tsProject = tsc.createProject({
  removeComments : false,
  noImplicitAny : false,
  target : "es5",
  module : "commonjs",
  declarationFiles : false,
  emitDecoratorMetadata : true,
  typescript: typescript
});
```

Once the compiler settings are ready, we can write a gulp task using the `gulp-typescript` plugin:

```
gulp.task("build-source", function() {
    return gulp.src(__dirname + "/file.ts")
            .pipe(tsc(tsProject))
            .js.pipe(gulp.dest(__dirname + "/"));
});
```

Annotations and decorators

Annotations are a way to add metadata to class declarations. The metadata can then be used by tools such as dependency injection containers.

The annotations API was proposed by the Google AtScript team but annotations are not a standard. However, decorators are a proposed standard for ECMAScript 7 by Yehuda Katz, to annotate and modify classes and properties at design time.

Annotations and decorators are pretty much the same:

> *Annotations and decorators are nearly the same thing. From a consumer perspective we have exactly the same syntax. The only thing that differs is that we don't have control over how annotations are added as metadata to our code. A decorator is rather an interface to build something that ends up as annotation.*
>
> *Over a long term, however, we can just focus on decorators, since those are a real proposed standard. AtScript is TypeScript and TypeScript implements decorators.*
>
> *- "The difference between Annotations and Decorators" by Pascal Precht*

We are going to use the following class to showcase how to work with decorators:

```
class Person {

  public name: string;
  public surname: string;

  constructor(name : string, surname : string) {
    this.name = name;
    this.surname = surname;
  }

  public saySomething(something : string) : string {
    return this.name + " " + this.surname + " says: " + something;
  }
}
```

There are four types of decorators that can be used to annotate: classes, properties, methods, and parameters.

The class decorators

The official TypeScript decorator proposal defines a class decorator as follows:

> *A class decorator function is a function that accepts a constructor function as its argument, and returns either undefined, the provided constructor function, or a new constructor function. Returning undefined is equivalent to returning the provided constructor function.*
>
> *- "Decorators Proposal – TypeScript" by Ron Buckton*

A class decorator is used to modify the constructor of class in some way. If the class decorator returns undefined, the original constructor remains the same. If the decorator returns, the return value will be used to override the original class constructor.

We are going to create a class decorator named `logClass`. We can start by defining the decorator as follows:

```
function logClass(target: any) {
  // ...
}
```

The class decorator above does not have any logic yet, but we can already apply it to a class. To apply a decorator, we need to use the at (@) symbol:

```
@logClass
class Person {
  public name: string;
  public surname: string;
  //...
```

If we have declared and applied a decorator, a function named __decorate will be generated by the TypeScript compiler, which will then compile our code in JavaScript. We are not going to examine the internal implementation of the __decorate function, but we need to understand that it is used to apply a decorator at runtime. We can see it in action by examining the JavaScript code that is generated when we compile the decorated `Person` class mentioned previously:

```
var Person = (function () {
    function Person(name, surname) {
        this.name = name;
        this.surname = surname;
    }
    Person.prototype.saySomething = function (something) {
        return this.name + " " + this.surname + " says: " +
        something;
    };
    Person = __decorate([
        logClass
    ], Person);
    return Person;
})();
```

Now that we know how the class decorator will be invoked, let's implement it:

```
function logClass(target: any) {

    // save a reference to the original constructor
    var original = target;

    // a utility function to generate instances of a class
    function construct(constructor, args) {
        var c : any = function () {
            return constructor.apply(this, args);
        }
        c.prototype = constructor.prototype;
        return new c();
    }

    // the new constructor behaviour
    var f : any = function (...args) {
        console.log("New: " + original.name);
        return construct(original, args);
    }

    // copy prototype so instanceof operator still works
    f.prototype = original.prototype;

    // return new constructor (will override original)
    return f;
}
```

The class decorator takes the constructor of the class being decorated as its only argument. This means that the argument (named `target`) is the constructor of the `Person` class.

The decorator starts by creating a copy of the class constructor, then it defines a utility function (named `construct`) that can be used to generate instances of a class.

Decorators are used to add some extra logic or metadata to the decorated element. When we try to extend the functionality of a function (methods or constructors), we need to wrap the original function with a new function that contains the additional logic and invokes the original function.

In the preceding decorator, we added extra logic to log in the console, the name of the class when a new instance is created. To achieve this, a new class constructor (named `f`) was declared. The new constructor contains the additional logic and uses the construct function to invoke the original class constructor.

At the end of the decorator, the prototype of the original constructor function is copied to the new constructor function to ensure that the instanceof operator continues to work when it is applied to an instance of the decorated class. Finally, the new constructor is returned and some code generated by the TypeScript compiler uses it to override the original class constructor.

After decorating the class constructor, a new instance is created:

```
var me = new Person("Remo", "Jansen");
```

On doing so, the following text appears in the console:

"New: Person"

The method decorators

The official TypeScript decorator proposal defines a method decorator as follows.

> *A method decorator function is a function that accepts three arguments:*
> *The object that owns the property, the key for the property (a string or a symbol),*
> *and optionally the property descriptor of the property. The function must return*
> *either undefined, the provided property descriptor, or a new property descriptor.*
> *Returning undefined is equivalent to returning the provided property descriptor.*
>
> *- "Decorators Proposal – TypeScript" by Ron Buckton*

The method decorator is really similar to the class decorator but it is used to override a method, as opposed to using it to override the constructor of a class.

If the method decorator returns a value different from undefined, the returned value will be used to override the property descriptor of the method.

> Note that a property descriptor is an object that can be obtained by invoking the Object.getOwnPropertyDescriptor() method.

Let's declare a method decorator named logMethod without any behavior for now:

```
function logMethod(target: any, key: string, descriptor: any) {
  // ...
}
```

We can apply the decorator to one of the methods in the `Person` class:

```
//...
@logMethod
public saySomething(something : string) : string {
  return this.name + " " + this.surname + " says: " + something;
}
// ...
```

The method decorator is invoked using the following arguments:

- The prototype of the class that contains the method being decorated is `Person.prototype`
- The name of the method being decorated is `saySomething`
- The property descriptor of the method being decorated is `Object.getOwnPropertyDescriptor(Person.prototype, saySomething)`

Now that we know the value of the decorator parameters, we can proceed to implement it:

```
function logMethod(target: any, key: string, descriptor: any) {

  // save a reference to the original method
  var originalMethod = descriptor.value;

  // editing the descriptor/value parameter
  descriptor.value = function (...args: any[]) {

      // convert method arguments to string
      var a = args.map(a => JSON.stringify(a)).join();

      // invoke method and get its return value
      var result = originalMethod.apply(this, args);

      // convert result to string
      var r = JSON.stringify(result);

      // display in console the function call details
      console.log(`Call: ${key}(${a}) => ${r}`);

      // return the result of invoking the method
      return result;
  }

  // return edited descriptor
  return descriptor;
}
```

Just like we did when we implemented the class decorator, we start by creating a copy of the element being decorated. Instead of accessing the method via the class prototype (`target["key"]`), we will access it via the property descriptor (`descriptor.value`).

We then create a new function that will replace the method being decorated. The new function invokes the original method but also contains some additional logic used to log in the console, the method name, and the value of its arguments every time it is invoked.

After applying the decorator to the method, the method name and arguments will be logged in the console when it is invoked:

```
var me = new Person("Remo", "Jansen");
me.saySomething("hello!");
// Call: saySomething("hello!") => "Remo Jansen says: hello!"
```

The property decorators

The official TypeScript decorator proposal defines a property decorator as follows:

> *A property decorator function is a function that accepts two arguments: The object that owns the property and the key for the property (a string or a symbol). A property decorator does not return.*

> - *"Decorators Proposal – TypeScript" by Ron Buckton*

A property decorator is really similar to a method decorator. The main differences are that a property decorator doesn't return a value and that the third parameter (the property descriptor) is not passed to the property decorator.

Let's create a property decorator named `logProperty` to see how it works:

```
function logProperty(target: any, key: string) {
  // ...
}
```

We can use it in one of the `Person` class's properties as follows:

```
class Person {
  @logProperty
  public name: string;
  // ...
```

As we have been doing so far, we are going to implement a decorator that will override the decorated property with a new property that will behave exactly as the original one, but will perform an additional task—logging the property value in the console whenever it changes:

```
function logProperty(target: any, key: string) {

  // property value
  var _val = this[key];

  // property getter
  var getter = function () {
    console.log(`Get: ${key} => ${_val}`);
    return _val;
  };

  // property setter
  var setter = function (newVal) {
    console.log(`Set: ${key} => ${newVal}`);
    _val = newVal;
  };

  // Delete property. The delete operator throws
  // in strict mode if the property is an own
  // non-configurable property and returns
  // false in non-strict mode.
  if (delete this[key]) {
    Object.defineProperty(target, key, {
      get: getter,
      set: setter,
      enumerable: true,
      configurable: true
    });
  }
}
```

In the preceding decorator, we created a copy of the original property value and declared two functions: `getter` (invoked when we change the value of the property) and `setter` (invoked when we read the value of the property) respectively.

In the previous decorator, the return value was used to override the element being decorated. Because the property decorator doesn't return a value, we can't override the property being decorated but we can replace it. We have manually deleted the original property and created a new property using the `Object.defineProperty` function and the previously declared getter and setter functions.

After applying the decorator to the `name` property, we will be able to observe any changes to its value in the console:

```
var me = new Person("Remo", "Jansen");
// Set: name => Remo
me.name = "Remo H.";
// Set: name => Remo H.
var n = me.name;
// Get: name Remo H.
```

The parameter decorators

The official decorator proposal defines a parameter decorator as follows:

> *A parameter decorator function is a function that accepts three arguments: The object that owns the method that contains the decorated parameter, the property key of the property (or undefined for a parameter of the constructor), and the ordinal index of the parameter. The return value of this decorator is ignored.*

> *Decorators Proposal – TypeScript" by Ron Buckton*

Let's create a parameter decorator named `addMetadata` to see how it works:

```
function addMetadata(target: any, key : string, index : number) {
  // ...
}
```

We can apply the property decorator to a parameter as follows:

```
public saySomething(@addMetadatasomething : string) : string {
  return this.name + " " + this.surname + " says: " + something;
}
```

The parameter decorator doesn't return, which means that we will not be able to override the method that contains the parameter being decorated.

We can use parameter decorators to add some metadata to the prototype (`target`) class. In the following implementation, we will add an array named `log_${key}_parameters` as a class property where `key` is the name of the method that contains the parameter being decorated:

```
function addMetadata(target: any, key : string, index : number) {
  var metadataKey = `_log_${key}_parameters`;
  if (Array.isArray(target[metadataKey])) {
    target[metadataKey].push(index);
  }
```

```
    else {
      target[metadataKey] = [index];
    }
  }
}
```

To allow more than one parameter to be decorated, we check whether the new field is an array. If the new field is not an array, we create and initialize the new field to be a new array containing the index of the parameter being decorated. If the new field is an array, the index of the parameter being decorated is added to the array.

A parameter decorator is not really useful on its own; it needs to be combined with a method decorator, so the parameter decorator adds the metadata and the method decorator reads it:

```
@readMetadata
public saySomething(@addMetadata something : string) : string {
  return this.name + " " + this.surname + " says: " + something;
}
```

The following method decorator works like the method decorator that we implemented previously in this chapter, but it will read the metadata added by the parameter decorator and instead of displaying all the arguments passed to the method in the console when it is invoked, it will only log the ones that have been decorated:

```
function readMetadata (target: any, key: string. descriptor: any) {

  var originalMethod = descriptor.value;
  descriptor.value = function (...args: any[]) {

    var metadataKey = `_log_${key}_parameters`;
    var indices = target[metadataKey];

    if (Array.isArray(indices)) {

      for (var i = 0; i < args.length; i++) {

        if (indices.indexOf(i) !== -1) {

          var arg = args[i];
          var argStr = JSON.stringify(arg) || arg.toString();
          console.log(`${key} arg[${i}]: ${argStr}`);
        }
      }
      var result = originalMethod.apply(this, args);
      return result;
```

```
        }
    }
    return descriptor;
}
```

If we apply the saySomething method:

```
var person = new Person("Remo", "Jansen");

person.saySomething("hello!");
```

The readMetadata decorator will display the value of the parameters that were added to the metadata (the class property named _log_saySomething_parameters) in the console by the addMetadata decorator:

```
saySomething arg[0]: "hello!"
```

> Note that, in the previous example, we used a class property to
> store some metadata. Later in this chapter, you will learn how to use
> the reflection metadata API; this API has been designed specifically
> to generate and read metadata and it is, therefore, recommended to
> use it when we need to work with decorators and metadata.

The decorator factory

The official decorator proposal defines a decorator factory as follows:

> *A decorator factory is a function that can accept any number of arguments, and*
> *must return one of the above types of decorator function.*

> *Decorators Proposal – TypeScript" by Ron Buckton*

You learned to implement class, property, method, and parameter decorators. In the majority of cases, we will consume decorators, not implement them. For example, in Angular 2.0, we will use an @view decorator to declare that a class will behave as a View, but we will not implement the @view decorator ourselves.

We can use the decorator factory to make decorators easier to consume. Let's consider the following code snippet:

```
@logClass
class Person {

    @logProperty
    public name: string;
```

```
      public surname: string;

      constructor(name : string, surname : string) {
        this.name = name;
        this.surname = surname;
      }

      @logMethod
      public saySomething(@logParameter something : string) : string {
        return this.name + " " + this.surname + " says: " + something;
      }
    }
```

The problem with the preceding code is that we, as developers, need to know that the logMethod decorator can only be applied to a method. This might seem trivial because the decorator naming used above makes it easier for us.

A better solution is to enable developers to use an @log decorator without having to worry about using the right kind of decorator:

```
    @log
    class Person {

      @log
      public name: string;
      public surname: string;

      constructor(name : string, surname : string) {
        this.name = name;
        this.surname = surname;
      }

      @log
      public saySomething(@log something : string) : string {
        return this.name + " " + this.surname + " says: " + something;
      }
    }
```

We can achieve this by creating a decorator factory. A decorator factory is a function that is able to identify what kind of decorator is required and return it:

```
    function log(...args : any[]) {
      switch(args.length) {
        case 1:
          return logClass.apply(this, args);
```

```
case 2:
  // break instead of return as property
  // decorators don't have a return
  logProperty.apply(this, args);
  break;
case 3:
  if(typeof args[2] === "number") {
    logParameter.apply(this, args);
  }
  return logMethod.apply(this, args);
default:
  throw new Error("Decorators are not valid here!");
}
}
```

As we can observe in the preceding code snippet, the decorator factory uses the number and type of arguments passed to the decorator to identify the required kind of decorator.

Decorators with arguments

We can use a special kind of decorator factory to allow developers to configure the behavior of a decorator. For example, we could pass a string to a class decorator as follows:

```
@logClass("option")
class Person {
// ...
```

In order to be able to pass some parameters to a decorator, we need to wrap the decorator with a function. The wrapper function takes the parameters of our choice and returns a decorator:

```
function logClass(option : string) {
  return function (target: any) {

    // class decorator logic goes here
    // we have access to the decorator parameters
    console.log(target, option);
  }
}
```

This can be applied to all the kinds of decorator that you learned about in this chapter.

The reflection metadata API

You learned that decorators can be used to modify and extend the behavior of a class's methods or properties. You also learned that we can use decorators to add metadata to the class being decorated.

For less experienced developers, the possibility of adding metadata to a class might not seem really useful or exciting but it is one of the greatest things that has happened to JavaScript in the past few years.

As we already know, TypeScript only uses types at design time. However, some features such as dependency injection, runtime type assertions, reflection, and testing are not possible without the type information being available at runtime. This is not a problem anymore because we can use decorators to generate metadata and that metadata can contain type information. The metadata can then be processed at runtime.

When the TypeScript team started to think about the best possible way to allow developers to generate type information metadata, they reserved a few special decorator names for this purposes.

The idea was that, when an element was decorated using these reserved decorators, the compiler would automatically add the type information to the element being decorated. The reserved decorators were the following:

TypeScript compiler will honor special decorator names and will flow additional information into the decorator factory parameters annotated by these decorators.

@type – The serialized form of the type of the decorator target

@returnType – The serialized form of the return type of the decorator target if it is a function type, undefined otherwise

@parameterTypes – A list of serialized types of the decorator target's arguments if it is a function type, undefined otherwise

@name – The name of the decorator target

- "Decorators brainstorming" by Jonathan Turner

Shortly after, the TypeScript team decided to use the reflection metadata API (one of the proposed ES7 features) instead of the reserved decorators.

The idea is almost identical but instead of using the reserved decorator names, we will use some reserved metadata keys to retrieve the metadata using the reflection metadata API. The TypeScript documentation defines three reserved metadata keys:

Type metadata uses the metadata key "design:type".

Parameter type metadata uses the metadata key "design:paramtypes".

Return type metadata uses the metadata key "design:returntype".

- Issue #2577 - TypeScript Official Repository at GitHub.com

Let's see how we can use the reflection metadata API. We need to start by referencing and importing the required `reflect-metadata` npm package:

```
/// <reference path="./node_modules/reflect-metadata/reflect-
metadata.d.ts"/>
import 'reflect-metadata';
```

We can then create a class for testing purposes. We are going to get the type of one of the class properties at runtime. We are going to decorate the class using a property decorator named `logType`:

```
class Demo {
  @logType
  public attr1: string;
}
```

Instead of using a reserved decorator, `@type`, we need to invoke the `Reflect.getMetadata()` method and pass the `design:type` key. The types are returned as functions, for example, for the type string, the `function String() {}` function is returned. We can use the `function.name` property to get the type as a string:

```
function logType(target: any, key: string) {
  var t = Reflect.getMetadata('design:type', target, key);
  console.log(`${key} type: ${t.name}`);
}
```

If we compile the preceding code and run the resulting JavaScript code in a web browser, we will be able to see the type of the `attr1` property in the console:

```
'attr1 type: String'
```

> Remember that, in order to run this example, the `reflect-medatada` library must be imported.

We can apply the other reserved metadata keys in a similar manner. Let's create a method with many parameters to use the `design:paramtypes` reserved metadata key to retrieve the types of the parameters

```
class Demo {
  @logParamTypes
  public doSomething(
    param1 : string,
    param2 : number,
    param3 : Foo,
    param4 : { test : string },
    param5 : IFoo,
    param6 : Function,
    param7 : (a : number) => void
  ) : number {

    return 1;
  }
}
```

This time, we will use the `design:paramtypes` reserved metadata key, and because we are querying the types of multiple parameters, the types will be returned as an array by the `Reflect.getMetadata()` function:

```
function logParamTypes(target : any, key: string) {
  var types = Reflect.getMetadata('design:paramtypes', target, key);
  var s = types.map(a => a.name).join();
  console.log(`${key} param types: ${s}`);
}
```

If we compile and run the preceding code in a web browser, we will be able to see the types of the parameters in the console:

```
'doSomething param types: String, Number, Foo, Object, Object,
Function, Function'
```

The types are serialized and follow some rules. We can see that functions are serialized as Function, objects literals (`{test : string}`) and interfaces are serialized as Object, and so on:

Type	Serialized
void	undefined
string	String
number	Number

Type	Serialized
boolean	Boolean
symbol	Symbol
any	Object
enum	Number
Class C{}	C
Object literal {}	Object
interface	Object

> Note that some developers have required the possibility of accessing the type of interfaces and the inheritance tree of a class via metadata. This feature is known as **complex type serialization** and is not available at the time of writing this book, but the TypeScript team has already started to work on it.

To conclude, we are going to create a method with a return type and use the design:returntype reserved metadata key to retrieve the types of the return type:

```
class Demo {
  @logReturntype
  public doSomething2() : string {
    return "test";
  }
}
```

Just like in the two previous decorators, we need to invoke the Reflect.getMetadata() function, passing the design:returntype reserved metadata key:

```
function logReturntype(target, key) {
  var returnType = Reflect.getMetadata('design:returntype', target,
  key);
  console.log(`${key} return type: ${returnType.name}`);
}
```

If we compile and run the preceding code in a web browser, we will be able to see the types of the return type in the console:

```
'doSomething2 return type: String'
```

Summary

In this chapter, you learned how to consume and implement the four available types of decorators (class, method, property, and parameter) and how to create a decorator factory to abstract developers from the decorator types when they are consumed.

You also learned how to use the reflection metadata API to access type information at runtime.

In the next chapter, you will learn about the architecture of a TypeScript application. You will also learn about how to work with some design patterns and how to create a single-page web application.

Application Architecture

9

In previous chapters, we have covered several aspects of TypeScript, and we should now feel confident enough to create a small application.

As we know, TypeScript was created by Microsoft to facilitate the creation of large-scale JavaScript applications. Some TypeScript features such as modules or classes can facilitate the process of creating large applications, but it is not enough. We need good application architecture if we want to succeed in the long term.

This chapter is divided into two main parts. In the first part, we are going to look at the **single-page application (SPA)** architecture and some design patterns that will help us create scalable and maintainable applications. This section covers the following topics:

- The single-page web application architecture
- The MV* architecture
- Models and collections
- Item views and collection views
- Controllers
- Events
- Router and hash navigation
- Mediator
- Client-side rendering and virtual DOM
- Data binding and data flow
- The web component and shadow DOM
- Choosing an MV* framework

In the second part of this chapter, we are going to put in to practice many of the theoretical concepts explored in the first part of this chapter. We are going to develop a single-page web application framework, from scratch, which will be used to create an application in *Chapter 10, Putting Everything Together*.

The single-page application architecture

We are going to start by exploring what **single-page applications** (**SPAs**) are and how they work. Numerous SPA frameworks are available that can help us develop applications with a good architecture.

We could jump directly into the use of one of these frameworks, but it is always a good thing to understand how a third-party software component works before we use it. For this reason, we are going use the first part of this chapter to study the internal architecture of an SPA. Let's start by understanding what an SPA is.

An SPA is a web application in which all the resources (HTML, CSS, JavaScript, and so on) are either loaded in one single request, or loaded dynamically without fully reloading the page. We use the term single-page to refer to this kind of application because the web page is never fully reloaded after the initial page load.

In the past, the Web was just a collection of static HTML files and hyperlinks; every time we clicked on a hyperlink, a new page was loaded. This affected web application performance negatively because many of the contents of the page (for example, page headers, page footers, side menus, scripts) were loaded again with each new page.

When AJAX support arrived for web browsers, developers started to load some of the page content via AJAX requests to avoid unnecessary page reloads and provide better user experience. AJAX applications and SPAs work in a very similar way. The significant difference is that AJAX applications load sections of the web application as HTML. These sections are ready to be appended to the DOM as soon as they finish loading. On the other hand, SPAs avoid loading the HTML; instead, they load data and client-side templates. The templates and data are processed and transformed into HTML in the web browser in a process known as **client-side rendering**. The data is usually in XML or JSON format, and there are many available client-side template languages.

Let's compare both approaches in detail. For example, to show a list of clients and orders in an HTML table using the AJAX application approach, we could load the initial page containing the list of clients in HTML format, ready to be displayed. In the table, we would use a row for each client:

```
<tr>
  <td>Client Name 1</td>
  <td>
    <a href="javascript: void(0);" class="orders_link" data-client-
id="1">
      View Orders
    </a>
  </td>
  <!-- more columns... -->
</tr>
```

> You don't need to create new folders or files for now. This is a theoretical example and is not mean to be implemented or executed.

We would also need some JavaScript code to load the client orders via AJAX when a user clicks on the View Orders link:

```
$(document).ready(){

  // load and display client orders
  function displayOrders(userId){
    $.ajax({
      method: "GET",
      url: `/client/orders.aspx?id=${userId}`,
      dataType: "html",
      success : function(html) {
        $("#page_container").html(html);
      },
      error : function(e) {
        var msg = "<h1>Sorry, there has been an error!</h1>";
        $("#page_container").html(msg);
      }
    });
  }

  // set click event
```

```
$('.orders_link').on('click', function(e) {
  var userId = $(e.currentTarget).data("client-id");
  displayOrders(userId);
});
}
```

> Refer to the Handlebars.js (http://handlebarsjs.com/) and
> JQuery AJAX (http://api.jquery.com/jquery.ajax/)
> documentation if you need additional help to understand the
> preceding example.

The preceding code snippet waits for the page to finish loading by using a
document-ready event handler. Then it adds an event handler for click events on
elements with a class attribute equal to orders_link.

The event handler takes the user ID from the data-client-id attribute and passes it
to the displayOrders function. The displayOrders function uses an AJAX request
to load the list of orders. The list of orders is in HTML format and can be inserted
into the DOM without changing its format.

In an SPA, the process is very similar. The initial HTML page (containing the list of
clients) is loaded just like in the AJAX application. In SPAs, the navigation to a new
page is also managed by JavaScript events, but it is usually managed by a component
known as **Router**.

Let's ignore navigation in SPAs for now and focus on the loading and rendering. In
an SPA, we will not load a list of orders in HTML format; we will load it using the
XML or JSON formats. If we use JSON, the response may look like the following one:

```
{
  "orders" : [
    {
      "order_id" : 32423234,
      "currency" : "EUR",
      "date" : "13-02-2015,
      "items" :[
        { "product_id" : 13223523, "price" : 150.00, "quantity": 2 }
        { "product_id" : 62352355, "price" : 50.00, "quantity": 1 }
      ]
    },
    {
      "order_id" : 32423786,
      "currency" : "EUR",
      "date": "13-02-2015,
```

```
  "items" : [
    { "product_id" : 13228898, "price" : 50.00, "quantity" : 1 }
  ]
}
    ]
}
```

We can use an AJAX request almost identical to the one that we used to load HTML in the AJAX application:

```
function getOrdersData(userId : number, cb){
  $.ajax({
    method: "GET",
    url: `/api/orders/${userId}`,
    dataType: "json",
    success : function(json) {
      cb(json);
    },
    error : function(e) {
      var msg = "<h1>Sorry, there has been an error!</h1>";
      $("#page_container").html(msg);
    }
  });
}
```

Before we can show the list of orders in the web browser, we need to transform it into HTML. To transform the JSON into HTML, we can use a template system. There are many template systems, but we are going use a Handlebars template for this example. Let's take a look at the syntax of one of these templates:

```
{{#each orders}}
  <tr>
    <td>{{order_id}}</td>
    <td>{{date}}</td>
    <td>
      <ul>
        {{#each items}}<li> {{product_id}} x {{quantity}}
        </li>{{/each}}
      </ul>
    </td>
  </tr>
{{/each}}
```

The elements of the Handlebars template language are wrapped with double brackets ({{ and }}). The preceding template starts with an `each` flow control statement. The `each` statement is used to repeat some instructions for each of the elements in an array. If we take a look at the JSON response, we will be able to see that the `orders` element is an array. The template will repeat the operations between `{{#each orders}}` and `{{/each}}` once for each object in the `orders` array.

Each repetition creates a new HTML table row. To display the value of one of the JSON fields in the HTML output, we just need to refer to the field wrapped around double brackets. For example, when we render the cell containing the order ID, we use `{{order_id}}`.

> When referring to a JSON field in a template, the field must be in the current scope. The scope can be explicitly accessed using the `this` keyword, for example, `{{this.order_id}}` is equal to `{{order_id}}`. The scope in a template changes when we use some of the available flow control sentences. For example, the `{{#each orders}}` statement assigns the current item in the array to the `this` keyword.

In order to use a Handlebars template, we need to load and compile it. We can load the template using a regular AJAX request:

```
function getOrdersTemplate(cb){
  $.ajax({
    method: "GET",
    url: "/client/orders.hbs",
    dataType: "text",
    success : function(templateSource) {
      var template = Handlebars.compile(source);
      cb(template);
    },
    error : function(e) {
      var msg = "<h1>Sorry, there has been an error!</h1>";
      $("#page_container").html(msg);
    }
  });
}
```

In the preceding example, we have loaded a template using an AJAX request and compiled it using the Handlebars compile method.

In a real production website, templates are usually precompiled by the continuous integration build. The templates are then ready to be used when they finish loading. Precompiling the templates can help to improve the application's performance.

We have created two functions: one to load the template and compile it and the other to load the JSON data. The last step is to create a function that puts together the template and the JSON data to generate the HTML table, which contains the list of client orders:

```
function displayOrders(userId){
  getOrdersData(userId, function(data) {
    getOrdersTemplate(data, function(template) {
      var html = template(json);
      $("#page_container").html(html);
    });
  });
}
```

It may seem like SPAs require much more work and that they could cause poor performance compared with AJAX applications because there are both more operations and requests to be performed in the web browser. However, that is far from the reality. To understand the benefits of SPAs, we need to understand why they were created in the first place.

The creation of SPAs was highly influenced by two events: the first one is the exponential increase of the popularity of mobile devices and tablets with Internet access and powerful hardware. The second event is the improvement of JavaScript performance that took place during the same period of time.

As mobile devices gained popularity, companies were forced to develop a mobile version of the same client application. Companies started developing web services to generate JSON and XML (instead of HTML pages) that could be consumed by each of these client applications. These web services could be used by all applications, thus allowing companies to reduce costs.

The problem was that the existing AJAX applications could not take advantage of the web services without a client-side rendering system. Template systems such as Mustache (the predecessor of Handlebars) were released for the first time to solve this problem.

One of the main advantages of SPAs is that we need an HTTP API. An HTTP API has many advantages over an application that renders HTML pages in the server side. For example, we can write unit tests for a web service with ease because asserting data is much easier than asserting some user interaction functionality. HTTP APIs can be used by many client applications, which can reduce costs and open new lines of business, such as selling the HTTP API as a product.

Another important advantage of SPAs is that because a lot of the work is performed in the web browser, the server performs fewer tasks and is able to handle a higher number of requests. Client-side performance is not negatively affected because personal computers and mobile devices have become really powerful and JavaScript performance has improved significantly over the last few years.

Network performance in SPAs can be both better and worse when compared to network performance in AJAX applications. The response formatted in the HTML format can sometimes be heavier than the data in JSON or XML formats.

The price to pay when using JSON or XML is that but we will perform an extra web request to fetch the template. We can solve these problems by pre-compiling the templates, implementing caching mechanisms and joining small template files into larger template files to reduce the number of requests.

The MV* architecture

As we have seen, many tasks that were traditionally performed on the server side are performed on the client side in SPAs. This has caused an increase in the size of JavaScript applications and the need for a better code organization.

As a result, developers have started using in the frontend some of the design patterns that have been used with success in the backend over the last decade. Among those, we can highlight the **Model-View-Controller** (**MVC**) design pattern and some of its derivative versions, such as **Model-View-ViewModel** (**MVVM**) and **Model-View-Presenter** (**MVP**).

Developers around the world started to share some SPA frameworks that somehow try to implement the MVC design pattern but do not necessarily follow the MVC pattern strictly. The majority of these frameworks implement Models and Views, but since not all of them implement Controllers, we refers to this family of frameworks as MV*.

> We will cover concepts such as MVC, Models, and Views later in this chapter.

We will now look at other architecture principles, design patterns, and components commonly present in MV* frameworks.

Common components and features in the MV* frameworks

We have seen that single-page web applications are usually developed using a family of frameworks known as MV*, and we have covered the basics of some common SPA architecture principles.

Let's delve further into some components and features that are commonly found in MV* frameworks.

> In this section, we will use some small code snippets from some of the most popular MV* frameworks. We are not attempting to learn how to use each of these frameworks, and no previous experience with an MV* framework is required.
>
> Our goal should be to understand the common components and features of an MV* framework and not focus on a particular framework.

Models

A **model** is a component used to store data. The data is retrieved from an HTTP API and displayed in the view. Some frameworks include a model entity that we, as developers, must extend. For example, in Backbone.js (a popular MV* framework), a model must extend the `Backbone.Model` class:

```
class TaskModel extends Backbone.Model{
  public created : number;
  public completed : boolean;
  public title : string;
  constructor() {
    super();
  }
}
```

A model inherits some methods that can help us interact with the web services. For example, in the case of a Backbone.js model, we can use a method named `fetch` to set the values of a model using the data returned by a web service. In some frameworks, models include logic to retrieve data from an HTTP API, while others include an independent component responsible for the communication with an HTTP API.

In other frameworks, models are plain entities, and it is not necessary to extend or instantiate one of the framework's classes:

```
class TaskModel {
  public created : number;
  public completed : boolean;
  public title : string;
}
```

Collections

Collections are used to represent a list of models. In the previous section, we saw an example of a model named `TaskModel`. While this model could be used to represent a single task in a list of things to do, a collection could be used to represent the list of tasks.

In the majority of MV* frameworks that support collections, we need to specify the model of the items of a collection when the collection is declared. For example, in the case of Backbone.js, the Task collection could look like the following:

```
class TaskCollection extends Backbone.Collection<TaskModel> {
  public model : TaskModel;
  constructor() {
    this.model = TodoModel;
    super();
  }
}
```

Just like in the case of models, some frameworks' collections are plain arrays, and we will not need to extend or instantiate one of the framework's classes. Collections can also inherit some methods to facilitate interaction with web services.

Item views

The majority of frameworks feature an item view (or just view) component. Views are responsible for rendering the data stored in the models as HTML. Views usually require a model, a template, and a container to be passed as a constructor argument, property, or setting.

- The model and the template are used to generate the HTML, as we discovered earlier on in this chapter
- The container is usually the selector of one of the DOM elements in the page; the selected DOM element is then used as a *container* for the HTML, which is inserted or appended to it

For example, in Marionette.js (a popular MV* framework based on Backbone.js), a view is declared as follows:

```
class NavBarItemView extends Marionette.ItemView {
    constructor(options: any = {}) {
        options.template = "#navBarItemViewTemplate";
        super(options);
    }
}
```

Collection views

A collection view is a special type of view. The relationship between collection views and views is somehow comparable with the relationship between collections and models. Collection views usually require a collection, an item view, and a container to be passed as a constructor argument, property, or setting.

A collection loops through the models in the specified collection, renders each of them using a specified item view, and then appends the results of the container.

> In the majority of frameworks, when a collection view is rendered, an item view is rendered for each item in the collection; this can sometimes create a performance bottleneck.
>
> An alternative solution is to use an item view and a model in which one of its attributes is an array. We can then use the {{#each}} statement in the view template to render a collection in one single operation, as opposed to one operation for each item in the collection.

The following code snippet is an example of a collection view in Marionette.js:

```
class SampleCollectionView extends Marionette.
CollectionView<SampleModel> {
  constructor(options: any = {}) {
    super(options);
  }
}
var view = new SampleCollectionView({
  collection : collection,
  el:$("#divOutput"),
  childView : SampleView
});
```

Controllers

Some frameworks feature Controllers. Controllers are usually in charge of handling the lifecycle of specific models and their associated views. They are responsible for instantiating connection models and collections with their respective views and collection views as well as disposing them before handling the control over to another controller.

Interaction in MVC applications is organized around controllers and actions. Controllers can include as many action methods as needed, and an action typically has one-to-one mapping with user interactions.

We are going to take a look at a small code snippet that uses an MV* framework known as **Chaplin**. Just like Marionette.js, Chaplin is a framework based on Backbone.js. The following code snippet defines a class that inherits from the base Controller class, which is defined by Chaplin:

```
class LikesController extends Chaplin.Controller {

    public beforeAction() {
      this.redirectUnlessLoggedIn();
    }

    public index(params) {
      this.collection = new Likes();
      this.view = new LikesView({collection: this.collection});
    }

    public show(params) {
      this.model = new Like({id: params.id});
      this.view = new FullLikeView({model: this.model});
    }
}
```

In the preceding code snippet, we can see that the controller is named LikesController, and it has two actions named index and show respectively. We can also observe a method named beforeAction that is executed by Chaplin before an action is invoked.

Events

An event is an action or occurrence detected by the program that may be handled by the program. MV* frameworks usually distinguish two kinds of events:

- **User events**: Applications allow users to interact with it by triggering and handling user events, such as clicking on a button, scrolling, or submitting a form. User events are usually handled in a view.

- **Application events**: The application can also trigger and handle events. For example, some frameworks trigger an `onRender` event when a view has been rendered or an `onBeforeRouting` event when a controller action is about to be invoked.

Application events are a good way to adhere to the Open/Close element of the SOLID principle. We can use events to allow developers to extend a framework (by adding event handlers) without having to modify the framework itself.

Application events can also be used to avoid direct communication between two components. We will cover more about them later in this chapter when we focus on a component known as Mediator.

Router and hash (#) navigation

The router is responsible for observing URL changes and passing the execution flow to a controller's action that matches the URL.

The majority of frameworks use a combination of a technique known as hash navigation and the usage of the HTML5 History API to handle changes in the URL without reloading the page.

In an SPA, the links usually contain the hash (#) character. This character was originally designed to set the focus on one of the DOM elements on a page, but it is used by MV* frameworks to navigate without needing to fully reload the web page.

In order to understand this concept, we are going to implement a really basic Router from scratch. We are going to start by taking a look at how a route—a plain object used to represent a URL—looks in the majority of MV* frameworks:

```
class Route {
  public controllerName : string;
  public actionName : string;
```

```
      public args : Object[];

      constructor(controllerName : string, actionName : string, args :
      Object[]){
        this.controllerName = controllerName;
        this.actionName = actionName;
        this.args = args;
      }
    }
```

The router observes the changes in the web browser's URL. When the URL changes, the router parses it and generates a new route instance.

A really basic router could look as follows:

```
class Router {
  private _defaultController : string;
  private _defaultAction : string;

  constructor(defaultController : string, defaultAction : string) {
    this._defaultController = defaultController || "home";
    this._defaultAction = defaultAction || "index";
  }

  public initialize() {

    // observe URL changes by users
    $(window).on('hashchange', () => {
      var r = this.getRoute();
      this.onRouteChange(r);
    });
  }

  // Encapsulates reading the URL
  private getRoute() {
    var h = window.location.hash;
    return this.parseRoute(h);
  }

  // Encapsulates parsing an URL
  private parseRoute(hash : string) {
    var comp, controller, action, args, i;
    if (hash[hash.length - 1] === "/") {
        hash = hash.substring(0, hash.length - 1);
    }
```

```
    comp = hash.replace("#", '').split('/');
    controller = comp[0] || this._defaultController;
    action = comp[1] || this._defaultAction;

    args = [];
    for (i = 2; i < comp.length; i++) {
        args.push(comp[i]);
    }
    return new Route(controller, action, args);
  }

  private onRouteChange(route : Route) {
    // invoke controller here!
  }
}
```

In the second part of this chapter, we are going to develop an entire SPA framework from scratch, and we will use an extended version of the preceding class.

The preceding class takes the name of the default constructor and the name of the default action as its constructor arguments. The controller named home and the action named index are used as the default values when no arguments are passed to the constructor.

The method named initialize is used to create an event listener for the hashchange event. Web browsers trigger this event when the window.location.hash value changes.

For example, let's consider the current URL to be http://localhost:8080. A user then clicks on the following link:

```
<a href="#tasks/index">View Tasks</a>
```

When the link is clicked, the window.location.hash value will change to "task/index". The URL in the browser navigation panel will change, but the hash character will prevent the page from fully reloading. The router will then invoke its getRoute method to transform the URL into a new instance of the Route class by using the parseRoute method.

The URL follows the following name convection:

```
#conrollerName/actionName/arg1/arg2/arg3/argN
```

This means that the `task/index` URL is transformed into:

```
new Route("task", "index", []);
```

> The majority of MV* frameworks use the HTML History API to hide the hash (#) character from the URL, but we will not implement this feature in our framework.

The instance of the `Route` class is passed to the `onRouteChange` method, which is responsible for invoking the controller that matches the route.

> We have omitted the implementation of the `onRouteChange` method on purpose but will refer to this function in the Mediator and Dispatcher sections later in this chapter.

This is basically how hash navigation and routers work. As we can expect, in a real framework, a router has many additional features, but the preceding example should help us gain a good understanding of how routing works in the majority of MV* frameworks.

Mediator

Some MV* frameworks introduce a component known as **Mediator**. The mediator is a simple object all other modules use to communicate with each other.

The mediator usually implements the publish/subscribe design pattern (also known as **pub/sub**). This pattern enables modules to not depend on each other. Instead of making direct use of other parts of the application, modules communicate through events.

Modules can listen for and react to events but also publish events of their own to give other modules the chance to react. This ensures loose coupling of application modules, while still allowing for ease of information exchange.

The mediator can also help us to allow developers to extend our framework (by subscribing to events) without actually having to modify the framework itself. As we saw in *Chapter 4, Object-Oriented Programming with TypeScript*, this is a good thing because it adheres to the Open/Close principle in the SOLID principles.

We are going to avoid the internal details of how a mediator works for now, but we can take a look at an example of the public interface of a mediator:

```
interface IMediator {
  publish(e : IAppEvent) : void;
  subscribe(e : IAppEvent) : void;
  unsubscribe(e : IAppEvent) : void;
}
```

In the previous section, we omitted the details about how the router invokes a controller because the framework that we are going to develop will use a mediator:

```
class Router {
  // ...
  private onRouteChange(route : Route) {
    this.meditor.publish(new AppEvent("app.dispatch", route, null));
  }
}
```

The preceding code snippet showcases how the router avoids invoking the controller's action directly, and instead, it publishes an event using a mediator.

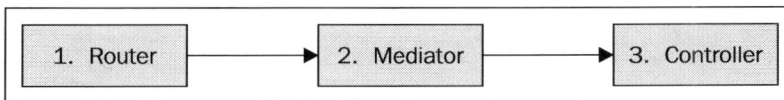

```
1. Router  →  2. Mediator  →  3. Controller
```

Dispatcher

There was something in the previous code snippet that may have caught your attention: the event name is app.dispatch.

The app.dispatch event refers to an entity known as **Dispatcher**. This means that the router is sending an event to the dispatcher and not to a controller:

```
class Dispatcher {
  // ...
  public initialize() {
    this.meditor.subscribe(
      new AppEvent("app.dispatch", null, (e: any, data? : any) => {
        this.dispatch(data);
```

```
    })
  );
}

// Create and dispose controller instances
private dispatch(route : IRoute) {
  // 1. Dispose previous controller
  // 2. Create instance of new controller
  // 3. Invoke controller action using Mediator
}
// ...
}
```

As we can see in this code snippet, the dispatcher is responsible for the creation of new controllers and the disposal of old controllers. When a router finishes parsing a URL, it will pass an instance of the Route class to the dispatcher using a mediator. The dispatcher then disposes the previous controller creates an instance of the new controller, and invokes the controller action using a mediator.

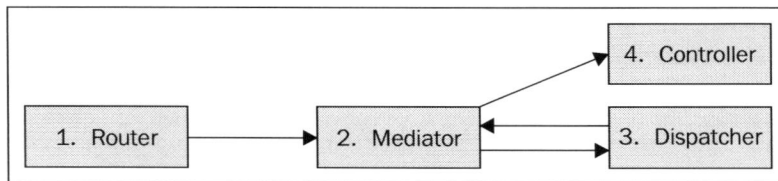

Client-side rendering and Virtual DOM

We are already familiar with the basics of client-side rendering. We know client-side rendering requires a template and some data to generate HTML as output, but we haven't mentioned some performance details that we need to consider when selecting an MV* framework.

Manipulating the DOM is one of the main potential performance bottlenecks in SPAs. For this reason, it is interesting to compare how frameworks render the views internally before we decide to work with one or another.

Some frameworks render a view whenever the model changes, and there are two possible ways to know when a model has changed:

- The first one is to check for changes using an interval (this operation is sometimes referred as a dirty check)
- The second option is to use an observable model

The observable approach is much more efficient than using a time interval because the observable model will only consume processing time when it has actually changed. On the other hand, the interval will consume processing time even when the model has not changed.

When to render is important, but we also need to consider how to render. Some frameworks manipulate the DOM directly and others use an in-memory representation of the DOM known as **Virtual DOM**. Virtual DOM is much more efficient because JavaScript is able to manipulate the in-memory representation of the DOM much faster than the DOM itself.

User interface data binding

User interface (**UI**) data binding is a design pattern that aims to simplify development of graphic UI applications. UI data binding binds UI elements to an application domain model.

A binding creates a link between two properties such that when one changes, the other one is updated to the new value automatically. Bindings can connect properties on the same object, or across two different objects. Most MV* frameworks include some sort of binding implementation between views and models.

One-way data binding

One-way data binding is a type of UI data binding. This type of data binding only propagates changes in one direction.

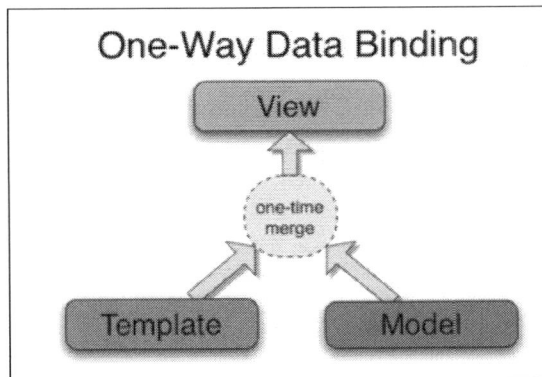

In the majority of MV* frameworks, this means that any changes in the model are propagated to the view. On the other hand, any changes in the view are not propagated to the model.

Two-way data binding

Two-way binding is used to ensure that any changes to the view are propagated to the model and any changes in the model are propagated to the view.

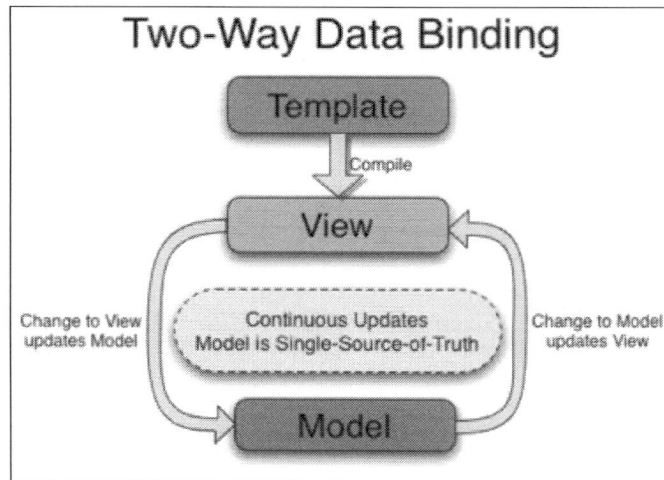

Data flow

Some of the latest MV* frameworks have introduced new approaches and techniques. One of these new concepts is the unidirectional data flow architecture (introduced by Flux).

This unidirectional data flow architecture is based on the idea that changing the value of a variable should automatically force recalculation of the values of variables that depend on its value.

In an MVC application, a controller handles multiple Models and Views. Sometimes, a View uses more than one model, and when two-way data binding is used, we can end up with a complicated flow of data to follow. The following diagram illustrates such a scenario:

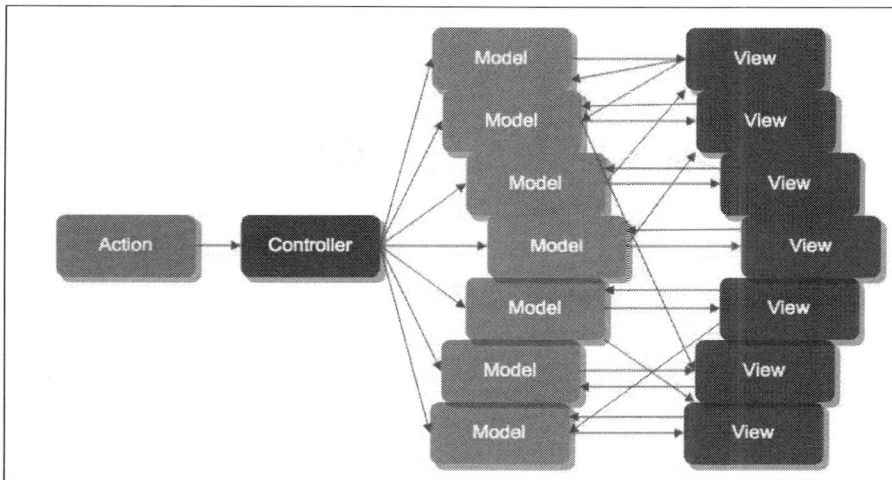

In this diagram, action does not refer to the actions in a controller. **Action** here refers to user or application events.

Dataflow architecture attempts to solve this problem by restricting the flow of data to one unique channel and direction. By doing so, the flow of data within the application components becomes much easier to follow. The following diagram illustrates the flow of data in an application that uses unidirectional data flow architecture:

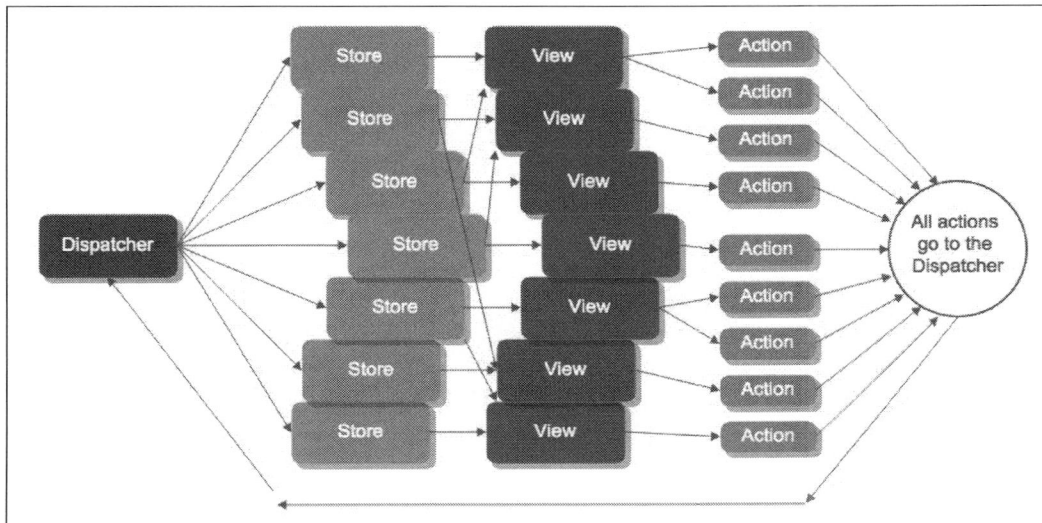

The preceding diagram illustrates how the data always moves in the same direction.

In Flux's unidirectional data flow architecture, all the actions are directed to the dispatcher. The dispatcher in Flux is like the dispatcher in our framework, but instead of passing the execution flow to a controller, it passes the execution flow to a store.

Stores are in charge of retrieving and manipulating data and can be compared with Models in MVC. Once the data has been modified in some way, it is passed to the views.

Views, just like in MVC, are responsible for rendering the data as HTML and handling user events (actions). If the event requires some data to be modified in some way, the Views will send an action to the dispatcher instead of manipulating its model, as would happen in an application with two-way data binding support.

The data always moves in the same direction and in circles, which makes the execution flow of a large dataflow application much easier to debug and predict than that of a two-way data binding MVC application.

Web components and shadow DOM

Some frameworks use the term web component to refer to reusable user interface widgets. Web components allow developers to define custom HTML elements. For example, we could define a new HTML `<map>` tag to display a map. Web components can import their own dependencies and use client-side templates to render their own HTML using a technology known as **shadow DOM**.

Shadow DOM allows the browser to use HTML, CSS, and JavaScript within a web component. Shadow DOM is useful when developing large applications because it helps to prevent CSS, HTML, and JavaScript conflicts between components.

> Some of the existing MV* frameworks (for example, Polymer) can be used to implement real web components. While other frameworks (for example, React) use the term web components to refer to reusable user interface widgets, those components cannot be considered real web components because they don't use the web components technology stack (custom elements, HTML templates, shadow DOM and HTML imports).

Choosing an application framework

We can create a SPA from scratch, but usually we pick up an existing framework before creating our own. One of the main problems of choosing a JavaScript SPA framework is that there are too many choices.

The latest and greatest JavaScript framework comes around every sixteen minutes.

- Allen Pike

I would personally recommend considering a framework or another depending on the features that you think that you will need to achieve your goals.

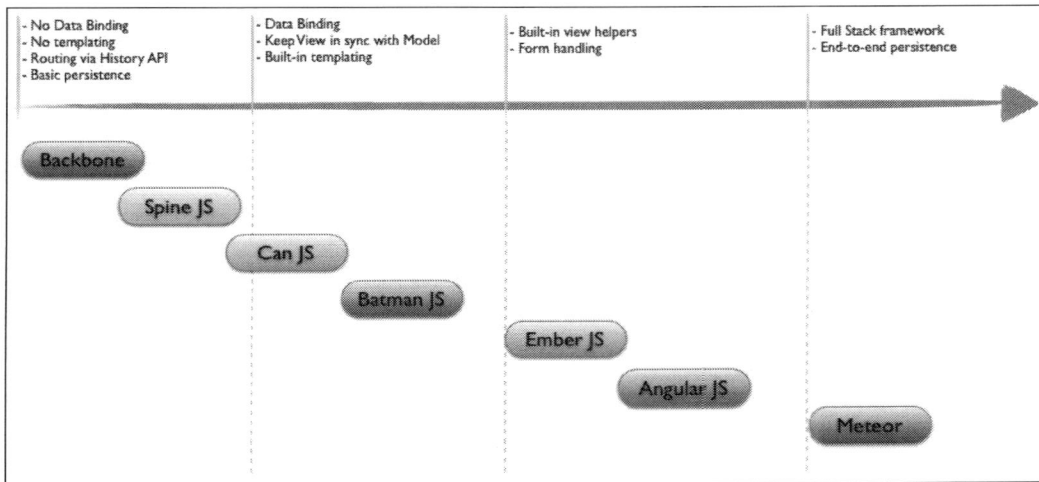

For example, if we are going to work on an application with not really complex views and forms, Backbone.js or one of its derivations (Marionette.js, Chaplin, and so on) should work for us. However, if our application is expected to have many forms and complex views, Ember.js or AngularJS might be a better option.

> If you need some extra help when choosing one framework over another, you should visit http://todomvc.com. TodoMVC is a project that offers the same application (a task manager) implemented using MV* concepts in most of the popular JavaScript MV* frameworks today.

Writing an MVC framework from scratch

Now that we have a good idea about the common components of an MV* application framework, we are going to try to implement our own framework from scratch.

> The framework that we are about to develop has not been designed to be used in a real professional environment. Real MV* frameworks have thousands of features and have been under intense development for months and even years before becoming stable.
>
> This framework has been developed not to be the most efficient or the most maintainable MV* framework available, but to be a good learning resource.

Our application will feature controllers, templates, views, and models as well as a router, a mediator, and a dispatcher. Let's take a look at the role of each of these components in our framework:

- **Application**: This is the root component of an application. The application component is in charge of the initialization of all the internal components of the framework (mediator, router, and dispatcher).

- **Mediator**: The mediator is in charge of the communication between all the other components in the application.

- **Application Events**: Application events are used to send information from one component to another. An application event is identified by an identifier known as a topic. The components can publish application events as well as subscribe and unsubscribe to application events.

- **Router**: The router observes the changes in the browser URL and creates instances of the Route class that are then sent to the Dispatcher using an application event.

- **Routes**: These are used to represent a URL. The URLs use naming conventions that can be used to identify which controller and action should be invoked.

- **Dispatcher**: The dispatcher receives instances of the Route class, which are used to identify the required controller. The dispatcher can then dispose the previous controller and create a new controller instance if necessary. Once the controller has been initialized, the dispatcher passes the execution flow to the controller using an application event.

- **Controllers**: Controllers are used to initialize views and models. Once the views and models are initialized, the controller passes the execution flow to one or more models using an application event.

- **Models**: Models are in charge of the interaction with the HTTP API as well as data manipulation in memory. This involves data formatting as well as operations such as the addition or deletion of data. Once the Model has finished manipulating the data, it is passed to one or more views using an application event.

- **Views**: Views are in charge of the load and compilation of templates. Once the template has been loaded, the views wait for data to be sent by the models. When the data is received, it is combined with the templates to generate HTML code, which is appended to the DOM. Views are also in charge of the binding and unbinding of UI events (click, focus, and so on).

The following diagram can help us to understand the interaction between the available components:

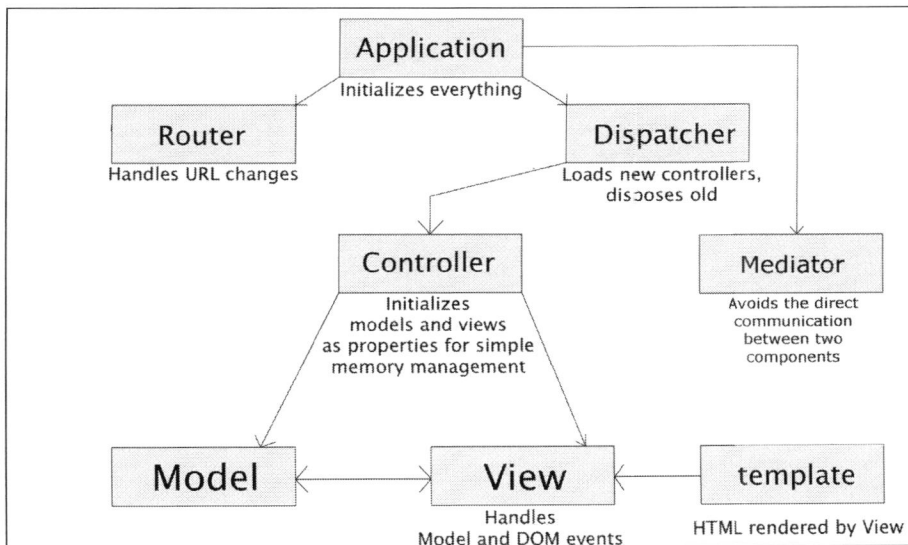

Now that we have a basic idea about the overall architecture of our framework, let's start a new project.

Prerequisites

Just like we have been doing in the previous chapters of this book, it is recommended to create a new project and configure an automated development workflow using Gulp.

You can try to create the framework and final application following the steps described in the following sections, or you can download the companion source code to get a copy of the finished application.

We are going to start by installing the following runtime dependencies with npm:

```
npm init

npm install animate.css bootstrap datatables handlebars jquery q --
save
```

We also need to install the following development dependencies:

```
npm browser-sync browserify chai gulp gulp-coveralls gulp-tslint
gulp-typescript gulp-uglify karma karma-chai karma-mocha karma-sinon
mocha run-sequence sinon vinyl-buffer vinyl-source-stream --save-dev
```

Now, let's install the required type definition files using `tsd`:

```
tsd init

tsd install jquery bootstrap handlebars q chai sinon mocha
jquery.dataTables highcharts --save
```

The application uses the following directory tree:

```
├── LICENSE
├── README.md
├── css
│   └── site.css
├── data
│   ├── nasdaq.json
│   └── nyse.json
├── gulpfile.js
├── index.html
├── karma.conf.js
├── node_modules
├── package.json
├── source
│   ├── app
│   │   └── // Chapter 10
│   └── framework
│       ├── app.ts
│       ├── app_event.ts
```

```
|        ├── controller.ts
|        ├── dispatcher.ts
|        ├── event_emitter.ts
|        ├── framework.ts
|        ├── interfaces.ts
|        ├── mediator.ts
|        ├── model.ts
|        ├── route.ts
|        ├── router.ts
|        ├── tsconfig.json
|        └── view.ts
├── test
├── tsd.json
└── typings
```

We will be working on the files located under the source folder during this chapter. In the next chapter, we will create an application using our framework. Most of the files of this application will be located under the app folder.

Now that we have a basic idea about the overall architecture of our framework, let's proceed to implement each of its components.

> The final version of the entire framework and application is included in the companion source code.

Application events

We are going to use application events that allow the communication between two components. For example, when a model finishes receiving the response of an HTTP API, the response of the request will be sent from the model to a view using an application event.

As we saw in *Chapter 4*, *Object-Oriented Programming with TypeScript*, one of the SOLID principles is the dependency inversion principle, which states that we should not depend upon concretions (classes) and should depend upon abstractions instead (interfaces). We are going to try to follow the SOLID principles, so let's get started by creating a new file named interfaces.ts inside the framework folder and declaring the IAppEvent interface:

```
interface IAppEvent {
  topic : string;
  data : any;
  handler: (e: any, data : any) => void;
}
```

An application event contains an identifier or topic and some data or an event handler. We will understand these properties better once we get to publish and subscribe to some events.

Let's continue by creating a new file named app_event.ts inside the framework folder and copy the following code into it:

```
/// <reference path="./interfaces"/>

class AppEvent implements IAppEvent {
  public guid : string;
  public topic : string;
  public data : any;
  public handler: (e: Object, data? : any) => void;

  constructor(topic : string, data : any, handler: (e: any, data? :
any) => void) {
    this.topic = topic;
    this.data = data;
    this.handler = handler;
  }
}
export { AppEvent };
```

The preceding code snippet declares a class named AppEvent which implements the IappEvent interface.

Mediator

As we already know, the mediator is a component that implements the pub/sub design pattern and is used to avoid the direct communication between two components.

Let's add a new interface to the interfaces.ts file:

```
interface IMediator {
  publish(e : IAppEvent) : void;
  subscribe(e : IAppEvent) : void;
  unsubscribe(e : IAppEvent) : void;
}
```

As we can see in this code snippet, the `IMediator` interface exposes the three methods necessary to implement the publish/subscribe design pattern, as follows:

- `publish`: This is used to trigger events. When we publish an event, all the event subscribers receive it.

- `subscribe`: This is used to subscribe to an event, or in other words, set an event handler for an event.

- `unsubscibe`: This is used to unsubscribe to an event, or in other words, remove an event handler for an event type.

Now, let's proceed to create a new file named `mediator.ts` under the framework folder and add the following code to it:

```
/// <reference path="./interfaces"/>

class Mediator implements IMediator {
  private _$ : JQuery;
  private _isDebug;

  constructor(isDebug : boolean = false) {
    this._$ = $({});
    this._isDebug = isDebug;
  }

  public publish(e : IAppEvent) : void {
    if(this._isDebug === true) { console.log(new Date().getTime(),
    "PUBLISH", e.topic, e.data); }
    this._$.trigger(e.topic, e.data);
  }

  public subscribe(e : IAppEvent) : void {
    if(this._isDebug === true) { console.log(new Date().getTime(),
    "SUBSCRIBE", e.topic, e.handler); }
    this._$.on(e.topic, e.handler);
  }

  public unsubscribe(e : IAppEvent) : void {
    if(this._isDebug === true) { console.log(new Date().getTime(),
    "UNSUBSCRIBE", e.topic, e.data); }
    this._$.off(e.topic);
  }
}
export { Mediator };
```

The preceding code snippet declares a class named `Mediator`, which implements the `IMediator` interface. The `Mediator` constructor has a default (`false`) parameter that is used to indicate if we are using the debug mode.

The debug mode is useful because when it is enabled, we will be able to observe all the calls to the `publish`, `subscribe`, and `unsubscribe` methods of the mediator without the need to use a debugger. In the following screenshot, we can observe the kind of information that we can expect to see in the browser console when the debug mode is enabled:

The `publish`, `subscribe`, and `unsubscribe` methods use the jQuery `trigger`, `on`, and `off` methods respectively to execute event listeners as well as create and remove event listeners when requested.

The default constructor also initializes a private property named `_$`. The value of this property is just an empty jQuery object in memory. This object is used by jQuery to add and remove event handlers when the trigger, on, and off method are invoked.

It important to mention that if the mediator is cleared from memory, its `_$` property will also be cleared from memory and all the application event handlers will be lost. In the following section, we will see how the `App` class ensures that the mediator is never cleared from memory.

Application

The application class is the root component of an application. The application class is in charge of the initialization of the main components of an application (router, mediator, and dispatcher).

We are going to start by declaring a couple of interfaces required by the application class, so let's add the following interfaces to the `interfaces.td` file:

```
interface IAppSettings {
  isDebug : boolean,
  defaultController : string;
  defaultAction : string;
  controllers : Array<IControllerDetails>;
  onErrorHandler : (o : Object) => void;
}

interface IControllerDetails {
  controllerName : string;
  controller : { new(...args : any[]): IController ;};
}
```

The `IAppSettings` interface is used to indicate the available application settings. We can use the application settings to enable the debug mode, set the name of the default controller and action, set the available controllers, and set a global error handler. Let's take a look at the actual implementation of the application class:

```
/// <reference path="./interfaces"/>

import { Dispatcher } from "./dispatcher";
import { Mediator } from "./mediator";
import { AppEvent } from "./app_event";
import { Router } from "./router";

class App {
  private _dispatcher : IDispatcher;
  private _mediator : IMediator;
  private _router : IRouter;
  private _controllers : IControllerDetails[];
  private _onErrorHandler : (o : Object) => void;

  constructor(appSettings : IAppSettings) {
    this._controllers = appSettings.controllers;
    this._mediator = new Mediator(appSettings.isDebug || false);
```

```
        this._router = new Router(this._mediator,
        appSettings.defaultController, appSettings.defaultAction);
        this._dispatcher = new Dispatcher(this._mediator,
        this._controllers);
        this._onErrorHandler = appSettings.onErrorHandler;
    }

    public initialize() {
        this._router.initialize();
        this._dispatcher.initialize();
        this._mediator.subscribe(new AppEvent("app.error", null, (e:
        any, data? : any) => {
            this._onErrorHandler(data);
        }));
        this._mediator.publish(new AppEvent("app.initialize", null,
        null));
    }
}
export { App };
```

The preceding code snippet declares a class named App that takes the implementation of IAppSettings as its only constructor argument. The class constructor initializes the class properties (dispatcher, mediator, router, controller and global error handler).

When we create a new application, it automatically creates a new mediator, and it is passed to both the router and the dispatcher. This means that one unique instance of the mediator is shared by all the components in the application, or in other words, the mediator is a singleton: it stays in memory for the entire application lifecycle.

After creating an instance of the App class, we must invoke the initialize method to start the execution of the application. We will later see that when the router is initialized, it uses the mediator to subscribe to the app.initialize event.

The initialize method calls the initialize method of some of the application components (router and dispatcher). It then sets an event handler for global errors and publishes the app.initialize event.

The mediator then invokes the event handler for the app.initialize event by the router. This explains how the execution flow is passed from the application class to the router class.

Route

In order to be able to understand the implementation of the router class, we need to learn about some of its dependencies first. The first of these dependencies is the Route class.

The Route class implements the Route interface. This interface was previously explained in this chapter, so we will not go into its details again.

```
interface IRoute {
  controllerName : string;
  actionName : string;
  args : Object[];
  serialize() : string;
}
```

We have also included the implementation of the Route class previously in this chapter, but the method named serialize was omitted on purpose. The serialize method transforms an instance of the Route class into a URL.

```
/// <reference path="./interfaces"/>

class Route implements IRoute {
  public controllerName : string;
  public actionName : string;
  public args : Object[];

  constructor(controllerName : string, actionName : string, args :
  Object[]){
    this.controllerName = controllerName;
    this.actionName = actionName;
    this.args = args;
  }

  public serialize() : string {
    var s, sargs;
    sargs = this.args.map(a => a.toString()).join("/");
    s = `${this.controllerName}/${this.actionName}/${sargs}`;
    return s;
  }
}
export { Route };
```

Event emitter

The router also has a dependency in the EventEmitter class. This class is particularly important because every single component (except the application component) in the entire framework extends it.

As we already know, all the components use a mediator to communicate with each other. The mediator is a singleton, which means that every single component in our application needs to be provided with access to the mediator instance.

The EventEmitter class is used to reduce the amount of boilerplate code that is necessary to achieve this and to provide developers with some helpers that facilitate the publication and subscription of multiple application events:

```
interface IEventEmitter {
  triggerEvent(event : IAppEvent);
  subscribeToEvents(events : Array<IAppEvent>);
  unsubscribeToEvents(events : Array<IAppEvent>);
}
```

Now, let's create a file named event_emitter.ts under the framework directory and copy the following code into it:

```
/// <reference path="./interfaces"/>

import { AppEvent } from "./app_event";

 class EventEmitter implements IEventEmitter{
   protected _metiator : IMediator;
   protected _events : Array<IAppEvent>;

   constructor(metiator : IMediator) {
     this._metiator = metiator;
   }

   public triggerEvent(event : IAppEvent){
     this._metiator.publish(event);
   }

   public subscribeToEvents(events : Array<IAppEvent>) {
     this._events = events;
     for(var i = 0; i < this._events.length; i++) {
       this._metiator.subscribe(this._events[i]);
     }
```

```
  }

  public unsubscribeToEvents() {
    for(var i = 0; i < this._events.length; i++) {
      this._metiator.unsubscribe(this._events[i]);
    }
  }
}
export { EventEmitter };
```

When the `subscribeToEvents` method is invoked, the `_events` property is used to store the events to which a component is subscribed.

When a component decides to remove its event handlers by using the `unsubscribeToEvents` method, we don't need to pass the full list of events again because the event emitter uses the `events` property to remember them.

Router

The router observes the URL for changes and generates instances of the `Route` class that are then passed to the dispatcher using an application event. The `Router` class implements the `IRouter` interface:

```
interface IRouter extends IEventEmitter {
  initialize() : void;
}
```

Let's take a look at the internal implementation of the `Router` class:

```
/// <reference path="./interfaces"/>

import { EventEmitter } from "./event_emitter";
import { AppEvent } from "./app_event";
import { Route } from "./route";

class Router extends EventEmitter implements IRouter {
  private _defaultController : string;
  private _defaultAction : string;

  constructor(metiator : IMediator, defaultController : string,
  defaultAction : string) {
    super(metiator);
    this._defaultController = defaultController || "home";
    this._defaultAction = defaultAction || "index";
```

```
  }

  public initialize() {

    // observe URL changes by users
    $(window).on('hashchange', () => {
      var r = this.getRoute();
      this.onRouteChange(r);
    });

    // be able to trigger URL changes
    this.subscribeToEvents([

      // used to trigger routing on app start
      new AppEvent("app.initialize", null, (e: any, data? : any)
      => {
        this.onRouteChange(this.getRoute());
      }),

      // used to trigger URL changes from other components
      new AppEvent("app.route", null, (e: any, data? : any) => {
      this.setRoute(data); }),
    ]);
  }

  // Encapsulates reading the URL
  private getRoute() {
    var h = window.location.hash;
    return this.parseRoute(h);
  }

  // Encapsulates writting the URL
  private setRoute(route : Route) {
    var s = route.serialize();
    window.location.hash = s;
  }

  // Encapsulates parsing an URL
  private parseRoute(hash : string) {
    var comp, controller, action, args, i;
    if (hash[hash.length - 1] === "/") {
        hash = hash.substring(0, hash.length - 1);
    }
```

```
    comp = hash.replace("#", '').split('/');
    controller = comp[0] || this._defaultController;
    action = comp[1] || this._defaultAction;

    args = [];
    for (i = 2; i < comp.length; i++) {
        args.push(comp[i]);
    }
    return new Route(controller, action, args);
  }

  // Pass control to the Dispatcher via the Mediator
  private onRouteChange(route : Route) {
    this.triggerEvent(new AppEvent("app.dispatch", route, null));
  }
}
export { Router };
```

We have seen this class previously in this chapter, but there are some significant differences here. This time the `Route` class extends the `EventEmitter` class takes a mediator and the names of the default controller and default action as its constructor arguments.

The `initialize` method now includes a call to the `subscribeToEvents` method, which is used to add an application event handler for the `app.initialize` event. This event is used to ensure that the router parses the URL when the application launches for the first time. The router observes the URL for changes, but when the application is launched for the first time, there are no changes in the URL, and the application does not invoke any controller. The router uses the `app.initialize` event handler to solve this problem.

The router is also subscribed to the `app.route` event. The event handler of this event uses a method named `setRoute` to set the browser's URL. The `app.route` application event is used to allow other components to navigate to a route.

Finally, we can find the method named `parseRoute`, which is used to transform a URL into an instance of the `Route` class, and the `onRouteChange` method, which is used to publish an `app.dispatch` application event.

Dispatcher

The dispatcher is a component used to create and dispose controllers when needed. Disposing controllers is important because a controller can use a large number of models and views, which can consume a considerable amount of memory.

If we have many controllers, the amount of memory consumed could become a performance issue. One of the main goals of the dispatcher is to prevent this potential issue.

The dispatcher implements the IDispatcher and IEventEmitter interfaces:

```
interface IDispatcher extends IEventEmitter {
  initialize() : void;
}
```

Let's take a look at the implementation of the dispatcher class:

```
/// <reference path="./interfaces"/>

import { EventEmitter } from "./event_emitter";
import { AppEvent } from "./app_event";

class Dispatcher extends EventEmitter implements IDispatcher {
  private _controllersHashMap : Object;
  private _currentController : IController;
  private _currentControllerName : string;

  constructor(metiator : IMediator, controllers :
  IControllerDetails[]) {
    super(metiator);
    this._controllersHashMap = this.getController(controllers);
    this._currentController = null;
    this._currentControllerName = null;
  }
```

We should be starting to become familiar with how the mediator works at this point. Every component inherits from the EventEmitter class and uses its methods to subscribe to some events in the method named initialize.

Later in this chapter, we will be able to observe that some classes (Controllers, Views, and Models) also have a method named dispose, which is used to unsubscribe to the methods to which the component subscribed in the initialize method.

```
// listen to app.dispatch events
public initialize() {
  this.subscribeToEvents([
```

```
      new AppEvent("app.dispatch", null, (e: any, data? : any) => {
        this.dispatch(data);
      })
    ]);
  }
```

This hash map is used to be able to find a controller as fast as possible when a new route needs to be dispatched The following method is used to generate a hash map that uses the controller name as the key and the controller constructor as values:

```
private getController(controllers : IControllerDetails[]) : Object {
    var hashMap, hashMapEntry, name, controller, l;

    hashMap = {};
    l = controllers.length;

    if(l <= 0) {
      this.triggerEvent(new AppEvent(
        "app.error",
        "Cannot create an application without at least one
        contoller.",
        null));
    }

    for(var i = 0; i < l; i++) {
      controller = controllers[i];
      name = controller.controllerName;
      hashMapEntry = hashMap[name];
      if(hashMapEntry !== null && hashMapEntry !== undefined) {
        this.triggerEvent(new AppEvent(
          "app.error",
          "Two controller cannot use the same name.",
          null));
      }
      hashMap[name] = controller.controller;
    }
    return hashMap;
  }
```

The following method is responsible for the creation, initialization, and disposal of controller instances; the code is commented to facilitate its understanding:

```
private dispatch(route : IRoute) {
    var Controller =
    this._controllersHashMap[route.controllerName];

    // try to find controller
```

```
if (Controller === null || Controller === undefined) {
  this.triggerEvent(new AppEvent(
    "app.error",
    `Controller not found: ${route.controllerName}`,
    null));
}
else {
  // create a controller instance
  var controller : IController = new
  Controller(this._metiator);

  // action is not available
  var a = controller[route.actionName];
  if (a === null || a === undefined) {
    this.triggerEvent(new AppEvent(
      "app.error",
      `Action not found in controller: ${route.controllerName}
      -  + ${route.actionName}`,
      null));
  }
  // action is available
  else {
    if(this._currentController == null) {
      // initialize controller
      this._currentControllerName = route.controllerName;
      this._currentController = controller;
      this._currentController.initialize();
    }
    else {
      // dispose previous controller if not needed
      if(this._currentControllerName !== route.controllerName) {
        this._currentController.dispose();
        this._currentControllerName = route.controllerName;
        this._currentController = controller;
        this._currentController.initialize();
      }
    }
    // pass flow from dispatcher to the controller
    this.triggerEvent(new AppEvent(
    `app.controller.${this._currentControllerName}
    .${route.actionName}`,
      route.args,
      null
    ));
```

```
            }
          }
        }
      }
    }
    export { Dispatcher };
```

After disposing the previous controller (if necessary) and creating a new controller, this controller is initialized. When a controller is initialized, its `initialize` method is invoked, and as we know, it is then that a component subscribes to some events.

When the dispatcher publishes the following application event, the controller is already subscribed to it and the execution flow is passed to the controller's event handler:

```
`app.controller.${this._currentControllerName}.
${route.actionName}`
```

Controller

Controllers are in charge of the initialization and disposal of views and models. Since controllers must be disposable by the dispatcher, a controller must implement the dispose method from the `IController` interface:

```
interface IController extends IEventEmitter {
  initialize() : void;
  dispose() : void;
}
```

The models and views are set as properties of the classes that extend the `Controller` class. The `Controller` class itself does not provide us with any functionality, as it is meant to be implemented by developers when working on an application.

```
/// <reference path="./interfaces"/>

import { EventEmitter } from "./event_emitter";
import { AppEvent } from "./app_event";

class Controller extends EventEmitter implements IController {

  constructor(metiator : IMediator) {
    super(metiator);
  }

  public initialize() : void {
```

```
      throw new Error('Controller.prototype.initialize() is abstract you
   must implement it!');
     }

   public dispose() : void {
      throw new Error('Controller.prototype.dispose() is abstract you
   must implement it!');
     }
   }
   export { Controller };
```

Even though it is not forced by the framework, it is recommended you use the mediator to pass the control to one of the models (not views) from the controller.

Model and model settings

Models are used to interact with a web service and transform the data returned by it. Models allow us to read, format, update, or delete the data returned by a web service. Models implement the `IModel` and `IEventEmitter` interfaces:

```
   interface IModel extends IEventEmitter {
     initialize() : void;
     dispose() : void;
   }
```

A model needs to be provided with the URL of the web service that it consumes. We are going to use a class decorator named `ModelSettings` to set the URL of the service to be consumed.

We could inject the service URL via its constructor, but it is considered a bad practice to inject data (as opposed to a behavior) via a class constructor. The decorator includes some comments to facilitate its understanding:

```
   /// <reference path="./interfaces"/>

   import { EventEmitter } from "./event_emitter";

   function ModelSettings(serviceUrl : string) {
     return function(target : any) {
       // save a reference to the original constructor
       var original = target;

       // a utility function to generate instances of a class
       function construct(constructor, args) {
         var c : any = function () {
```

```
      return constructor.apply(this, args);
    }
    c.prototype = constructor.prototype;
    var instance =  new c();
    instance._serviceUrl = serviceUrl;
    return instance;
  }

  // the new constructor behaviour
  var f : any = function (...args) {
    return construct(original, args);
  }

  // copy prototype so intanceof operator still works
  f.prototype = original.prototype;

  // return new constructor (will override original)
  return f;
  }
}
```

In the next chapter, we will be able to apply the decorator as follows:

```
@ModelSettings("./data/nasdaq.json")
class NasdaqModel extends Model implements IModel {
//...
```

Let's take a look at the internal implementation of the Model class:

```
class Model extends EventEmitter implements IModel {

  // the values of _serviceUrl must be set using the ModelSettings
  decorator
  private _serviceUrl : string;

  constructor(metiator : IMediator) {
    super(metiator);
  }

  // must be implemented by derived classes
  public initialize() {
    throw new Error('Model.prototype.initialize() is abstract and
    must implemented.');
  }

  // must be implemented by derived classes
```

```
public dispose() {
  throw new Error('Model.prototype.dispose() is abstract and
  must implemented.');
}

protected requestAsync(method : string, dataType : string, data) {
  return Q.Promise((resolve : (r) => {}, reject : (e) => {}) => {
    $.ajax({
      method: method,
      url: this._serviceUrl,
      data : data || {},
      dataType: dataType,
      success: (response) => {
        resolve(response);
      },
      error : (...args : any[]) => {
        reject(args);
      }
    });
  });
}

protected getAsync(dataType : string, data : any) {
  return this.requestAsync("GET", dataType, data);
}

protected postAsync(dataType : string, data : any) {
  return this.requestAsync("POST", dataType, data);
}

protected putAsync(dataType : string, data : any) {
  return this.requestAsync("PUT", dataType, data);
}

protected deleteAsync(dataType : string, data : any) {
  return this.requestAsync("DELETE", dataType, data);
}
}
export { Model, ModelSettings };
```

Just like in the case of the controllers, the initialize and dispose methods are meant to be implemented by the derived models, so they don't contain any logic here.

The `requestAsync` method is used to retrieve data from a web service or static file. As we can see, the method uses the jQuery AJAX API and Q's Promises.

The class also includes the `getAsync`, `postAsync`, `putAsync`, and `deleteAsync` methods, which are helpers to perform GET, POST, PUT, and DELETE requests respectively.

Even though it is not forced by the framework, it is recommended you use the mediator to pass the control to one of the views from the model.

View and view settings

Views are used to render templates and handle UI events. Just like the rest of the components in our application, the `View` class extends the `EventEmitter` class:

```
interface IView extends IEventEmitter {
  initialize() : void;
  dispose() : void;
}
```

A view needs to be provided with the URL of the template that it consumes. We are going to use a class decorator named `ViewSettings` to set the URL of the template to be consumed.

We could inject the template URL via its constructor, but it is considered a bad practice to inject data (as opposed to a behavior) via a class constructor. The decorator includes some comments to facilitate its understanding:

```
/// <reference path="./interfaces"/>

import { EventEmitter } from "./event_emitter";
import { AppEvent } from "./app_event";

function ViewSettings(templateUrl : string, container : string) {
  return function(target : any) {
    // save a reference to the original constructor
    var original = target;

    // a utility function to generate instances of a class
    function construct(constructor, args) {
      var c : any = function () {
        return constructor.apply(this, args);
      }
      c.prototype = constructor.prototype;
```

```
          var instance =  new c();
          instance._container = container;
          instance._templateUrl = templateUrl;
          return instance;
      }

      // the new constructor behaviour
      var f : any = function (...args) {
        return construct(original, args);
      }

      // copy prototype so instanceof operator still works
      f.prototype = original.prototype;

      // return new constructor (will override original)
      return f;
    }
}
```

In the next chapter, we will be able to apply the decorator as follows:

```
@ViewSettings("./source/app/templates/market.hbs", "#outlet")
class MarketView extends View implements IView {
//...
```

Let's take a look at the `View` class. Just like in the case of the controllers and models, the `initialize` and `dispose` methods are meant to be implemented by the derived views, so they don't contain any logic here.

```
class View extends EventEmitter implements IView {

    // the values of _container and _templateUrl must be set using
    the ViewSettings decorator
    protected _container : string;
    private _templateUrl : string;

    private _templateDelegate : HandlebarsTemplateDelegate;

    constructor(metiator : IMediator) {
      super(metiator);
    }

    // must be implemented by derived classes
    public initialize() {
      throw new Error('View.prototype.initialize() is abstract and
      must implemented.');
```

```
    }

    // must be implemented by derived classes
    public dispose() {
      throw new Error('View.prototype.dispose() is abstract and must
      implemented.');
    }
```

The view class includes two new methods (named `bindDomEvents` and `unbindDomEvents`) that must be implemented by their derived classes. As we can guess from their names, these methods should be used to set (`bindDomEvents`) and unset (`unbindDomEvents`) UI event handlers:

```
    // must be implemented by derived classes
    protected bindDomEvents(model : any) {
      throw new Error('View.prototype.bindDomEvents() is abstract
      and must implemented.');
    }

    // must be implemented by derived classes
    protected unbindDomEvents() {
      throw new Error('View.prototype.unbindDomEvents() is abstract
      and must implemented.');
    }
```

The following asynchronous methods use promises and are used to load a template (`loadTemplateAsync`), compile it (`compileTemplateAsync`), cache it (`getTemplateAsync`), and render it (`renderAsync`)—all the methods are private except `renderAsync`, which is mean to be used by the derived views:

```
    // asynchroniusly loads a template
    private loadTemplateAsync() {
      return Q.Promise((resolve : (r) => {}, reject : (e) => {}) => {
        $.ajax({
          method: "GET",
          url: this._templateUrl,
          dataType: "text",
          success: (response) => {
            resolve(response);
          },
          error : (...args : any[]) => {
            reject(args);
          }
        });
      });
```

```
    }

    // asynchroniusly compile a template
    private compileTemplateAsync(source : string) {
      return Q.Promise((resolve : (r) => {}, reject : (e) => {}) => {
        try {
          var template = Handlebars.compile(source);
          resolve(template);
        }
        catch(e) {
          reject(e);
        }
      });
    }
    // asynchroniusly loads and compile a template if not done
    already
    private getTemplateAsync() {
      return Q.Promise((resolve : (r) => {}, reject : (e) => {}) => {
        if(this._templateDelegate === undefined ||
          this._templateDelegate === null) {
          this.loadTemplateAsync()
              .then((source) => {
                return this.compileTemplateAsync(source);
              })
              .then((templateDelegate) => {
                this._templateDelegate = templateDelegate;
                resolve(this._templateDelegate);
              })
              .catch((e) => { reject(e); });
        }
        else {
          resolve(this._templateDelegate);
        }
      });
    }

    // asynchroniusly renders the view
    protected renderAsync(model) {
      return Q.Promise((resolve : (r) => {}, reject : (e) => {}) => {
        this.getTemplateAsync()
            .then((templateDelegate) => {
              // generate html and append to the DOM
              var html = this._templateDelegate(model);
```

```
            $(this._container).html(html);

            // pass model to resolve so it can be used by
            // subviews and DOM event initializer
            resolve(model);
          })
          .catch((e) => { reject(e); });
      });
    }
  }
export { View, ViewSettings };
```

Framework

The framework file is used to provide access to all the components in the framework from one single file. This means that when we implement an application using our framework, we will not need to import a different file for each component:

```
/// <reference path="./interfaces"/>

import { App } from "./app";
import { Route } from "./route";
import { AppEvent } from "./app_event";
import { Controller } from "./controller";
import { View, ViewSettings } from "./view";
import { Model, ModelSettings } from "./model";

export { App, AppEvent, Controller, View, ViewSettings, Model,
ModelSettings, Route };
```

Summary

In this chapter, we understood what a single-page web application is, what its common components are, and what the main characteristics of this architecture are.

We also created our own MV* framework. This practical experience and knowledge will help us to understand many of the available MV* frameworks.

In the next chapter, we will try to put in practice many of the concepts that we have learned in this book by creating a full SPA using the framework that we created in this chapter.

10
Putting Everything Together

In this chapter, we are going to put into practice the majority of the concepts that we have covered in the previous chapters.

We will develop a small single-page web application using the SPA framework that we developed in *Chapter 9, Application Architecture*.

This application will allow us to find out how the NASDAQ and NYSE stocks are doing on a particular day. It will not be a very large application, but it will be big enough to demonstrate the advantages of working with TypeScript and using a good application architecture.

We will write some classes and several functions. Some of these functions will be asynchronous (*Chapter 1, Introducing TypeScript*; *Chapter 3, Working with Functions*; *Chapter 4, Object-Oriented Programming with TypeScript*; and *Chapter 5, Runtime*). We will also consume some decorators provided by our SPA framework (*Chapter 8, Decorators*).

To complete the chapter, we will create an automated build to facilitate the development process (*Chapter 2, Automating Your Development Workflow*), improve the application performance (*Chapter 6, Application Performance*), and ensure that it works correctly by writing some unit and integration tests (*Chapter 7, Application Testing*).

In this chapter, we will aim to help you gain confidence with TypeScript and the SPA architecture. We need to focus on the SOLID principles and the separation of concerns. Our goal is to create an application that is maintainable and testable, and an application that can grow over time and which components can be reused in future applications.

Prerequisites

In this application, we will use the tools and the directory tree that we created in the previous chapter. You can use the `tsd.json` and `package.json` files included in the companion source code to install the required npm packages and type definition files. Refer to the prerequisites section under the *Writing an MVC framework from scratch* section in *Chapter 9, Application Architecture*, for additional information about the prerequisites of this application.

The application's requirements

We will develop a small application that will allow users to see a list of stock symbols. A stock symbol represents a company that trades its shares on a stock exchange.

The application home page will display stock symbols from two popular stock exchanges: **NASDAQ (National Association of Securities Dealers Automated Quotations)** and **NYSE (New York stock exchange)**.

As you can see in the following screenshot, the web application requires a top menu containing links that allow the user to see the stock symbols in one of the aforementioned stock exchanges. The list of stock symbols will be displayed in a table, which will include some basic details about the stocks, such as the price of a share in the last sale or the name or the company:

The last column in the table contains some buttons that will allow users to navigate to a second screen that displays a stock quote. A stock quote is just a summary of the pricing performance details of the stock for a given period of time.

The stock quote screen will display a line graph that is used by the brokers to see how the price of the shares (the *y* axis) has evolved over time (the *x* axis). We can display multiple lines to visualize the evolution of the opening price (the price of the shares at the beginning of the day), the closing price (the price of a share at the end of the day), the high price (the highest selling price of the share in a given day), and the low price (the lowest selling price of the share in a given day).

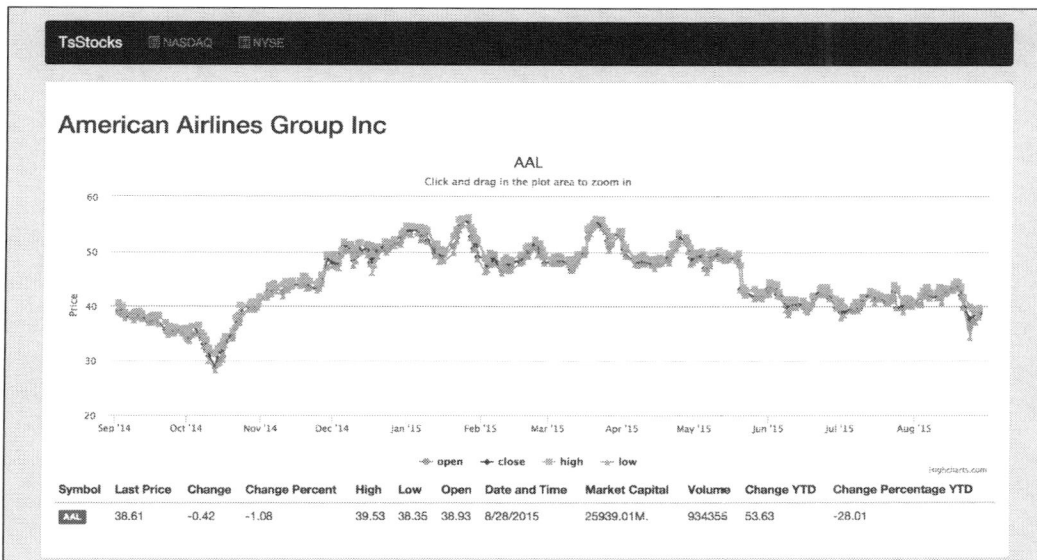

American Airlines Group Inc

Symbol	Last Price	Change	Change Percent	High	Low	Open	Date and Time	Market Capital	Volume	Change YTD	Change Percentage YTD
AAL	38.61	-0.42	-1.08	39.53	38.35	38.93	8/28/2015	25939.01M.	934356	53.63	-28.01

The application's data

As we explained in the previous chapter, we need an application backend that allows us to query the data from a web browser using AJAX requests in order to develop an SPA. This means that we are going to need an HTTP API.

We will use a freely available public HTTP API that will allow us to obtain real stock quote data. For the list of available stock symbols, we will use static JSON files. These JSON files have been generated by transforming a CSV file available on the NASDAQ website. The external HTTP API will also provide the line graph data.

In total, we will be using three sets of data:

- **Market data**: This data is stored in static JSON files. These files have been generated from a CSV file provided by the NASDAQ official website and can be found in the companion example.

- **Stock quote data**: This has been provided by an external web service. The external data provider that we will use in this example is a company called **Markit**, specializing in financial information services. We will use their market data API (v2), which is available for free and has been well documented at `http://dev.markitondemand.com/`.

- **Chart data**: This is also provided in a web service by Markit.

The application's architecture

We will develop an SPA using our own framework. As we saw in the previous chapter, our framework can map a URL with an action in a controller.

Our application will have three main screens. Each screen uses a different URL, as follows:

- `#market/nasdaq` displays stocks in the NASDAQ stock market

- `#market/nyse` displays stocks in the NYSE stock market

- `#symbol/quote/{symbol}` displays a stock quote for the selected stock symbol

Each of the main URLs mentioned earlier will be implemented as a controller's action in our application. In the previous chapter, you saw that URLs adhere to the following naming convention: `#controllerName/actionName/arg1/arg2/argN`.

If we extrapolate this naming convention to the URLs mentioned in the preceding list, we can deduce that our application will have two controllers: `MarketController` and `SymbolController`.

The `MarketController` controller will be implemented using two models and one view:

- **NasdaqModel**: This loads a list of NASDAQ stocks from a static JSON file

- **NyseModel**: This loads a list of NYSE stocks from a static JSON file

- **MarketView**: This renders the list of either the NASDAQ or NYSE stocks

Each component communicates with the other using application events and the mediator. The execution order of the market screen looks as follows:

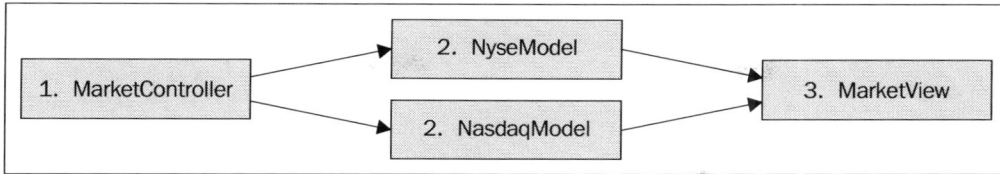

The `SymbolController` controller will be implemented using two models and two views:

- **QuoteModel**: This loads a stock quote for the selected symbol
- **ChartModel**: This loads symbol performance data points for the last year
- **ChartView**: This displays stock performance in an interactive chart
- **SymbolView**: This displays the last price change for the selected symbol

Each component communicates with the other using application events and the mediator. The execution order of the stock quote screen looks as follows:

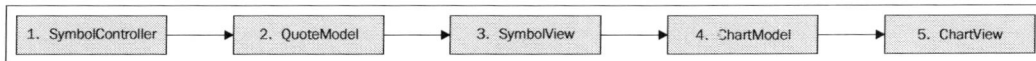

The application's file structure

Presented in this section is the folder structure of the application we are going to build. In the root directory, you can find the application access point (index.html), as well as some of the automation tools' configuration files (gulpfile.js, karma.conf.js, package.json, and so on). You can also observe the typings folder, which contains some type definition files.

Just as in the previous chapters, the application source code is located under the source directory. The unit and integration tests are located in the test folder. The following is the folder structure of the application:

```
├── LICENSE
├── README.md
├── css
│   └── site.css
├── data
│   ├── nasdaq.json
```

```
|       └── nyse.json
├── gulpfile.js
├── index.html
├── karma.conf.js
├── node_modules
├── package.json
├── source
|   ├── app
|   |   ├── controllers
|   |   |   ├── market_controller.ts
|   |   |   └── symbol_controller.ts
|   |   ├── main.ts
|   |   ├── models
|   |   |   ├── chart_model.ts
|   |   |   ├── nasdaq_model.ts
|   |   |   ├── nyse_model.ts
|   |   |   └── quote_model.ts
|   |   ├── templates
|   |   |   ├── market.hbs
|   |   |   └── symbol.hbs
|   |   └── views
|   |       ├── chart_view.ts
|   |       ├── market_view.ts
|   |       └── symbol_view.ts
|   └── framework
|       └── framework.ts (Chapter 9)
├── test
|   ├── app
|   └── framework
├── tsd.json
└── typings
```

Under the source directory, you can observe two folders, named app and framework. We created all the files under the framework directory in the previous chapter. This time, we will focus on the application, which means we will be working under the app directory most of the time.

Inside the app directory, you can find some directories named controllers, models, templates, and views. As you can guess, these directories are used to store controllers, models, templates, and views respectively.

You can also find the main.ts file inside the app directory. This file is the application's entry point, but because we are going to use ES6 modules, we are not going to be able to load this file in a web browser using a <script/> tag.

Configuring the automated build

Just as we did in *Chapter 2, Automating Your Development Workflow,* we need to create a configuration file to configure the desired Gulp tasks. So let's create a file named `gulpfile.js` and import the required Gulp plugins:

```
var gulp        = require("gulp"),
    browserify  = require("browserify"),
    source      = require("vinyl-source-stream"),
    buffer      = require("vinyl-buffer"),
    tslint      = require("gulp-tslint"),
    tsc         = require("gulp-typescript"),
    karma       = require("karma").server,
    coveralls   = require('gulp-coveralls'),
    uglify      = require("gulp-uglify"),
    runSequence = require("run-sequence"),
    header      = require("gulp-header"),
    browserSync = require("browser-sync"),
    reload      = browserSync.reload,
    pkg         = require(__dirname + "/package.json");
```

We need to remember that before we can import one of these packages, we must first install them using npm.

Once the plugins have been imported, we can proceed to write our first task, which is used to check for some basic name convention rules and to avoid some bad practices (the TypeScript files are under the `source` and `tests` directories):

```
gulp.task("lint", function() {
  return gulp.src([
               "source/**/**.ts",
               "test/**/**.test.ts"
             ])
             .pipe(tslint())
             .pipe(tslint.report("verbose"));
});
```

We also need another task to compile our TypeScript code into JavaScript code. As we are working with decorators, we need to ensure that we are using TypeScript 1.5 or higher and that the `experimentalDecorators` compiler settings and target are configured as in the following code snippet:

```
var tsProject = tsc.createProject({
  target : "es5",
  module : "commonjs",
```

```
      experimentalDecorators: true,
      typescript: typescript
});
```

Once we have set up the compiler options, we can proceed to write some tasks. The first one will compile the application code:

```
gulp.task("build", function() {
    return gulp.src("src/**/**.ts")
               .pipe(tsc(tsProject))
               .js.pipe(gulp.dest("build/source/"));
});
```

The second one will compile the unit test and integration test code. We need to use a new project object to avoid potential runtime issues:

```
var tsTestProject = tsc.createProject({
    target : "es5",
    module : "commonjs",
    experimentalDecorators: true,
    typescript: typescript
});

gulp.task("build-test", function() {
    return gulp.src("test/**/*.test.ts")
               .pipe(tsc(tsTestProject))
               .js.pipe(gulp.dest("/build/test/"));
});
```

The two previous tasks should be enough to generate JavaScript, but because we are using CommonJS modules, we need to write a task to bundle the CommonJS modules into a package that can be loaded and executed in a web browser. As we saw in *Chapter 2, Automating Your Development Workflow*, we will create a few Gulp tasks that use Browserify for this purpose.

We need a task to bundle the application code:

```
gulp.task("bundle-source", function () {
    var b = browserify({
        standalone : 'TsStock',
        entries: "build/source/app/main.js",
        debug: true
    });

    return b.bundle()
        .pipe(source("bundle.js"))
```

```
    .pipe(buffer())
    .pipe(gulp.dest("bundled/source/"));
});
```

We further need a task to bundle the application's unit tests:

```
gulp.task("bundle-unit-test", function () {
  var b = browserify({
    standalone : 'test',
    entries: "build/test/bdd.test.js",
    debug: true
  });

  return b.bundle()
    .pipe(source("bdd.test.js"))
    .pipe(buffer())
    .pipe(gulp.dest("bundled/test/"));
});
```

We need a final task to bundle the application's integration tests:

```
gulp.task("bundle-e2e-test", function () {
  var b = browserify({
    standalone : 'test',
    entries: "build/test/e2e.test.js",
    debug: true
  });

  return b.bundle()
    .pipe(source("e2e.test.js"))
    .pipe(buffer())
    .pipe(gulp.dest("bundled/e2e-test/"));
});
```

We will return to the `gulpfile.js` configuration file later in this chapter to add some additional tasks that will be in charge of running the application and its automated tests, as well as some optimizations.

> Until now, we have been working on the configuration of an automated development workflow. From now on, we will focus on the application components. A component is composed of four core elements: template, style rules, services, and the component's logic. You will be able to find the style rules and templates in the companion code samples, but we will mainly focus on the TypeScript files (services and the component's logic) here.

The application's layout

Let's create a new file, named `index.html`, under the application's root directory. The following code snippet is an altered version of the real `index.html` page, which is included with the companion source code:

```html
<ul class="nav navbar-nav">
  <li>
    <a href="#market/nasdaq">NASDAQ</a>
  </li>
  <li>
    <a href="#market/nyse">NYSE</a>
  </li>
</ul>
<div id="outlet">
  <!-- HTML GENERATED BY VIEWS GOES HERE -->
</div>
```

As you can see in the preceding HTML snippet, the code has two important elements. The first significant element is the URL of the two links. These links include the hash character (#), and they will be processed by the application's router.

The second significant element is the element that uses `outlet` as ID. This node is used by our framework as a container where the DOM of each new page is dynamically generated and added to the page.

Implementing the root component

As you saw in the previous chapter, the root component of our custom MVC framework is the `App` component. So, let's create a new file, named `main.ts`, under the `source/app` directory.

We can access all the interfaces in the framework by adding a reference to the `source/interfaces.ts` as follows:

```
/// <reference path="../framework/interfaces"/>
```

We can then access all the components in the framework by importing the `framework/framework.ts` file:

```
import { App, View } from "../framework/framework";
```

Our application will have two controllers. The files don't exist yet but we can add the two import statements anyway:

```
import { MarketController } from
"./controllers/market_controller";
import { SymbolController } from
"./controllers/symbol_controller";
```

At this point, we need to create an object literal that implements the `IAppSettings` interface. This object allows us to set some basic configuration, such as the name of the default controller or action, or a global error handler. However, the most important field in the object literal is the `controller` field, which must be an array of `IControllerDetails`. If you need additional details about the `IControllerDetails`, refer to the previous chapter.

```
var appSettings : IAppSettings = {
  isDebug : true,
  defaultController : "market",
  defaultAction : "nasdaq",
  controllers : [
    { controllerName : "market", controller : MarketController },
    { controllerName : "symbol", controller : SymbolController }
  ],
  onErrorHandler : function(e : Object) {
    alert("Sorry! there has been an error please check out the console
for more info!");
    console.log(e.toString());
  }
};
```

We can then create the `App` instance and invoke the `initialize` method to start executing it:

```
var myApp = new App(appSettings);
myApp.initialize();
```

At this point, our code does not compile because we have not defined the `MarketController` and `SymbolController` controllers yet. Let's define our first controller.

Implementing the market controller

Let's create a new file named `market_controller.ts` under the `app/controllers` directory. We need to import the `Controller` and `AppEvent` entities from the framework along with some entities that are not available yet (`NyseModel`, `NasdaqModel` and `MarketView`).

```
/// <reference path="../../framework/interfaces"/>

import { Controller, AppEvent } from "../../framework/framework";
import { MarketView } from "../views/market_view";
import { NasdaqModel } from "../models/nasdaq_model";
import { NyseModel } from "../models/nyse_model";
```

In an application that uses our framework, a controller must extend the base `Controller` class and implement the `IController` class:

```
class MarketController extends Controller implements IController {
```

We are not forced to declare the views and models used by the controller as its properties, but it is recommended:

```
private _marketView : IView;
private _nasdaqModel : IModel;
private _nyseModel : IModel;
```

It is also recommended that you set the value of all the controller's dependencies inside the controller constructor:

```
constructor(metiator : IMediator) {
  super(metiator);
  this._marketView = new MarketView(metiator);
  this._nasdaqModel = new NasdaqModel(metiator);
  this._nyseModel = new NyseModel(metiator);
}
```

> Instead of setting the value of all the controller's dependencies inside the controller constructor, it would be even better to use an IoC container to automatically inject the controller's dependencies via its constructor. Though, implementing an IoC container is not a simple task, it is beyond the scope of this book.

We must implement the `initialize` method. The `initialize` method is the place where a controller should do the following:

- Subscribe to one application event for each action available in the controller. In this case, the controller has two actions (the `nasdaq` and `nyse` methods).

- Initialize views by invoking the `View.initialize()` method. In this case, there is only one view (`marketView`).

- Initialize models by invoking the `Model.initialize()` method. In this case, there are two models (`nasdaqModel` and `nyseModel`).

```
public initialize() : void {

    // subscribe to controller action events
    this.subscribeToEvents([
        new AppEvent("app.controller.market.nasdaq", null, (e, args
        : string[]) => { this.nasdaq(args); }),
        new AppEvent("app.controller.market.nyse", null, (e, args :
        string[]) => { this.nyse(args); })
    ]);

    // initialize view and models events
    this._marketView.initialize();
    this._nasdaqModel.initialize();
    this._nyseModel.initialize();
}
```

The `dispose` method is the opposite of the `initialize` method. If an event handler was created in the `initialize` method, it should be destroyed in the `dispose` method. The `unsubscribeToEvents` helper will unsubscribe all the events that were subscribed using the `subscribeToEvents` helper:

```
// dispose views/models and stop listening to controller actions
public dispose() : void {

    // dispose the controller events
    this.unsubscribeToEvents();

    // dispose views and model events
    this._marketView.dispose();
    this._nasdaqModel.dispose();
    this._nyseModel.dispose();
}
```

As you saw in the previous chapter, the dispatcher uses the controller's `initialize` and `dispose` methods to free some memory when it is not needed any more. If we forget to dispose one of the views used by the controller in its `dispose` method, the view could end up staying in memory forever.

The actions of a controller should not perform any kind of data manipulation (models should be in charge of that) or user interface events management (views should be in charge of that). Ideally, a controller's actions should only publish one or more application events so the execution flow goes from the controller to one or more models.

In the case of the `nasdaq` action, the controller publishes one of the events to which the `nasdaq` model subscribed when the `initialize` method of NasdaqModel was invoked:

```
// display NASDAQ stocks
public nasdaq(args : string[]) {
  this._metiator.publish(new AppEvent("app.model.nasdaq.change",
  null, null));
}
```

In the case of the `nyse` action, the controller publishes one of the events to which the `nyse` model was subscribed when the `initialize` method of NyseModel was invoked:

```
// display NYSE stocks
public nyse(args : string[]) {
  this._metiator.publish(new AppEvent("app.model.nyse.change",
  null, null));
  }
}
export { MarketController };
```

Implementing the NASDAQ model

Let's create a new file named nasdaq_model.ts under the app/models directory. We can then import the Model, AppEvent, and ModelSettings from our framework and declare a new class named NasdaqModel. The new class must extend the base Model class and implement the IModel interface.

We will also use the ModelSettings decorator to indicate the path of a web service or static data file. In this case, we will use a static data file, which can be found in the companion source code:

```
/// <reference path="../../framework/interfaces"/>

import { Model, AppEvent, ModelSettings } from "../../framework/
```

```
framework";
@ModelSettings("./data/nasdaq.json")
class NasdaqModel extends Model implements IModel {

  constructor(metiator : IMediator) {
    super(metiator);
  }
}
```

The model will subscribe to the `app.model.nasdaq.change` event when the `initialize` method is invoked. This is actually the event that the controller's action published to pass the execution flow from the controller to the model:

```
// listen to model events
public initialize() {
  this.subscribeToEvents([
    new AppEvent("app.model.nasdaq.change", null, (e, args) => {
    this.onChange(args); })
  ]);
}
```

Just like in the previous controller, the `unsubscribeToEvents` helper will unsubscribe all the events that were subscribed using the `subscribeToEvents` helper:

```
// dispose model events
public dispose() {
  this.unsubscribeToEvents();
}
```

This is the event handler of the `app.model.nasdaq.change` event. The event handler uses the `getAsync` method to load the data from the service URL that we previously specified using the `ModelSettings` decorator. The `getAsync` method is inherited from the base `Model` class, which we implemented in the previous chapter.

The `getAsync` method returns a promise; if the promise is fulfilled, the data is formatted and then passed to a view:

```
private onChange(args) : void {
  this.getAsync("json", args)
    .then((data) => {

      // format data
      var stocks = { items : data, market : "NASDAQ" };

      // pass controll to the market view
      this.triggerEvent(new AppEvent("app.view.market.render",
      stocks, null));
    })
```

```
          .catch((e) => {
            // pass control to the global error handler
            this.triggerEvent(new AppEvent("app.error", e, null));
          });
      }
  }
  export { NasdaqModel };
```

Implementing the NYSE model

Let's create a new file named `nyse_model.ts` under the `app/models` directory.
The `NyseModel` class is almost identical to the `NasdaqModel` class, so we will not
go into too much detail:

```
@ModelSettings("./data/nyse.json")
class NyseModel extends Model implements IModel {
  // ...
}
export { NyseModel };
```

All we need to do is copy the contents of the `nasdaq_model.ts` file into the
`nyse_model.ts` file and replace (case sensitive) `nasdaq` with `nyse`.

> This kind of code duplication is known as a code smell. A code smell
> indicates that something is wrong and we need to refactor (improve)
> it. We could avoid a lot of code duplication by using Generic types.
> However generic types were not used here because we though that
> showcasing the usage of decorators would be more valuable for the
> readers of this book.

Implementing the market view

Let's create a new file named `market_view.ts` under the `app/views` directory.
We can then import the `AppEvent`, `ViewSettings`, and `Route` components from
our framework and declare a new class named `MarketView`. The new class must
extend the base `View` class and implement the `IView` interface.

We will also use the `ViewSettings` decorator to indicate the path, a Handlebars
template, and a selector, which is used to find the DOM element that will be used
as the parent node of the view's HTML:

```
/// <reference path="../../framework/interfaces"/>

import { View, AppEvent,ViewSettings, Route } from "../../framework/
framework";
```

```
@ViewSettings("./source/app/templates/market.hbs", "#outlet")
class MarketView extends View implements IView {

  constructor(metiator : IMediator) {
    super(metiator);
  }
```

This view is subscribed to the `app.view.market.render` event and its handler invokes the `renderAsync` method, which has been inherited from the base `view` class. This method returns a promise, which is fulfilled if the template passed to the `ViewSettings` decorator has been loaded and compiled successfully.

For the promise to be fulfilled, the view must be successfully rendered and appended to the DOM element that matches the selector passed to the `ViewSettings` decorator:

```
initialize() : void {
  this.subscribeToEvents([
    new AppEvent("app.view.market.render", null, (e, args : any)
    => {
      this.renderAsync(args)
          .then((model) => {
            // set DOM events
            this.bindDomEvents(model);
          })
          .catch((e) => {
            // pass control to the global error handler
            this.triggerEvent(new AppEvent("app.error", e,
            null));
          });
    }),
  ]);
}
```

Just like in the previous controller and model, the `unsubscribeToEvents` helper will unsubscribe all the events that were subscribed to using the `subscribeToEvents` helper:

```
public dispose() : void {
  this.unbindDomEvents();
  this.unsubscribeToEvents();
}
```

Views are responsible for the management of user events. The components in our framework use the `initialize` method to subscribe to application events, and the `dispose` method to unsubscribe to application events. In the case of user events, we will use the `bindDomEvents` method to set the user events, and the `unbindDomEvents` method to dispose of them:

```
// initializes DOM events
protected bindDomEvents(model : any) {
  var scope = $(this._container);
  // handle click on "quote" button
  $(".getQuote").on('click', scope, (e) => {
    var symbol = $(e.currentTarget).data('symbol');
    this.getStockQuote(symbol);
  });

  // make table sortable and searchable
  $(scope).find('table').DataTable();
}

// disposes DOM events
protected unbindDomEvents() {
  var scope = this._container;
  $(".getQuote").off('click', scope);
  var table = $(scope).find('table').DataTable();
  table.destroy();
}
```

One of the user events observes clicks on the `quote` buttons. When the event is triggered, the following event handler is invoked:

```
private getStockQuote(symbol : string) {
  // navigate to route using route event
  this.triggerEvent(new AppEvent(
    "app.route",
    new Route("symbol", "quote", [symbol]),
    null));
  }
}
```

As you can see, this event handler creates a new route and publishes an `app.route` event. This will cause the router to navigate to the quote action in the `SymbolController: export { MarketView };`

Implementing the market template

The template loaded and compiled by `MarketView` looks as follows:

```
<div class="panel panel-default fadeInUp animated">
  <div class="panel-body">
    <h2>{{market}}</h2>
    <table class="table table-responsible table-condensed">
      <thead>
        <tr>
          <th>Symbol</th>
          <th>Name</th>
          <th>Last Sale</th>
          <th>Market Capital</th>
          <th>IPO year</th>
          <th>Sector</th>
          <th>industry</th>
          <th>Quote</th>
        </tr>
      </thead>
      <tbody>
        {{#each items}}
          <tr>
            <td><span class="label label-
            default">{{Symbol}}</span></td>
            <td>{{{Name}}}</td>
            <td>{{LastSale}}</td>
            <td>{{MarketCap}}</td>
            <td>{{IPOyear}}</td>
            <td>{{Sector}}</td>
            <td>{{industry}}</td>
            <td>
              <button class="btn btn-primary btn-sm getQuote"
              data-symbol="{{Symbol}}">
                <span class="glyphicon glyphicon-stats" aria-
                hidden="true"></span>
                Quote
              </button>
            </td>
          </tr>
        {{/each}}
      </tbody>
    </table>
  </div>
</div>
```

Implementing the symbol controller

Let's create a new file named `symbol_controller.ts` under the `app/controllers` directory. This file will contain a new controller named `SymbolController`. The implementation of this controller is largely similar to the implementation of the `MarketController` controller, so we are going to avoid going into too much detail.

The main difference between this controller and the previous controller is that the new controller uses two new models (`QuoteModel` and `ChartModel`) and two new views (`SymbolView` and `ChartView`):

```
/// <reference path="../../framework/interfaces"/>

import { Controller, AppEvent } from "../../framework/framework";
import { QuoteModel } from "../models/quote_model";
import { ChartModel } from "../models/chart_model";
import { SymbolView } from "../views/symbol_view";
import { ChartView } from "../views/chart_view";

class SymbolController extends Controller implements IController {
  private _quoteModel : IModel;
  private _chartModel : IModel;
  private _symbolView : IView;
  private _chartView : IView;

  constructor(metiator : IMediator) {
    super(metiator);
    this._quoteModel = new QuoteModel(metiator);
    this._chartModel = new ChartModel(metiator);
    this._symbolView = new SymbolView(metiator);
    this._chartView = new ChartView(metiator);
  }

  // initialize views/ models and strat listening to controller
  actions
  public initialize() : void {

    // subscribe to controller action events
    this.subscribeToEvents([
      new AppEvent("app.controller.symbol.quote", null, (e, symbol
      : string) => { this.quote(symbol); })
    ]);
```

```
    // initialize view and models events
    this._quoteModel.initialize();
    this._chartModel.initialize();
    this._symbolView.initialize();
    this._chartView.initialize();
}

// dispose views/models and stop listening to controller actions
public dispose() : void {

    // dispose the controller events
    this.unsubscribeToEvents();

    // dispose views and model events
    this._symbolView.dispose();
    this._quoteModel.dispose();
    this._chartView.dispose();
    this._chartModel.dispose();
}
```

It is also important to notice that the `quote` action passes the control to the `QuoteModel` model:

```
public quote(symbol : string) {
    this.triggerEvent(new AppEvent("app.model.quote.change",
    symbol, null));
}
}
export { SymbolController };
```

Implementing the quote model

Let's create a new file named `quote_model.ts` under the `app/models` directory. This is the third model that we have implemented so far. This means that you should be familiar with the basics already, but there are some minor additions in this particular model. The first thing that you will notice is that the web service is no longer a static file:

```
/// <reference path="../../framework/interfaces"/>

import { Model, AppEvent, ModelSettings } from "../../framework/
framework";
```

```
@ModelSettings("http://dev.markitondemand.com/Api/v2/Quote/jsonp")
class QuoteModel extends Model implements IModel {

  constructor(metiator : IMediator) {
    super(metiator);
  }

  // listen to model events
  public initialize() {
    this.subscribeToEvents([
      new AppEvent("app.model.quote.change", null, (e, args) => {
      this.onChange(args); })
    ]);
  }

  // dispose model events
  public dispose() {
    this.unsubscribeToEvents();
  }
```

The second thing that you should notice is that the onChange function invokes a new function (formatModel) when the promise returned by getAsync is fulfilled:

```
private onChange(args) : void {
  // format args
  var s = { symbol : args };
  this.getAsync("jsonp", s)
      .then((data) => {

        // format data
        var quote = this.formatModel(data);

        // pass controll to the market view
        this.triggerEvent(new AppEvent("app.view.symbol.render",
        quote, null));
      })
      .catch((e) => {
        // pass control to the global error handler
        this.triggerEvent(new AppEvent("app.error", e, null));
      });
}
```

The new function just formats the response of the web services to be displayed in a user-friendly manner. We could have done this formatting inside the promise fulfillment callback. Using a separate function makes the code significantly cleaner.

```
    private formatModel (data) {
      data.Change = data.Change.toFixed(2);
      data.ChangePercent = data.ChangePercent.tcFixed(2);
      data.Timestamp = new
      Date(data.Timestamp).toLocaleDateString();
      data.MarketCap = (data.MarketCap / 1000000).toFixed(2) + "M.";
      data.ChangePercentYTD = data.ChangePercentYTD.toFixed(2);
      return { quote : data };
    }
  }
}
export { QuoteModel };
```

Implementing the symbol view

Let's create a new file named symbol_view.ts under the app/views directory. The SymbolView view receives the stock data formatted by the QuoteModel model through the mediator using the app.view.symbol.render event:

```
/// <reference path="../../framework/interfaces"/>

import { View, AppEvent,ViewSettings } from "../../framework/
framework";

@ViewSettings("./source/app/templates/symbol.hbs", "#outlet")
class SymbolView extends View implements IView {

  constructor(metiator : IMediator) {
    super(metiator);
  }
```

This view is just like MarketView; it subscribes to some events using the initialize method, and later disposes of those events using the dispose method. The SymbolView view can also initialize and dispose of user events using the bindDomEvents and unbindDomEvents methods.

However, there is one significant difference between SymbolView and MarketView. After the promise returned by renderAsync has been fulfilled and the user events have been initialized, the execution flow is passed to another model via the app. model.chart.change event. At this point, the stock quote screen is visible but it is missing the chart.

```
initialize() : void {
  this.subscribeToEvents([
    new AppEvent("app.view.symbol.render", null, (e, model :
    any) => {
      this.renderAsync(model)
          .then((model) => {
            // set DOM events
            this.bindDomEvents(model);

            // pass control to chart View
            this.triggerEvent(new
             AppEvent("app.model.chart.change", model.quote.Symbol,
             null));
          })
          .catch((e) => {
            this.triggerEvent(new AppEvent("app.error", e,
            null));
          });
    }),
  ]);
}

public dispose() : void {
  this.unbindDomEvents();
  this.unsubscribeToEvents();
}

// initializes DOM events
protected bindDomEvents(model : any) {
  var scope = $(this._container);
  // set DOM events here
}

// disposes DOM events
protected unbindDomEvents() {
  var scope = this._container;
  // kill DOM events here
}
}
export { SymbolView };
```

Implementing the chart model

Let's create a new file named `chart_model.ts` under the `app/models` directory.
This is the last model that we will implement:

```
/// <reference path="../../framework/interfaces"/>

import { Model, AppEvent, ModelSettings } from "../../framework/
framework";

@ModelSettings("http://dev.markitondemand.com/Api/v2/InteractiveChart/
jsonp")
class ChartModel extends Model implements IModel {

  constructor(metiator : IMediator) {
    super(metiator);
  }

  // listen to model events
  public initialize() {
    this.subscribeToEvents([
      new AppEvent("app.model.chart.change", null, (e, args) => {
      this.onChange(args); })
    ]);
  }

  // dispose model events
  public dispose() {
    this.unsubscribeToEvents();
  }
```

This time, we will need to format both the request and the response. We need to
encode the request parameter because the web service requires a group of settings
that cannot be sent as parameters in the URL without encoding it first.

The `onChange` method uses the browser's `JSON.stringify` function to transform
the required web service arguments (a JSON object) into a string. The string is then
encoded using the browser's `encodeURIComponent` function so it can be used as a
parameter in the URL.

The response is formatted using a method named `formatModel`:

```
private onChange(args) : void {

    // format args (more info at http://dev.markitondemand.com/)
    var p = {
      Normalized : false,
      NumberOfDays : 365,
      DataPeriod : "Day",
      Elements :[
        { Symbol : args , Type : "price", Params :["ohlc"] }
      ]
    };
    var queryString = "parameters=" +
    encodeURIComponent(JSON.stringify(p));

    this.getAsync("jsonp", queryString)
        .then((data) => {

            // format data
            var chartData = this.formatModel(args, data);

            // pass controll to the market view
            this.triggerEvent(new AppEvent("app.view.chart.render",
            chartData, null));
        })
        .catch((e) => {
            // pass control to the global error handler
            this.triggerEvent(new AppEvent("app.error", e, null));
        });
}
```

This function is used to format the response from `dev.markitondemand.com`, so it can be used by Highcharts with ease. Highcharts is a library that allow us to render graphs on the client side:

```
private formatModel(symbol, data) {
    // more info at http://dev.markitondemand.com/
    // and http://www.highcharts.com/demo/line-time-series
    var chartData = {
      title : symbol,
      series : []
    };
```

```
        var series = [
          { name : "open", data :
          data.Elements[0].DataSeries.open.values },
          { name : "close", data :
          data.Elements[0].DataSeries.close.values },
          { name : "high", data :
          data.Elements[0].DataSeries.high.values },
          { name : "low", data :
          data.Elements[0].DataSeries.low.values }
        ];

        for(var i = 0; i < series.length; i++) {
          var serie = {
            name: series[i].name,
            data: []
          }

          for(var j = 0; j < series[i].data.length; j++){
            var val = series[i].data[j];
            var d = new Date(data.Dates[j]).getTime();
            serie.data.push([d, val]);
          }

          chartData.series.push(serie);
        }
        return chartData;
      }
    }
    export { ChartModel };
```

Implementing the chart view

Let's create a new file named `chart_view.ts` under the `app/views` directory. This is the last view that we will implement. This view is almost identical to the previous ones, but there is one significant difference. As the chart is rendered by Highcharts and not Handlebars, we will avoid passing a template URL to the `ViewSettings` decorator:

```
/// <reference path="../../framework/interfaces"/>

import { View, AppEvent,ViewSettings } from "../../framework/
framework";
```

```
@ViewSettings(null, "#chart_container")
class ChartView extends View implements IView {

  constructor(metiator : IMediator) {
    super(metiator);
  }
```

The `ChartView` view is subscribed to the `app.view.chart.render` event. The event handler is invoked when the `ChartModel` model has been loaded and formatted, but since we don't need to render a Handlebars template, we will not invoke the `renderAsync` method here (as we did in all the previous views), and we will invoke a method named `renderChart` instead:

```
  initialize() : void {
    this.subscribeToEvents([
      new AppEvent("app.view.chart.render", null, (e, model : any) =>
{
        this.renderChart(model);
        this.bindDomEvents(model);
      }),
    ]);
  }

  public dispose() : void {
    this.unbindDomEvents();
    this.unsubscribeToEvents();
  }

  // initializes DOM events
  protected bindDomEvents(model : any) {
    var scope = $(this._container);
    // set DOM events here
  }

  // disposes DOM events
  protected unbindDomEvents() {
    var scope = this._container;
    // kill DOM events here
  }
```

The `renderChart` method uses the Highcharts API (`http://api.highcharts.com/highcharts`) to transform the data returned by `ChartModel` into a nice looking interactive chart:

```
private renderChart(model) {
  $(this._container).highcharts({
    chart: {
      zoomType: 'x'
    },
    title: {
      text: model.title
    },
    subtitle: {
      text : 'Click and drag in the plot area to zoom in'
    },
    xAxis: {
      type: 'datetime'
    },
    yAxis: {
      title: {
        text: 'Price'
      }
    },
    legend: {
      enabled: true
    },
    tooltip: {
      shared: true,
      crosshairs: true
    },
    plotOptions: {
      area: {
        marker: {
          radius: 0
        },
        lineWidth: 0.1,
        threshold: null
      }
    },
    series: model.series
  });
}
}
export { ChartView };
```

Testing the application

We can test this application using the same set of tools that we used in the previous chapters of this book. As you already know, in order to run our unit test, we need to create a Gulp task like the following one:

```
gulp.task("run-unit-test", function(cb) {
  karma.start({
    configFile : "karma.conf.js",
    singleRun: true
  }, cb);
});
```

We have used the Karma test runner, and we need to set its configuration using the `karma.conf.js` file. The `karma.conf.js` file is almost identical to the one that we used in *Chapter 7, Application Testing*, and will not be included here for the sake of brevity.

We also need a task to run some end-to-end tests:

```
gulp.task('run-e2e-test', function() {
  return gulp.src('')
    .pipe(nightwatch({
      configFile: 'nightwatch.json'
    }));
});
```

The `nightwatch.json` file is almost identical the one that we used in *Chapter 7, Application Testing*, and thus will not be included here.

Refer to the companion source code to see the content of `nightwatch.json` and the `karma.conf.js` file, as well as some examples of unit tests and E2E tests.

Preparing the application for a production release

Now that the application has been implemented and tested, we can prepare it for release in a production environment.

In this section, we will implement two Gulp tasks. The first task is used to compress the output JavaScript code. Compressing the JavaScript code will improve both the loading and execution performance of our application:

```
gulp.task("compress", function() {
  return gulp.src("bundled/source/bundle.js")
             .pipe(uglify({ preserveComments : false }))
             .pipe(gulp.dest("dist/"))
});
```

The second Gulp task that we will implement is used to add a copyright header. The task uses some of the fields from the npm configuration file (`package.json`) to generate a string, which contains the copyright details. The string is then added to the top of the compressed JavaScript file that was generated by the previous task:

```
gulp.task("header", function() {

  var pkg = require("package.json");

  var banner = ["/**",
    " * <%= pkg.name %> v.<%= pkg.version %> - <%= pkg.description
    %>",
    " * Copyright (c) 2015 <%= pkg.author %>",
    " * <%= pkg.license %>",
    " * <%= pkg.homepage %>",
    " */",
    ""].join("\n");

  return gulp.src("dist/bundle.js")
             .pipe(header(banner, { pkg : pkg } ))
             .pipe(gulp.dest("dist/"));
});
```

We could also create some extra Gulp tasks to improve the performance of our application further. For example, we could create a task to generate a cache manifest (a simple text file that lists the resources the browser should cache for offline access) to implement client-side caching.

Summary

In this chapter, we created an MVC application that allowed us to find out how the NASDAQ and NYSE stocks were doing on a particular day. This application is a single-page web application, and its architecture makes its components easy to extend, reuse, maintain, and test.

The application showcases many of the concepts that we covered in the previous chapters. We created an automated build, and we used many functions, classes, modules, and other core language features. We also used modules and worked with some asynchronous functions, and we used some decorators. The automated build performs some tasks that will help us to improve the application performance and ensures that it works correctly.

This application is not a very large JavaScript application. However, the application is large enough to showcase the ways in which TypeScript can help us develop complex applications that are ready to grow and adapt to changes with ease.

I hope you enjoyed this book and feel eager to learn more about TypeScript.

If you are up for a challenge and you would like to reinforce your TypeScript skills, try the following:

You can try to achieve 100 percent test coverage in the application that we have developed over the last two chapters. You can improve our custom SPA the framework and introduce features such as using an IoC container or using a unidirectional dataflow.

You can also visit the TodoMVC website (`http://todomvc.com/`) to find examples of integration between TypeScript and popular MV* frameworks, such as Ember.js or Backbone.js, to learn how to use a production-ready SPA framework.

Index

Symbols

@name decorator 245
@parameterTypes decorator 245
@returnType decorator 245
@type decorator 245

A

action 271
after() function 215
aggregation 105
Akamai
  URL 175
AMD modules 133
annotations
  about 233
  and decorators 232
  class decorators 233-235
  decorator factory 242, 243
  decorators with arguments 244
  method decorators 236-238
  parameter decorators 240-242
  property decorators 238, 239
  reflection metadata API 245-248
Any type 8
application 281, 282
application events 274-278
application programming interface
    (API) 125
apply method 145, 146
applyMixins method 114
architecture, single-page application (SPA)
  about 304
  MarketController controller,
    implementing 304

arithmetic operators 13
arrow function 84, 85
assertion 194
assignment operators 15, 16
association 105
asynchronous code
  testing 217, 218
asynchronous flow control, types
  composite 96
  concurrent 95
  series 95
  waterfall 95
asynchronous functions
  about 97
  async 97, 98
  await 97, 98
asynchronous module definition (AMD) 99
asynchronous programming
  about 83
  arrow functions 84-86
  asynchronous functions 97, 98
  callback hell 86-90
  callbacks 83
  generators 96
  higher order functions 83
  promises 90-95
Atom
  about 30-32
  URL 30, 31

B

beforeEach() function 215, 223
before() function 215

behavior-driven development (BDD)
  about 201
  URL 201
bind method 147
BitBucket
  URL 34
bitwise operators 14, 15
Bower
  about 41
  URL 41
browserified function 49
Browserify
  URL 135, 136
Browser Object Model (BOM) 12, 140
BrowserSync
  URL 57

C

callback 83
callback hell 86-90
call method 145
Central Processing Unit (CPU) 166
Chai
  about 198
  TDD, versus BDD 219
  URL 219
  used, for creating specs 213-217
  used, for creating suites 213-217
  used, for creating test assertions 213-217
Chaplin 262
chart model, single-page application (SPA)
  implementing 325, 326
circular dependency
  about 136-138
  URL 138
class 101
class decorators 233-235
client-side rendering 252
closures
  about 158-160
  private members, using with 162-164
  static variables, using with 160-162
collections 260
collection views 261
CommonJS modules
  runtime 134

comparison operators 13, 14
complex type serialization 248
components, TypeScript
  compiler 4
  IDE integration 4
  language 4
  language services 4
composition 105, 106
configuration testing 189
constructor 101
Continuous Integration (CI) tools 58
controller 262, 275, 292
createElement property 73

D

data, single-page application (SPA)
  about 303
  chart data 304
  market data 304
  stock quote data 304
data types
  any 9
  array 8
  Boolean 8
  enum 8
  number 8
  string 8
  void 9
declaration files 42
decorator factory 242-244
decorators
  and annotations 232
  prerequisites 231
  with arguments 244
DefinitelyTyped
  about 42
  URL 43
dependency inversion (DI) principle
  about 126
  URL 127
depth of inheritance tree (DIT) 109
design time code 2
development workflow
  about 29
  Continuous Integration (CI) tools 58
  package management tools 38

M

mark phase 186
mark-and-sweep algorithm 186
market controller, single-page
      application (SPA)
  implementing 312-314
market template, single-page
      application (SPA)
  implementing 319
market view, single-page application (SPA)
  implementing 316-318
Markit
  about 304
  URL 304
mediator 266, 274, 278-280
memory leak
  about 183
  issues, preventing 186
method decorators
  about 236-238
  invoking 237
method overriding 108
mixin 109, 110 111
Mocha
  about 198
  TDD, versus BDD 219
  used, for creating specs 213-217
  used, for creating suites 213-217
  used, for creating test assertions 213-216
mocks 196
model
  about 259, 292-295
  settings 292-295
Model-View-Controller (MVC) 258
Model-View-Presenter (MVP) 258
Model-View-ViewModel (MVVM) 258
Modernizr
  about 140
  URL 140
module loader
  about 129
  Browserify 130
  RequireJS 130
  SystemJS 130

modules
  about 25, 129, 130
  AMD modules 133
  CommonJS modules 134
  ES6 modules 131, 132
  external modules 132
  SystemJS modules 136
  UMD modules 135
multiple inheritance 109
multiple-selection structure (switch) 17, 18
MV* architecture 258
MVC framework
  prerequisites 276, 277
  writing, from scratch 274, 275
MVC framework components
  application 274, 281, 282
  application events 274, 277, 278
  controller 291, 292
  controllers 275
  dispatcher 288-291
  event emitter 284, 285
  framework 299
  mediator 274-280
  models 275, 292-295
  model settings 292-295
  router 274, 285, 287
  routes 274, 283
  view 295-297
  views 275
  view settings 295-297
MV* frameworks
  application framework, selecting 273
  client-side rendering 268
  collections 260
  collection views 261
  components 259
  controllers 262
  data flow 270-272
  dispatcher 267, 268
  events 263
  features 259
  hash (#) navigation 263-266
  item views 260
  mediator 266, 267
  model 259

Visual Studio (VS)
  about 3
  URLs 31

W

web components 272
web performance analysis
  prerequisites 166
  resources 166
web workers 143
while expression 19

Y

YSlow
  URL 177

Thank you for buying
Learning TypeScript

About Packt Publishing

Packt, pronounced 'packed', published its first book, *Mastering phpMyAdmin for Effective MySQL Management*, in April 2004, and subsequently continued to specialize in publishing highly focused books on specific technologies and solutions.

Our books and publications share the experiences of your fellow IT professionals in adapting and customizing today's systems, applications, and frameworks. Our solution-based books give you the knowledge and power to customize the software and technologies you're using to get the job done. Packt books are more specific and less general than the IT books you have seen in the past. Our unique business model allows us to bring you more focused information, giving you more of what you need to know, and less of what you don't.

Packt is a modern yet unique publishing company that focuses on producing quality, cutting-edge books for communities of developers, administrators, and newbies alike. For more information, please visit our website at www.packtpub.com.

About Packt Open Source

In 2010, Packt launched two new brands, Packt Open Source and Packt Enterprise, in order to continue its focus on specialization. This book is part of the Packt Open Source brand, home to books published on software built around open source licenses, and offering information to anybody from advanced developers to budding web designers. The Open Source brand also runs Packt's Open Source Royalty Scheme, by which Packt gives a royalty to each open source project about whose software a book is sold.

Writing for Packt

We welcome all inquiries from people who are interested in authoring. Book proposals should be sent to author@packtpub.com. If your book idea is still at an early stage and you would like to discuss it first before writing a formal book proposal, then please contact us; one of our commissioning editors will get in touch with you.

We're not just looking for published authors; if you have strong technical skills but no writing experience, our experienced editors can help you develop a writing career, or simply get some additional reward for your expertise.

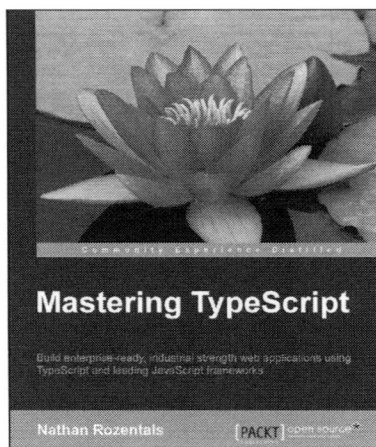

Mastering TypeScript

ISBN: 978-1-78439-966-5   Paperback: 364 pages

Build enterprise-ready, industrial strength web applications using TypeScript and leading JavaScript frameworks

1. Focus on test-driven development to help build quality applications that are modular, scalable, maintainable, and adaptable.

2. Practical examples that show you how to use TypeScript with popular JavaScript frameworks including Backbone, Angular, Node.js, require. js, and Marionette.

3. Enhance your TypeScript knowledge with in-depth discussions on language features, third-party libraries, declaration files, and so on using practical scenarios.

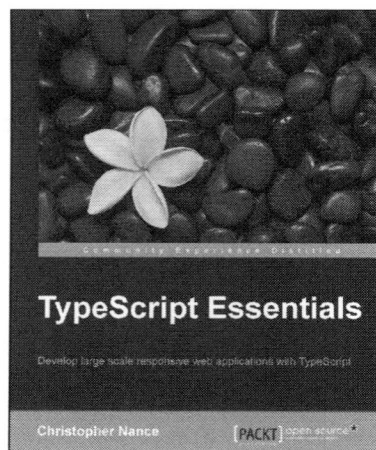

TypeScript Essentials

ISBN: 978-1-78398-576-0   Paperback: 182 pages

Develop large scale responsive web applications with TypeScript

1. Explore the key features of TypeScript to develop web applications of your own.

2. Take advantage of the static typing system to improve the web development experience and add stability to your code.

3. Discover how to effectively use type annotations, declaration files, and ECMA script integration with lots of code and examples.

Please check **www.PacktPub.com** for information on our titles

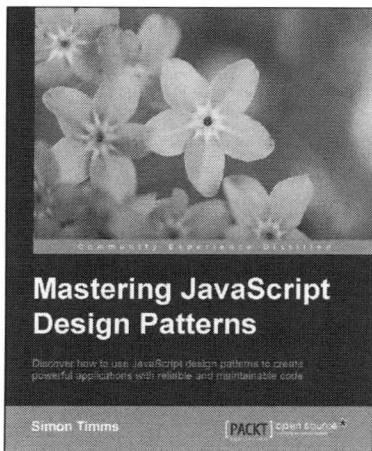

Mastering JavaScript Design Patterns

ISBN: 978-1-78398-798-6   Paperback: 290 pages

Discover how to use JavaScript design patterns to create powerful applications with reliable and maintainable code

1. Learn how to use tried and true software design methodologies to enhance your Javascript code.

2. Discover robust JavaScript implementations of classic as well as advanced design patterns.

3. Packed with easy-to-follow examples that can be used to create reusable code and extensible designs.

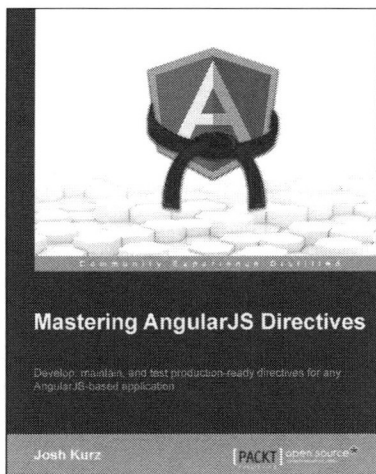

Mastering AngularJS Directives

ISBN: 978-1-78398-158-8   Paperback: 210 pages

Develop, maintain, and test production-ready directives for any AngularJS-based application

1. Explore the options available for creating directives, by reviewing detailed explanations and real-world examples.

2. Dissect the life cycle of a directive and understand why they are the base of the AngularJS framework.

3. Discover how to create structured, maintainable, and testable directives through a step-by-step, hands-on approach to AngularJS.

Please check **www.PacktPub.com** for information on our titles

Printed in Great Britain
by Amazon